EXPLORING MORE SIGNATURE PEDAGOGIES

EXPLORING MORE SIGNATURE PEDAGOGIES

Approaches to Teaching Disciplinary Habits of Mind

Edited by

Nancy L. Chick, Aeron Haynie, and Regan A.R. Gurung

Foreword by Anthony A. Ciccone

STERLING, VIRGINIA

Published by Stylus Publishing, LLC
22883 Quicksilver Drive
Sterling, Virginia 20166-2102

Library of Congress Cataloging-in-Publication-Data
Exploring more signature pedagogies : approaches to teaching disciplinary habits of mind / edited by Nancy L. Chick, Aeron Haynie, and Regan A.R. Gurung ; foreword by Anthony A. Ciccone.—1st ed.
p. cm.
Includes bibliographical references and index.
ISBN 978-1-57922-475-2 (cloth : alk. paper)
ISBN 978-1-57922-476-9 (pbk. : alk. paper)
ISBN 978-1-57922-766-1 (library networkable e-edition)
ISBN 978-1-57922-767-8 (consumer e-edition)
1. College teaching. 2. Universities and colleges—Curricula. 3. Interdisciplinary approach in education. I. Chick, Nancy L., 1968– II. Haynie, Aeron, 1964– III. Gurung, Regan A. R.
LB2331.E946 2012
378.1′25—dc23 2011028782

13-digit ISBN: 978-1-57922-475-2 (cloth)
13-digit ISBN: 978-1-57922-476-9 (paper)
13-digit ISBN: 978-1-57922-766-1 (library networkable e-edition)
13-digit ISBN: 978-1-57922-767-8 (consumer e-edition)

Printed in the United States of America

All first editions printed on acid free paper that meets the American National Standards Institute Z39-48 Standard.

First Edition, 2012

10 9 8 7 6 5 4 3 2

CONTENTS

ACKNOWLEDGMENTS

The editors, once again, thank the University of Wisconsin System's Office of Professional and Instructional Development (OPID) for introducing them to the scholarship of teaching and learning and for their outstanding work encouraging and facilitating collaboration. Each of us has benefited from being a part of such an excellent state university system. We dedicate this volume to our collective hope that such state institutions are allowed to continue.

FOREWORD

Several years ago, I had the pleasure of team teaching a graduate course with my colleague Fred Eckman, a recognized expert in the field of second language acquisition. Team teaching is the defining feature of the graduate program in foreign language and linguistics at University of Wisconsin–Milwaukee; all the required core seminars use it. Whereas other colleagues might have practiced "turn teaching," Fred and I team taught with a vengeance: I immersed myself in unfamiliar linguistics-based research, while he studied the classroom-based research on methods that I was more conversant with. We challenged ourselves to lead seminar discussions on the other's topics: He critiqued articles from the canon of foreign language pedagogy and practice, while I discussed his work on "markedness" from a classroom perspective. We grappled with, and forced our students to confront, the ultimate question for foreign language teachers—does language instruction actually make a difference in language acquisition? It's a question that researchers ask so naturally and teachers usually take for granted. Our version of team teaching modeled the conversation between theory and practice that we hoped our students (practicing foreign language teachers or graduate students in linguistics) would engage in, in their own teaching or research. In short, we chose and implemented a pedagogy that would show how practitioners connect two critical components of their field in a way that respects and challenges the insights of both. In signature pedagogy terms, we modeled an important habit of mind, demonstrated reflective practice, and, perhaps to a lesser degree, socialized future teacher-researchers to the field through our own collegiality.

Team teaching, however, is hardly a signature pedagogy, especially in graduate education. It is not widespread, can be done in many different ways in many different fields, and connects only partly to the habits of head, heart, and hand needed by the foreign language professional. But even this cursory reflection on my experience with it hints at the value inherent in exploring teaching and learning from the signature pedagogies viewpoint. In trying to do it well, Fred and I discovered that reflecting on the implicit values of a pedagogy ultimately benefits the instructor and the students, in addition to advancing the field. I'd like to explore the value of this continuing work on signature pedagogies from this perspective. Signature pedagogies . . . so what?

This second volume of *Exploring Signature Pedagogies* significantly advances what we know about the subject by expanding the number of disciplines now in the discussion. More professions, interdisciplinary fields, and disciplines are included. Perhaps more importantly, however, each author carefully describes and evaluates the current connections (and disconnections) between what a field or discipline values and how it instills (or not) those values in its future practitioners through the teaching and learning experiences it designs. In so doing, the authors make many useful distinctions and observations that expand our thinking about individual fields or disciplines, the concept of a signature pedagogy itself, and the role this concept can play in helping us frame an agenda for research and development in teaching and learning.

In asking where signature pedagogies come from and how they can and should evolve, the authors remind us that the epistemology, practices, and values of a profession or discipline are not immutable and that changes in these dispositions should lead to changes in pedagogical practice. Where do these changes come from? In some cases, they lie in the evolving relationship between a field's practitioners and their clients; the author of the chapter on disability studies provides an excellent example of this when highlighting the shift from a medical to a social perspective on disability. In other cases, occupational therapy, for instance, the expansion of the field and the necessary use of instructional technology have challenged the discipline to reconceptualize a signature pedagogy that would remain faithful to its core principles of relational, affective, and contextualized learning. In second language teaching, the current signature pedagogy, the communicative approach, arose from research findings, teacher experience and reflection, and, most importantly, an evolving understanding of what proficient language speakers actually do. Reflecting on the nature and value of practitioner–client interaction, aligning emerging pedagogical trends with core principles, recognizing and responding to a new way to understand learner needs and abilities—this is where exploring signature pedagogies can lead us.

The signature pedagogies perspective also highlights tensions and controversies in a field and thus helps frame discussions about priorities and emerging trends. When Jeffrey L. Bernstein suggests that the field of political science and its practitioners now seek to understand the behaviors of goal-seeking actors, he can argue for a new signature pedagogy, simulation, that enables students to think and behave like the actors they are trying to understand. Similarly, Mark Maier, KimMarie McGoldrick, and Scott P. Simkins, in seeking the signature pedagogy of economics, find instead an "expedient, model-oriented, analytical, and lecture-based" pedagogy that reflects the narrowness of graduate education, to the detriment of the development of the professional economist, who will face "multifaceted, interdisciplinary, and global challenges." This allows them to argue for a pedagogy based on experimental and behavioral economics that would encourage students at all levels to perform economic analysis "in ways that mimic what economists actually do." In short, looking for signature pedagogies often sharpens the widening gap between advancing the knowledge of a field and developing the habits of head, heart, and hand that the field's professionals will need, that is, between academic and professional preparation. What better place to start when change is needed?

The signature pedagogies perspective, as I noted in my foreword to the earlier volume, can advance discussion of important theoretical and practical questions about the scholarship of teaching and learning. The interdisciplines, I believe, can play a crucial role here. Like the scholarship of teaching and learning itself, the interdisciplines often confront conflicting "rules of evidence," or a clash between their values and their methods. The authors of the chapter on women's studies point this out quite clearly that as a field, women's studies questions the "objective paradigm" that would separate the rational from the emotional or the "large *n*" from the individual story, yet it often must use traditional social science methods to make a case. This tension appears especially in the pedagogical research of the field; if women's studies seeks to transform the student by encouraging the development of a "feminist consciousness that is carried beyond the classroom," humanistic protocols for evidence and interpretation would seem more appropriate. Similarly, the scholarship of teaching and learning often looks for the elusive "transformative learning"—ethical and moral development, lifelong learning—that requires an openness to protocols from more than one discipline. The authors point to humanistic values and methods—close reading of student work, students and faculty as codesigners of research—as a way to bridge the gap in women's studies pedagogical research. The lesson for the scholarship of teaching and learning as a field? Embrace discipline-specific study while making sure that the methods and results are appropriate to the question, speak across fields, and, if possible, raise important issues about what is worth knowing and doing.

Even where a signature pedagogy has emerged, much can be gained by asking why a scholarship of teaching and learning has not yet flourished in some of those fields. Is the signature pedagogy itself not conducive to a systematic inquiry into student learning? Stephen Bloch-Schulman makes this case for philosophy when he argues that the Socratic method and the field's "penchant for the armchair" discourages observing, predicting, and testing the method's results. Understanding how argument and "truth" are created in the abstract could be keeping the field from examining "what *students* find easy or hard to comprehend," and thus from gaining a deeper knowledge of how and when learning occurs in the philosophy classroom.

The authors of the chemistry chapter make a similar case, but for a pedagogy that has clearly worked well. Undergraduate research is the "premier way to engage in the situated learning and cognitive apprenticeship of chemistry," but its obvious value as a pedagogy could have limited the field's understanding of how exactly it encourages students to think, know, and do as chemists. In examining this broader issue, the authors of this chapter not only discover significant and testable heuristics (role-modeling by mentors, etc.) for connecting undergraduate research to the desired dispositions of the field, they also point us toward other pedagogies (science writing heuristic, discovery-based lab experiments, process-oriented guided inquiry) that also encourage the desired dispositions. In short, studying why we believe in something clarifies the belief, outlines a research agenda, and opens us to other similarly directed pedagogies.

If the quest for a field's signature pedagogy leads us to examine classroom practice, the evolving circumstances of teaching in the field, the intersection of the field with the larger community, and the relationship between the field's pedagogy and the values and dispositions it would instill in its students, it can also lead us to questions about intellectual and moral development that go beyond any one field or discipline. Translating the cycle of experience, reflection, action, and evaluation from the *Spiritual Exercises* of St. Ignatius into a pedagogy that prepares students for good work in *all* professions and undergirds good learning in *all* disciplines seems a challenge worth taking on. (In the interest of full disclosure, I graduated from a Jesuit high school and a Jesuit college.) A pedagogy grounded in the development of the entire person seems a good model for *any* pedagogy.

I was never a better teacher than when I team taught with a colleague. Why? Because in trying to do it well, I had to ask myself what were the connections between this possible signature pedagogy of my field and the habits of heart, head, and hand that my field purports to develop in our students. When we ask this question of alignment between the knowledge, skills, and dispositions we want to develop in our students and the pedagogy we currently use, we ask perhaps the most crucial question we can ask as academic professionals. In so doing, we question the values of our field, the way we teach, and what and how students learn. We create a research agenda for teaching and learning in the field that is grounded in what we value for our students. The authors of this volume and my editor colleagues from Wisconsin have significantly advanced this agenda again, while encouraging all of us to sign on to the work from our own disciplinary perspectives. I thank them for this opportunity to introduce their work here.

Anthony A. Ciccone
University of Wisconsin–Milwaukee

1

SIGNATURE PEDAGOGIES IN THE LIBERAL ARTS AND BEYOND

Aeron Haynie, Nancy L. Chick, and Regan A. R. Gurung

In 2010 *The New York Times Magazine* ran the provocative article, "Can Good Teaching Be Learned?" (Green, 2010). The article highlighted recent developments in teacher education, in particular, the clash between those like Doug Lemov, who believe that mastering a "taxonomy of effective teaching practices" will improve teaching, and education experts like Deborah Loewenberg Ball, who argue for the importance of content knowledge.[1] Although these debates focus on teaching effectiveness in K–12 schools, the debate over good generic teaching skills versus deep knowledge in the discipline occurs in higher education as well.

The Ongoing Tension Between Generic Teaching Practices and Pedagogical Content Knowledge

Professors are hired for their extensive, specialized disciplinary knowledge; however, often this expert knowledge means that they take the basic skills, values, and methods of their disciplines for granted. Professors' abilities to teach groups of students, especially disciplinary novices, vary widely. Unfortunately, academia's rewards are still structured around traditional definitions of scholarship and untenured faculty might worry (and rightly so) that their scholarship of teaching and learning (SoTL) work will not count toward promotion, or worse, might diminish their credibility as scholars in their fields. In addition, because SoTL is a new field, few of us were mentored by faculty who combined research in their disciplinary field with scholarship of teaching and learning. Traditional methods of recognizing teaching, such as faculty teaching awards, generally do not measure the effectiveness of student learning; instead, they often reward charisma or professional accomplishments and rarely are based on any verifiable analysis of what students have learned.

How can college professors be educated so that their students' learning is deepened, increased, and stimulated? Shulman (1995) and Graff (2006), among others, have proposed changes in graduate education to better prepare graduate students for the teaching work of their careers as educators. Pace and Middendorf's groundbreaking *Decoding the Disciplines* (2004) continues to be at the center of most discussions of how to begin thinking about what Shulman (1987) calls "pedagogical content knowledge" (p. 8)—the understanding and skill to teach the discipline, especially its difficulties or what Pace and Middendorf call its "bottlenecks" (p. 4).

However, for those already in their professional careers, what can be done? The ever-growing movement of SoTL suggests that many in higher education are indeed taking effective teaching and student learning more seriously, as does the proliferation of university teaching and learning centers. So there are solutions, and there is reason to be hopeful for those with the time, energy, and willingness to work hard to fill in the teaching gaps in their own educational backgrounds. According to research on the habits of the most successful physicians, teachers, and therapists, specific techniques might not be as effective as the habits of deliberate practice, such as measuring one's baseline performance, seeking feedback, and ongoing reflection (Miller, Hubble, & Duncan, 2007). These are the very habits that the scholarship of teaching and learning seeks to foster.

Signature Pedagogies: Then and Now

After the publication of *Exploring Signature Pedagogies: Approaches to Teaching Disciplinary Habits of Mind* (Gurung, Chick, & Haynie, 2008), we coeditors were asked when we would do a second volume, one that might allow the authors to take their work a step farther and publish SoTL studies documenting the student work using the identified signature pedagogies. (There was no room for that in the first book, which we conceived of as more theoretical—or as Shulman [2009] called it, creating "conceptual and empirical bridges" between SoTL and signature pedagogies—and the beginning of the conversation, with further discussions in each field and the SoTL studies to follow independently.) Would we make it a collection of responses to the chapters in the first book? Would we fill in the disciplinary gaps from the first book? As much as we believe all of the projects to be worthy, we decided to use this second volume to do the latter.

Our first book extended the discussion of teaching and learning in the disciplines in new, more conceptual directions through Shulman's notion of signature pedagogies. What seemed most significant to us, though, was the consideration within the variety of disciplines—largely new ground in each. Thus, what we felt most was the absence of some disciplines, so that became our primary aim with this follow-up. Additionally, voices from around the world would broaden the discussion even further, so we called for authors from well beyond the first book's Wisconsin authors. We sent the call across the United States but also to Canada, the United Kingdom and the rest of Europe, Australia, and elsewhere, through as many international venues as possible. Now, we are pleased to include authors from all across the United States, Ireland, and Australia.

Riding SoTL's "Second Wave"

Much is written about the history of SoTL (e.g., Bender, 2005; Hutchings, Huber, & Ciccone, 2011; Shulman, 2011), the prevalence of SoTL (e.g., Gurung, Ansburg, Alexander, Lawrence, & Johnson, 2008; Huber & Hutchings, 2005), the potential benefit to faculty who engage in SoTL efforts (e.g., Goodburn & Savory, 2009; Weimer, 2006), and even the demographics of SoTL (Liddell, 2008; McKinney, 2008; McKinney & Chick, 2010). The last 10 years in particular has seen an increased focus on examining how different disciplines vary in thinking.

In what can be seen as the "second wave of SoTL" (Gurung et al., 2008, p. xvii; Gurung & Schwartz, 2010), many scholars have taken an almost metacognitive look at the scholarship in their disciplines. First, Donald (2002) took into account the different ways learning occurs in various academic disciplines, starting a trend of looking at one's discipline in the light of other disciplines and refining one's pedagogies based on the uniqueness of each discipline. This trend was boosted by Shulman's (2005) introduction of the notion of signature pedagogies, the way each discipline teaches students to think like the professionals in that discipline. Then Pace and Middendorf's (2004) *Decoding the Disciplines* gave a more thorough look at student learning within a discipline. This book, like Donald (2002), noted how student learning differs significantly across disciplines and that this notion is rarely presented to students explicitly. Their notion of "bottlenecks," or conceptual or procedural obstacles to learning, illustrates how experts would work on these impediments and then model the thinking for students. Similarly, in the UK, Meyer and Land (2005) worked to identify the different concepts within disciplines that prevent students from moving on and continuing with additional deep learning in the discipline.

We entered this discussion in 2008 with *Exploring Signature Pedagogies: Approaches to Teaching Disciplinary Habits of Mind* (Gurung et al., 2009). As Calder (2009) noted, "Here we see more evidence that the scholarship of teaching and learning can no longer be described as an 'emergent' field, but is well into its prime and yielding some of the most exciting and potentially transformative discoveries in higher education today." Authors of the first collection provided a description of the unique content and characteristic methods of learning in their disciplines, as well as the default pedagogies most often used in the fields' classrooms. They then reviewed and evaluated the pedagogical research related to their discipline, paying special attention to how faculty collect evidence of effective teaching and learning, and highlighted what future pedagogical research is needed. Some focused on what the pedagogical literature of the discipline suggests are the best ways to teach material in that field—and verify that learning. Finally, authors assessed how the common pedagogies within their disciplines reflect and engage students in the ways of knowing, the habits of mind, and the values used by experts in the field—or don't—and articulated a signature pedagogy that might more effectively reflect and engage these core elements of the discipline. In this volume, we extend the work into different disciplines in the liberal arts and sciences, in some interdisciplinary fields, and in the professions.

Chapter Overview and Synthesis

Traditionally, scholarship of teaching and learning has not drawn as much participation from scholars in the humanities as in the various sciences (Chick, 2009, 2011). Our first book even documented the greater presence of the social and natural sciences, with only two chapters representing the humanities (even fewer than the three in the fine arts) and nine chapters representing the sciences and mathematics. Therefore, we are pleased that the first section of this volume begins with an examination of the signature pedagogies of five humanities and fine arts disciplines: philosophy, foreign languages, communication, art and design, and arts entrepreneurship. In chapter 2, Bloch-Schulman begins by tracing the history of the discipline back to its ancient roots in Plato's writings about Socrates as a way to examine its main values and its core practice: the open dialogue and "elenchus," or argumentation through hypothesis, refutation, and cross-examination. Bloch-Schulman questions the teacher-centered way that the Socratic dialogue has been performed in many instances and urges the development of a Socratic dialogue *between* students and as a form of student self-reflection. In addition, Bloch-Schulman calls for the development of more scholarship into the teaching and learning of philosophy, urging those in his profession to build on recent scholarly work in other fields in their examination of how best to teach students the habits of a philosophical method.

In chapter 3, Ham and Schueller offer a rich history of foreign language programs and trace changes in teaching methods from the early translation-focused model to post–World War II imitative "audolingualism" and finally to the current communicative approach favored by most instructors today. Ham and Schueller argue that foreign language offers unique challenges for instructors, because it asks students to renegotiate their sense of self and transform into global citizens, not just with an understanding of technical aspects of another language, but also with a deep knowledge of another culture and an increased awareness of their own.

In his chapter on communications, Williamson first explores the field as a multidisciplinary, multimedia, multicontextual one that leads to a variety of professional possibilities, invoking the term *pluralist* several times to describe the challenge of describing the discipline's signature pedagogy. However, he also comes back to the significance of the classroom itself as a site for "communication in action," a key context where communication educators should focus students' attention—not simply applying theories to media and communication actions outside of the classroom but recognizing the classroom itself as an ideal site to "apply theoretical categories in structured learning situations."

This section concludes with two chapters that focus on the intersection between creative arts and the marketplace: art and design and arts entrepreneurship. Both chapters trace the many ways that instructors work to increase students' creativity—both in creating and in marketing their art. In their chapter on art entrepreneurship, Hong, Essig, and Bridgstock explain how arts entrepreneurship programs teach students how to use their creativity to generate business opportunities in nonprofit and for-profit ventures. Sims and Shreeve contextualize their discussion of art and design pedagogy within the changing landscape of higher education reform in the United Kingdom and outline the standard ways that design is taught: the studio, the brief (or assignment), critique, sketchbook, research, and discussion. Expanding on Klebesadel and Kornetsky's (2008) examination of the role of the critique in arts education, Sims and Shreeve raise their own questions on the effectiveness of traditional critiques. Finally, the authors worry that budget constraints could cause institutions to question the value of maintaining studios, a practice that this chapter maintains is central in allowing emerging design students to learn the core habits of their discipline.

The second section contains descriptions of signature pedagogies in the social and natural sciences: political science, economics, and chemistry. Bernstein succinctly states the overarching goal of teaching political science: for students to take on the perspective of various "political actors" and thereby understand their motivations and predict future behavior. According to research Bernstein cites, this transformation of student understanding can best be accomplished by using more active learning, such as simulations and academic service-learning projects, rather than by relying on the default pedagogy of lecture. In order for students to learn to think like political scientists, they must have opportunities to "do" political science.

Maier, McGoldrick, and Simkins argue that most economics courses currently use an "expedient" rather than a signature pedagogy: Introductory courses employ lectures based on deductive reasoning, thus producing an "unwarranted certainty" in the methods of modern economics. Instead, the authors call for a teaching of economics through interdisciplinary classroom experiments that would allow students to respond to recent economic events and that nurture students' abilities to think more creatively about economic issues. In many ways, this chapter represents a critique, not just of teaching styles, but of the values of the discipline in general, as the authors suggest a need to reform how economists think.

Gravelle and Fisher's chapter on chemistry argues that students best understand chemistry when they perform undergraduate research through labs or, because labs are costly and time-consuming, through "process-oriented guided research inquiry."

Section three includes three chapters on interdisciplinary fields: Ignatian pedagogy, women's studies, and disability studies. In their chapter, "Reflection in Action: A Signature Ignatian Pedagogy for the 21st Century," Nowacek and Mountin outline the distinguishing values of a Jesuit education: a "cycle of experience, reflection, action, and evaluation." Although many Jesuit institutions have become centers for SoTL, according to Nowacek and Mountin, there has been little attention paid to articulating and measuring best practices in specifically Jesuit teaching.

Both women's and disability studies connect their pedagogies to political activism and discuss ways that their courses can teach students to challenge social norms. Hassel and Nelson discuss the particular mission of women's studies: to connect the personal to the political, theory to praxis. They describe a women's studies pedagogy based on shared experience, inclusivity, and collaboration. Although they explain the reasons why women's studies has been uneasy with notions of objective measurements, they urge women's studies scholars to use qualitative assessment to measure how well these forms of pedagogy accomplish their goals.

According to O'Driscoll, disability studies rejects the medical model and instead teaches students to understand disabilities within their social and political contexts, often challenging students' preconceived notions of disability. Drawing distinctions among the ways disability studies is taught in the United States, the United Kingdom, and elsewhere, this chapter delineates a signature pedagogy of disability studies that uses problem-based learning and personal narratives of disabled people to help students see disability studies as part of a larger social critique.

Signature pedagogies in the professions should be more easily discernible; after all, these fields train students for specific, identifiable jobs, which is why the notion of signature pedagogies originated in the professions. However, as the four chapters in our final section suggest, developing signature pedagogies in the professions might change as the nature of the professions shift and morph and as practitioners in the fields debate values. For example, in Long et al.'s chapter on nursing education, the authors point out the challenges of preparing students for a field in which the core information is continually being updated. The high demand for nurses, occupational therapists, and social workers, as the next chapters explore, and the subsequent growth of these programs, means an increased pressure to deliver classes online and use newly trained instructors. Therefore, these professions' signature pedagogies must appropriately go beyond content and instead teach the core values of the profession. In nursing, these values are empathy, ethics, and social justice. To these ends, nursing programs employ both practicums and clinical simulation and encourage study abroad as a way for nursing students to learn about cultural diversity. A similar sensitivity to cultural differences is stressed in Cornell-Swanson's chapter on teaching social work, which explains the importance of a "strengths-based perspective" or assuming that a client's behavior is adaptive in some way. She argues that the capstone field placement is incomplete as the traditionally identified signature pedagogy, because although it applies the field's practices most effectively, social work students' learning events before field placement are critical to teaching the field's values and ways of thinking. Occupational therapy programs likewise are facing challenges as online courses diminish the strong "relational" focus found in traditional mentoring. However, the authors recognize that new technology also brings opportunities for relational learning through video narratives and online discussions.

In our final chapter, Crafton and Albers address the controversial topic of teacher education, a field that is much beleaguered of late. In their provocative chapter, they take issue with traditional approaches to "training" teachers—an approach that assumes the neutrality of content knowledge and treats teaching as the simple acquisition of skills. Instead, the authors argue, teacher educators need to focus on *how* students learn. Citing the burnout rate of new teachers, the authors argue for a supportive community that would help teachers "practice, develop, and form their identities." The chapter also encourages a broader understanding of semiotics to include ways of making meaning beyond traditional literacy and highlights education's broadest goal: democratic learning.

Next Steps: Signature Pedagogies and Student Learning

As suggested earlier, the next step—in addition to encouraging disciplines and professionals still unrepresented here to explore such questions—is to seek evidence from our students. What does their thinking about our disciplines and professions look like as we practice these signature pedagogies? What values do these practices express? What practices do they begin to use? In other words, we need SoTL work applying the discipline's signature SoTL practices in order to gather the best evidence for the effectiveness of these signature pedagogies and perhaps raise the conversation to a "third wave." For instance, the think-aloud method or protocol (Calder & Carlson, 2002; Maarten, Barnard, & Sandberg, 1994) is a method in which the student says aloud everything he or she is thinking while working on a learning task to help make thinking visible, offering a rich way to, as Calder and Carlson explain, "open a fascinating window into the thinking patterns of students." These windows are just out of reach for many assessment and data-gathering methods when it comes to seeking evidence of the deeper processes of what students value and think, not just do—all of which are woven into the hopes of signature pedagogies.

Note

1. See also Crafton and Albers in this book for a thoughtful reframing of this either/or debate in teacher education.

References

Bender, E. (2005, September/October). CASTLs in the air. *Change, 37*(5), 40–49.

Calder, L. (2009). Back cover of R. A. R. Gurung, N. Chick, & A. Haynie (Eds.), *Exploring signature pedagogies: Approaches to teaching disciplinary habits of mind.* Sterling, VA: Stylus.

Calder, L., & Carlson, S. (2002). *Using "Think Alouds" to evaluate deep understanding.* Retrieved from http://www.uwlax.edu/sotl/tutorial/designingaresearchplan.htm#sample

Chick, N. L. (2009, October). *In search of the humanities in (IS)SOTL: A panel of the ISSOTL interest group for the humanities.* Panel Presentation at the Conference of the International Society for the Scholarship of Teaching and Learning, Bloomington, Indiana.

Chick, N. L. (2011). Difference, power, and privilege in the scholarship of teaching and learning: The value of humanities SoTL. In K. McKinney (Ed.), *Ebs, Flows, and Ripps: The Scholarship of Teaching and Learning in and Across the Disciplines.* Bloomington: Indiana University Press.

Donald, J. G. (2002). *Learning to think: Disciplinary perspectives.* San Francisco, CA: Jossey-Bass.

Goodburn, A., & Savory, P. (2009). Integrating SoTL into instructional and institutional processes. *MountainRise, the International Journal of the Scholarship of Teaching and Learning, 5*, 1–14.

Graff, G. (2006). Toward a new consensus: The PhD in English. In C. M. Golde, G. E. Walker, & Associates (Eds.), *Envisioning the future of doctoral education: Preparing stewards of the discipline. Carnegie essays on the doctorate* (pp. 370–389). San Francisco, CA: Jossey-Bass.

Green, E. (2010, March 7). Can good teaching be learned? *New York Times Magazine*, March 7.

Gurung, R. A. R., Ansburg, P. I., Alexander, P. A., Lawrence, N. K., & Johnson, D. E. (2008). The state of scholarship of teaching and learning in psychology. *Teaching of Psychology, 35*, 249–261.

Gurung, R. A. R., Chick, N., & Haynie, A. (Eds.). (2008). *Exploring signature pedagogies: Approaches to teaching disciplinary habits of mind.* Sterling, VA: Stylus.

Gurung, R. A. R., & Schwartz, B. M. (2010). Riding the third wave of SoTL. *International Journal for the Scholarship of Teaching and Learning, 4*(2), 1–6.

Huber, M. T., & Hutchings, P. (2005). *The advancement of learning: Building the teaching commons.* San Francisco, CA: Jossey-Bass.

Hutchings, P., Huber, M. T., & Ciccone, A. (2011). Getting there: An integrative vision of the scholarship of teaching and learning. *International Journal for the Scholarship of Teaching and Learning, 5*(1). Retrieved from http://academics.georgiasouthern.edu/ijsotl

Klebesadel, H., & Kornetsky, L. (2008). Critique as signature pedagogy in the arts. In R. A. R. Gurung, N. Chick, & A. Haynie (Eds.), *Exploring signature pedagogies: Approaches to teaching disciplinary habits of mind* (pp. 121–138). Sterling, VA: Stylus.

Liddell, J. (2008). On increasing representation of people of color in SoTL. *The International Commons, 3*(1), 8.

McKinney, K. (2008). On increasing representation of people of color in SoTL: A response. *The International Commons, 3*(2), 4–5.

McKinney, K., & Chick, N. (2010). SoTL as women's work: What do existing data tell us? *International Journal for the Scholarship of Teaching and Learning, 4*(2), 1–14.

Meyer, J. H. F., & Land, R. (2005). Threshold concepts and troublesome knowledge (2): Epistemological considerations and a conceptual framework for teaching and learning. *Higher Education, 49*(3), 373–388.

Miller, S., Hubble, M., & Duncan, B. (2007). Supershrinks. *Psychotherapy Network, 31*(6), 26–35, 56.

Pace, D., & Middendorf, J. (2004). *Decoding the disciplines: Helping students learn disciplinary ways of thinking.* San Francisco, CA: Jossey-Bass.

Shulman, L. S. (1987). Knowledge and teaching: Foundations of the new reform. *Harvard Educational Review, 57*, 1–22.

Shulman, L. S. (1995). The pedagogical colloquium: Three models. *AAHE Bulletin, 47*(9), 609.

Shulman, L. S. (2005, Summer) Signature pedagogies in the professions. *Daedalus, 134*, 52–59.

Shulman, L. S. (2008). Back cover of R. A. R. Gurung, N. Chick, & A. Haynie (Eds.), *Exploring signature pedagogies: Approaches to teaching disciplinary habits of mind.* Sterling, VA: Stylus.

Shulman, L. S. (2011). The scholarship of teaching and learning: A personal account and reflection. *International Journal for the Scholarship of Teaching and Learning,* 5(1). Retrieved from http://academics.georgiasouthern.edu/ijsotl

van Someren, M. W., Barnard, Y. F., & Sandberg, J. A. C. (1994). *The think-aloud method: A practical guide to modelling cognitive processes.* London, UK: Academic Press.

Weimer, M. (2006). *Enhancing scholarly work on teaching and learning: Professional literature that makes a difference.* San Francisco, CA: Jossey-Bass.

PART ONE

HUMANITIES AND FINE ARTS

2

THE SOCRATIC METHOD

Teaching and Writing About Philosophy's Signature Pedagogy[1]

Stephen Bloch-Schulman

People often point to Socrates' dialogues as the quintessential method of philosophical thinking and teaching.

—Nahmias, 2005

From its very beginning and throughout almost all of its history, philosophers have given incredible attention to the question of how and why to teach philosophy. To show the importance of these issues, one need look no farther than Plato's work—work that is central to just about all of Western Philosophy—which is almost all either explicitly or implicitly about how one learns and how one teaches philosophy. The protagonist in almost all of Plato's writing and his philosophical hero, Socrates, was condemned to death largely because he was accused of corrupting the youth by teaching them things that were considered harmful. In fact, the question of how and what to teach is likely contemporaneous with philosophy itself.[2] The warning of the danger of teaching philosophy is equally old and well known. It would, therefore, seem an easy case to make that philosophy has a long and glorious history of doing the scholarship of teaching and learning (SoTL).

Despite philosophy's age-old concern with pedagogy, describing the past and current state of SoTL in philosophy, if there is such a thing, is actually a particularly vexed task. Asking whether there is a *scholarship* of teaching and learning in philosophy seems strange, given the prominent role pedagogical questions have played in the history of philosophy; even so, answering such a question is, in fact, quite difficult.

Is There a *Scholarship* of Teaching and Learning in Philosophy?

To explain why this is such a difficult question to answer, a bit of a background is needed. In his work, *The Philosophy of Philosophy*, Williamson (2007) asks, as a way to come to understand philosophy's methods, "What can be pursued in an armchair?" (p. 1). He frames his inquiry with this question because the methods traditionally used in philosophy "consist of thinking, without any special interaction with the world beyond the chair, such as measurement, observation, or experiment would typically involve" (p. 1). He also offers this clarification: Because philosophers think in conversation with other philosophers, this armchair-work is likely done not in one armchair but in many. Finally, he explains why it is in the armchair that philosophers work: "For good or for ill, few philosophers show much appetite for the risky business of making predictions and testing them against observation, whether or not their theories in fact have consequences that could be so tested" (p. 1). What does this penchant for the armchair mean for how philosophers talk, write, and think about teaching and learning philosophy?

The answer can be found, in part, in a book review by Michael Goldman, the then editor of *Teaching Philosophy* (Goldman, 2005). In the review, he describes philosophy pedagogy as rather primitive, noting, in particular, that in this work, little is said about what constitutes improved learning or how one measures it, and when techniques are purported to work, we are rarely told why they work. He goes on to suggest:

> It would be unreasonable to ask for much more. As philosophers we are not, and cannot be, experts in educational theory or the related disciplines that help provide the psychological underpinning for such theory. . . . What we *can* do, however, is create clear and measurable (or at least observable) criteria for success . . . and familiarize ourselves with existing literature on assessment, cognitive development, and cognitive domains. . . . [T]here is little evidence that *anyone* working in the scholarship of philosophical pedagogy has done this" (emphasis in the original). (p. 278)

As I will show, what was true of philosophy pedagogy when Goldman wrote this critique remains true today. There is still little evidence that philosophers have clear criteria for success or familiarity with cognitive development or other fields that might illuminate the way learning occurs, and, therefore, little evidence that philosophers can or are in a position to have measurable criteria for success for their pedagogical innovations. Furthermore, as Williamson notes, even if philosophers did, they would be unlikely to do the "risky" work of observing, predicting, and testing.

It is thus because of the methods that they choose that philosophers do not, and are not in a good position to, "create clear and measurable (or at least observable) criteria for success," and without that, the scholarship of teaching and learning in philosophy, if one would say that there is one, takes on a bit of a strange tenor. In addition, one might reasonably suspect that there is actual observation (if not testing) going on. It is hard to think that these philosophers do not pay attention at all to their students and how their students perform in their courses, what questions they ask, and how they respond to what it taught. Yet whatever evidence there might be is either not presented at all or presented through anecdotes, as if these offered self-evident justification in need of no further exploration.[3] What, then, *is* going on in the philosophy pedagogy literature?

To get a fair picture of what philosophers are doing, it might make sense to look at one very common way of proceeding for those who write about philosophy pedagogy: They explain a complex philosophical argument in a way that the author is convinced makes it easier to understand, more accessible, more direct, and thus would be more likely to be used in the classroom and more accessible for students (see, for examples, Brod, 2007; Hardwig, 2007; Passell, 2000). The unstated goal is to render clear for the reader of the article, presumably an instructor of philosophy, an argument that is intended to inform how she or he teaches that same argument. The unstated assumption is that one becomes a better teacher (primarily or to a large extent) by being able to make arguments for students in clear and precise language, such that they can see the relevance, assumptions, and implications of the argument; thus, articles about philosophy pedagogy tend to offer arguments that can be so passed on. That is, the argument as made by the author is intended to be repeated by the reader for his or her students. Because there is little evidence of what *students* find easy or hard to comprehend, embedded in this method is the assumption that what is clearer to the author will be clearer to the reader/philosopher and will also be clearer to her or his students, although what makes an argument clearer is never described.

Thus, it is not that these philosophers say nothing at all about criteria, but that they say little about their students and their students' learning. They also rarely use other scholarship that could connect their work to student learning. Thus, when it comes time for the philosophers to produce careful and convincing evidence that their innovation or ideas work *for actual students*, they have said little (or nothing at all).[4] In addition, the articles contain an almost total lack of discussion of the concrete circumstances and contexts in which their authors work, and thus, in which the pedagogical innovations have been used (this is noted, as well, in Goldman [2005]). The reader almost never knows how large the classes are, how well prepared the students are, what the purpose of the courses are, or how they fit into the program of study. There remain serious questions about the assumptions these authors make about the transferability of their work. I think the best way to describe these articles, in this regard, is as "transfer unfriendly"; that is, the authors do not take care to provide readers any clear or obvious way to link the suggestions to their own teaching context.

The same problem thus exists in philosophy that Bass and Linkon (2008) have identified in literary analysis in their examination of the journal *Pedagogy*. As they explain, as opposed to "articles in other venues for the scholarship of teaching and learning, where there is greater focus on student work as evidence of learning," in *Pedagogy*, the "focus of analysis" is "the teacher's practice, its intentions and process" (p. 249). Without knowing it, the real focus of the articles in *Teaching Philosophy* can thus be summed up where Biondi (2008), referring to insights of Heather Reid, writes that "it is Reid who suggests that we should pay additional attention not only to what Socrates does, but also what *instructors* do" (emphasis in the original, p. 122; see Reid, 1998). The impression, therefore, intended or not, is that philosophers offer a "what works" (see Hutchings, 2000), but that this "what works" remains entirely cut off from the learning of actual students, and because there are very few citations in these articles, it is cut off from the work of other scholars (who might do the dirty empirical work philosophers tend to shy away from).[5] To put it another way: It is as if philosophers are concerned not with what *actually* works but with what *ought to* work, and the *ought* here is built primarily on theoretical rather than empirical evidence. Together, without citation of appropriate sources that could ground the work in the empirical and go beyond the anecdotal, what appears in these articles might, in fact, be an expanded analogue to "pedagogical narcissism" (Chick, 2009, p. 42). We see a certain form of self-regard that ignores other scholars and assumes others will find clear what the author finds clear and ignores actual students and their learning. Together, I think this can best be described as a scholarly myopia. If these articles are scholarship, they appear to be solely a scholarship of teaching, *not* the scholarship of teaching and learning.

Finally, let me make one other observation: Philosophers have turned to Socrates and his method of teaching for thousands of years, and yet, quite famously, in almost all of the Platonic texts in which Socrates appears, he fails as a teacher. As Scott (2000) notes: "Despite his ceaseless efforts to purge his fellow citizens of their unfounded opinions and bring them to care for what he believes are the most important things, Plato's Socrates rarely seems to succeed. . . . More often than not, his target interlocutors leave their conversation with the philosopher wholly unchanged by the experience" (p. 1). It is hard to miss the irony here. I cannot help but wonder if there is a relationship among the pedagogical hero of philosophers, his own evident failures as a teacher, and how the work about him and his teaching method is taken up and written about by philosophers.

The Socratic Method: At What Price?

There are different conceptions of what the Socratic Method is, and here I will focus on descriptions as they have appeared between 2000 and 2010 in *Teaching Philosophy*.[6] I turn to *Teaching Philosophy* because it is by far the most prominent venue for philosophy pedagogy. Although this type of work might appear occasionally in other places (e.g., *Arts and Humanities in Higher Education*) and there are journals that have as a larger part of their mission publishing work in philosophy (e.g., *The Journal of Ethics Across the Curriculum* and the British journal *Discourse: Learning and Teaching in Philosophical and Religious Studies*), there are only a few sources devoted solely to publishing work about the teaching of philosophy. There are the newsletters of the American Association of Philosophy Teachers and the American Philosophical Association Committee on the Teaching of Philosophy, and there is *Teaching Philosophy*. This journal, which was started in 1975, is widely and rightly regarded as the best of all of these outlets.[7] Seventeen articles have appeared in the decade of the 2000's in *Teaching Philosophy* focused on Socrates and his Method, and from these, one can glean a clear picture of how philosophers think about their teaching.[8] It is, therefore, to those articles, in particular, that I turn in this investigation, although I will use other work to analyze what is found therein.

Before describing the Method they do highlight, it is helpful to note, first, that there is a consistent distancing by philosophers from the conception of the *Socratic Method* as these philosophers understand the term—and the pedagogy that goes by the term—used in law schools. In the conception of the Socratic Method practiced in law schools, faculty "aggressively question . . . randomly called-on students," as exemplified in the *Paper Chase* (Biondi, 2008, p. 119), with the goal of preparing students for the highly charged atmosphere that "legal encounters entail" (Shulman, 2005, p. 55).

Philosophers' conceptions of the Socratic Method are many and various; they can be seen on a spectrum from a minimalist conception that takes only the most basic elements from Socrates to others that emulate his teaching much more precisely. The most common conception of the Socratic Method, what Biondi calls the "traditional Socratic pedagogical model," which is generally agreed upon in something like a similar form, is described by Biondi (2008) in this way: "I believed that it was important to educate students by asking questions and engaging in open dialogue, thereby allowing them to think for themselves. I took this, along with the method of *elenchus*, to be the essence of the Socratic method" (p. 120). Here, *elenchus* is understood to be a form of "refutation and cross-examination" (Boghossian, 2002, p. 348) where, "a thesis is debated by question and answer for the purpose of finding the truth" (p. 347).[9] Whereas some philosophers identify (or focus on) the Socratic Method as only referring to a form of open dialogue, most define it and focus on the fuller, twofold meaning Biondi describes: open dialogue and the hypothesis/refutation/cross-examination of *elenchus*. So conceived, the Socratic Method focuses on one's desire not to contradict oneself and thus allows the teacher to compel the student to examine her or his internal incoherences.

There are, in addition, some philosophers that hew closer to the Socrates they see in the dialogues, thus refining the method of *elenchus*. This more rigorous view includes all that Biondi describes as the "traditional" model and more; these are rarer, but still in evidence in the literature. Boghossian

(2002), for example, advocates for a more specific and formal form of *elenchus*, which begins in wonder and moves through the formation of a thesis from the follower, leading to the formation of counter-theses that the leader argues from and that are formulated in such a way that they gain assent from the follower, and finally arriving at the use of these counter-theses and their entailments to refute the original thesis (p. 348). Another example of a more rigorous view is held by Passell (2000), who focuses on the task of defining terms as key to *elenchus* and thus conceives of *elenchus* as starting from and centering on this task.

An unstated assumption about the central goal of the Socratic Method seems to run through the descriptions of the Method in these articles. As Williamson (2007) explains: "David Lewis once wrote that 'what we accomplish in philosophical argument' is to 'measure the price' of maintaining a philosophical claim" (p. 8). From what I see in these articles, the Socratic Method is taken to be an exceptionally powerful tool in doing just that, because it focuses students on the price of their views and forces students to look at their long-held views and critique them in the name of coherence.[10] In this way, the Socratic Method helps students learn core philosophical skills, teaching them fundamental ways to "think like" a philosopher (Shulman, 2005, p. 55).

However, holding on to a Socratic vision of teaching tends to encourage teachers to see themselves as the hero of the drama and envisions students as the dupes. Plato, whose writings have almost entirely defined how we think of Socrates, was Socrates' student and portrays his mentor in almost all of his own work as the hero. This hero worship is so profound that Plato puts in Socrates' mouth what must have been to the Greeks who heard it a blasphemous analogy: Socrates compares himself favorably to Achilles (Plato, *Apology*, 28b3–28d5, in Plato, 2002, 32–33). In addition, Plato rarely spares much in making Socrates' interlocutors look like fools, idiots, sycophants, and impostors; as noted before, almost none of Socrates' interlocutors is shown to have learned from the conversation. In addition, my students regularly get mad at Socrates' interlocutors, seeing how silly they look in the conversation. My point here is that, to the extent that we have Socrates in mind when we think of ourselves as teachers, we are likely to bring along—maybe not consciously, maybe quite intentionally—the view that we are the heroes of the classroom and students are the bystanders of the real activity. At times, this can be seen in what philosophers write about their use of the Socratic

Method. For a telling example, Passell (2000) describes the challenge of getting students to understand in the following way: "Notice that even when the means for interpretation are provided, the student may fail. Think of Euthyphro who after an hour's inquiry into the nature of piety seems unaware that he doesn't get it!" (p. 316). Although I do not know his students, I am quite sure that many of my students would be rightly insulted were I to compare them to Euthyphro.

Furthermore, thinking of our teaching in these traditional Socratic terms can hide better uses of the Socratic Method. For example, it often hides the multiplicity of roles that students can and should play in the classroom. First, thinking within the traditional model, the faculty member ignores (or is likely to undervalue) the role that students can play for each other. Rather than exploring student–student *elenchus*, there is barely a mention of what role students play in their peers' learning in any of these articles—no surprise, given the model used. Second, the Socratic Method, as described here, often (although not always) ignores the possibility that students will come to play this Socratic/critical role for themselves. Although self-examination is often mentioned as a goal of the Socratic Method, what is needed is not merely to be put in a position to answer questions, but to be taught and get practice in how to formulate philosophically rich questions and, in particular, practice asking the difficult questions of oneself (Arendt, 2003). I recognize that doing this is quite difficult, but it is something that we can scaffold and teach. By learning how to ask questions of other students and of themselves, students would not be learning merely to follow someone else's lead, but to lead others and to lead themselves in critical analysis—to act like philosophers.

Conclusion

I am not suggesting here that these articles about philosophical teaching are not helpful, well considered, and informative. Many are. I will and have used them in thinking about my own classes. What I am suggesting, though, is that even the best of them remain less helpful, less well-considered, less informative than they might be by following scholarly practices, for example, by citing other relevant work on the topic and by offering concrete details of where the ideas were used and why we should believe that they worked so we can determine if they will work in our own context.

In part, I take the problem to be methodological: If one does not observe, measure, predict, or test, or cite work that does, there are few options for including student experience and student learning in philosophy pedagogy. One option is to turn to experimentation and observation, as the newly emerging "Experimental" strain of philosophy does. But it is unlikely that most philosophers will do this, and this type of philosophy is often dismissed by those who question its philosophical *bono fides*. Another option, and one that would not require most philosophers to abandon their core methodologies is possible, although at the moment it is entirely underutilized: Given that philosophers work in conversation with others, their interlocutors and collaborators could be students, and research in philosophy pedagogy could take into account student learning through these collaborations. Although possible and done in other fields, this remains quite rare in philosophy, and there is no evidence that philosophers have done that in these articles.[11]

I am also not suggesting that the use of the Socratic Method be abandoned. But, rather, I write to highlight the price we pay when we use the Socratic Method uncritically, so that we might be in a better position to counteract problems and weaknesses when they arise.

Notes

1. I would like to thank David Concepcion for his helpful suggestions.

2. Thales, who is often considered the first philosopher, was quite concerned with teaching, specifically, with teaching others the value of philosophy.

3. For more on the problem of anecdote as evidence, see Salvatori (2002).

4. A completely nonscientific set of numbers I uncovered is incredibly suggestive: The word *student(s)* is used but 16 times in Hardwig (2007), which runs 9 pages, 14 times in the 9 pages of Brod (2007), and the words *student(s)* and *learn* do not appear anywhere in Hankamer (2006), although *teach* does appear once. This is generally the case, however, it is not true across the board. There were articles with 65 uses of the word *student(s)* (Shah, 2008) and 97 such uses (Mullis, 2009). But it seems telling to me that any articles can be included in *Teaching Philosophy* that do not ever use the word *student(s)*.

5. Many of the articles fail to even cite relevant sources in the same journal. Though I find their standards in need of some adjustment within the context of the discipline of philosophy, Salvatori and Donahue's (2010) point about the role of citation in scholarly work is an excellent and apt one here.

6. My experience in reading philosophy pedagogy tells me that these articles are quite typical and thus can stand in nicely for the general state of the field today.

There are some exceptions to be found, but they are quite rare and do not speak to the state of where the field currently is, although they might speak well to where it might and ought to be heading.

7. As Nik Jewell describes it, writing for The Higher Education Academy Subject Center for Philosophical and Religious Studies, given the paucity of other venues for this type of work, *Teaching Philosophy* "constitutes the main resource for establishing the teaching of philosophy as a research discipline in its own right" (Jewell, 2010).

8. In this chapter, I will be focusing exclusively on the Socratic Method and Socrates as used in the contemporary discussion of teaching and learning, leaving aside many other thorny historical and philosophic questions, such as: To what extent does the Socrates portrayed in Plato's dialogues accurately represent the historical Socrates? Have the philosophers who are writing about the Socratic Method accurately represented the Socrates of Plato's dialogues? Is there really a Socratic Method at all?

9. Although Boghossian defines *elenchus* more narrowly as the testing of the hypothesis through "refutation and cross-examination," most others see it more broadly as the hypothesis as well as the testing of the hypothesis (Boghossian, 2002, p. 348).

10. On the role and importance of teaching for coherence, see Concepcion and Eflin (2009). There are, however, problems with many forms of coherence as an appropriate pedagogical goal, although there is not space here to delve into these issues.

11. Although very rare, there is philosophy pedagogy research elsewhere that is done through faculty and student collaboration; see, for example, Manor et al. (2010), Decyk et al. (2010) and Schulman et al. (2008).

References

Arendt, H. (2003). *Responsibility and judgment*, edited and with an introduction by Jerome Kohn. New York, NY: Schocken.

Bass, R., & Linkon, S. (2008). On the evidence of theory: Close reading as a disciplinary model for writing about teaching and learning. *Arts and Humanities in Higher Education*, *7*(3), 245–261.

Biondi, C. (2008). Socratic teaching: Beyond *The Paper Chase*. *Teaching Philosophy*, *31*(2), 119–140.

Boghossian, P. (2002). The Socratic Method (or, having a right to get stoned). *Teaching Philosophy*, *25*(4), 345–359.

Brod, H. (2007). Euthyprho, Foucault, and baseball: Teaching the *Euthyphro*. *Teaching Philosophy*, *30*(3), 249–258.

Chick, N. L. (2009). Unpacking a signature pedagogy in literary studies. In R. A. R. Gurung, N. L. Chick, & A. Haynie (Eds.), *Exploring signature pedagogies: Approaches to teaching disciplinary habits of mind* (pp. 36–55). Sterling, VA: Stylus.

Concepcion, D., & Eflin, J. (2009). Enabling change: Transformative and trangressive learning in feminist ethics and epistemology. *Teaching Philosophy, 32*(2), 177–198.

Decyk, B., Murphy, M., Currier, D. G., & Long, D. T. (2010). Challenges and caveats. In C. Werder & M. Otis (Eds.), *Engaging student voices in the study of teaching and learning* (pp. 49–65). Sterling, VA: Stylus.

Goldman, M. (2005). Book review of *Teaching philosophy: Theoretical reflections and practical suggestions*, edited by Tziporah Kasachkoff. *Teaching Philosophy, 28*(3), 277–279.

Hankamer, E. (2006). Re: Is the unexamined life not worth living? *Teaching Philosophy, 29*(1), 37–39.

Hardwig, J. (2007). Socrates' conception of piety: Teaching the *Euthyphro. Teaching Philosophy, 30*(3), 259–268.

Hutchings, P. (2000). Introduction. In *Opening lines: Approaches to the scholarship of teaching and learning* (pp. 1–10). Menlo Park, CA: The Carnegie Foundation for the Advancement of Teaching.

Jewell, N. (2010). The Journal *Teaching Philosophy.* For The Higher Education Academy Subject Center for Philosophical and Religious Studies. Retrieved March 5, 2011, from http://www.prs.heacademy.ac.uk/philosophy

Manor, C., Bloch-Schulman, S., Flannery, K., & Felten, P. (2010). Foundations of student-faculty partnerships in the scholarship of teaching and learning. In C. Werder & M. Otis (Eds.), *Engaging student voices in the study of teaching and learning* (pp. 3–15). Sterling, VA: Stylus.

Mullis, E. (2009). On being a Socratic philosophy instructor. *Teaching Philosophy, 32*(4), 345–359.

Nahmias, E. (2005). Practical suggestions for teaching small philosophy classes. *Teaching Philosophy, 28*(1), 59–65.

Passell, D. (2000). Plato's "Introduction to Philosophy." *Teaching Philosophy, 23*(4), 315–328.

Plato (2002). *Five dialogues*, translated by G. M. A. Grube, revised by John M. Cooper (2nd ed.). Indianapolis, IN: Hackett.

Reid, H. (1998). *The Educational Value of Plato's Early Socratic Dialogues.* Twentieth World Congress of Philosophy, Boston, MA. Retrieved August 20, 2011, from www.bu.edu/wcp/Papers/Teac/TeacReid.htm

Reid, H. (2003). Book review of *Plato's Socrates as educator*, by Gary Alan Scott. *Teaching Philosophy, 26*(2), 188–192.

Salvatori, M. (2002). The scholarship of teaching: Beyond the anecdotal. *Pedagogy, 2*(3), 297–310.

Salvatori, M., & Donahue, P. (2010). Citation difficulties. *International Journal for the Scholarship of Teaching and Learning, 4*(1), 1–5.

Schulman, S., McGarry, C., Duggins, K., Bright, C., & Flannery, K. (2008). Student/Faculty partnerships in course re-design: Learning about who students are to transform them. *Bridges: An Interdisciplinary Journal of Theology, Philosophy, History and Science, 15*(2), 181–204.

Scott, G. A. (2000). *Plato's Socrates as educator*. New York, NY: SUNY.

Shah, M. (2008). The Socratic teaching method: A therapeutic approach to learning. *Teaching Philosophy, 31*(3), 267–275.

Shulman, L. (2005). Signature pedagogies in the professions. *Daedalus, 134*(3), 52–55.

Williamson, T. (2007). *The philosophy of philosophy*. Oxford, UK: Blackwell.

3

TRADITIONS AND TRANSFORMATIONS

Signature Pedagogies in the Language Curriculum

Jennifer Ham and Jeanne Schueller

> Learning to speak another's language means taking one's place in the human community. It means reaching out to others across cultural and linguistic boundaries. Language is far more than a system to be explained. It is our most important link to the world around us. Language is culture in motion. It is people interacting with people.
>
> —Savignon, 1983

Significant misunderstandings often exist on college campuses about the nature of the work of language programs. Although long seen in the United States as mere "service departments," responsible solely for providing students and presumably more essential disciplines with secondary language skills, language curricula today actually share a much broader mission, one progressing from educating students in beginning language study toward literary and cultural proficiency, and ultimately global citizenship. Because many of the learning goals in upper-level courses in the discipline align with those in other disciplines, for example, close reading of literary texts, critical thinking and knowledge of history, politics, and cultural diversity, this chapter will focus explicitly on the teaching of second languages. Beginning with an illustration of once robust approaches to language teaching, we investigate some of the guiding principles and practices of the current signature pedagogy, map some of the transformative shifts in the pedagogical landscape, and explore some contemporary issues in the profession and their relationship to the scholarship of teaching and learning (SoTL).

Traditional Approaches

The teaching of second and foreign languages has a rich history spanning over a century that includes myriad pedagogical approaches, methods, and techniques. Although hard to imagine, especially for language professionals, the teacher-centered model of a single talking teacher and listening students favored in Greek and Roman times continued to dominate language instruction throughout the 18th and 19th centuries, when the study of modern languages was first introduced to the academic curriculum in Europe, until around the 1950s. Heavily influenced by methods derived earlier for ancient languages, most notably for Latin, instruction in modern languages also involved mostly silent students memorizing dehydrated linguistic forms, studying grammatical rules and completing written translations of canonical texts taken mostly from the fields of literature and philosophy. From the start, language instruction was characterized largely by teacher talk, an emphasis on "high culture," and this "grammar translation" approach to language acquisition.

On the heels of World War II, the aim of language learning shifted away from a focus on translating these well-worn academic texts to equipping students as well as soldiers, tourists, and professionals with "survival" knowledge of spoken language useful in everyday contexts. Although this more democratic and utilitarian pedagogy provided a more balanced valuation of both the mouth (lingual) and the ear (audio), that is, of both active production as well as receptive consumption, much of the surface pedagogy was still imitative, concentrating on memorization of scripted dialogs, and modeled on the behaviorist theory from psychology that language learning was primarily a matter of habit formation. In many ways, contemporary approaches to language instruction are, for better or worse, still responding to this inherent tension between these traditional default pedagogies of grammar translation and audiolingualism (Ciccone, 2009, p. xi), on the one hand, and the need for pedagogical innovation and transformation, on the other.

Language pedagogy in the 20th and 21st centuries has indeed seen significant change, due in part to language teachers' seemingly endless "quest for better methods" (Richards & Rodgers, 2001, p. 1).[1] Likewise, Omaggio Hadley (2001) finds more controversy than consensus over the decades as the profession, driven by the "method concept," continues searching for "the best way—'the one true way' (Strasheim, 1976)—to teach a foreign language . . . an ideal method which, once discovered, will unlock the door to language proficiency for all learners and will make the learning process swift and effortless" (p. 86).

For many years, pedagogical instinct drove foreign language teaching. Prior to the 1960s, when classroom research was first used to inform postsecondary language teaching, "language teachers were enjoying a period of unprecedented confidence" in their audiolingual method (Allwright, 1983, p. 194). Audiolingualism was considered successful both in practice and in theory (Allwright, 1983, p. 195). Perceived success was determined not by a student's ability to produce original and meaningful communication in the target language, but rather whether he or she developed "correct habits," was able to "mimic" models, and could "answer automatically without stopping to think" (Larsen-Freeman, 2000, p. 43). Classroom-based research in the 1960s and 1970s challenged this proclamation and found that audiolingualism was, in fact, not "superior to its competitors" (Allwright, 1983, p. 195) and also questioned the efficacy of using such forms of pseudo-communication in the classroom (Krashen & Terrell, 1983).

Toward a Signature Pedagogy

Since the early 1980s, first- and second-year language curricula have moved away from a focus on discrete linguistic components within sentence-level contexts, to the goal of developing communicative competence—that is, "knowing when and how to say what to whom" (Larsen-Freeman, 2000, p. 121). This *communicative approach*, which might be better described as a grouping of underlying assumptions about the nature of language rather than a single narrowly defined method, has been serving broadly as the current signature pedagogy of the field for decades, especially in the United States. In practice, communicative language instructors typically integrate techniques culled from a range of methods, resulting in an eclectic signature teaching style. According to Horwitz (2008), "most language teachers find it impossible to adhere to a single teaching approach due to the variety of student needs that they encounter, and even teachers who claim to follow a particular language teaching method tend to modify it to better fit their teaching situations" (p. 59). Although a unified method might not exist, certain guiding principles and practices, or "habits of mind and heart," are certainly associated with effective language teaching in the communicative classroom.

At the core of the communicative approach is the belief that the purpose of learning another language is to communicate in relevant ways with native and nonnative speakers. With its emphasis on meaningful and personalized use of the target language, communicative language teaching marked a dramatic shift in the discipline, both in terms of pedagogy as well as what language experts value. Whereas the audiolingual method emphasized imitation and language as a system of structural elements and defined mastery primarily in terms of accuracy, the communicative approach underscores the interactive functions of language as vehicles for conveying meaning and accomplishing tasks and defines proficiency in terms of successful communication. Perhaps language educators are still attempting to address the problem of pragmatics World War II exposed and audiolingualism attempted to address, namely, how to get learners communicating, not just mimicking accurately, but actually using language to create and accomplish. Instead of classrooms dominated by repetition and memorization, where learners internalized written dialogues and formed new linguistic habits through textbook patterning and instructor-led substitution exercises, the communicative approach values a student-centered immersion classroom, where learners practice using the target language to communicate their own ideas, desires, and meanings in conversations. Communicative classrooms typically present students in groups or pairs with real-life situations that require them to cooperate and negotiate in the language to accomplish specific tasks, for example, to conduct a class survey, interview a native speaker, or pool their expertise in other areas to collectively solve a problem. This applied learning, where learners use authentic oral and written input intended for native speakers to perform in actual real-world contexts, not only takes students out of their passive roles but also serves to decentralize the role of the instructor and the textbook as the only sources of information about the target language and culture. Frequent group work maximizes class time by providing ample opportunities for cooperative learning and oral practice and makes learners more accountable to themselves and their peers.

In a world where demographic shifts are the norm, the border between native and nonnative is becoming not only less clearly drawn, but generally speaking, also less significant. Communicative language teaching references this reality by emphasizing fluency over accuracy and by regarding errors in communication as natural. Language acquisition research has overwhelmingly demonstrated a direct correlation between improved proficiency and both the amount of contact with the target language (Krashen, 1982) and the intensity of that encounter (Met & Rhodes, 1990). Both have been found to significantly impact students' rate of acquisition and have important implications for language curriculum design. Such research has resulted in classes being conducted exclusively in the target language. Although surveys have shown that the main reason students enroll in language classes is to learn to communicate in the target language (Arendt & Hallock, 1979), most are still unprepared for this near-immersion experience, where they are, in fact, learning another language through another language. Faced with such a challenge, students who fear being corrected or are simply uncomfortable speaking in front of their classmates often avoid speaking in whole-group activities. Thus, communicative language teachers need to draw on a range of implicit and explicit error feedback techniques depending on the context. Whereas explicit feedback is typically used for grammar- or accuracy-oriented activities, an instructor will use implicit correction to respond to miscommunications, that is, to errors that affect the student's ability to make themselves comprehensible. In such performative classrooms, special care must also be taken to lower the affective filter in class so that students' emotions, such as anxiety, do not interfere with their ability or motivation to learn.

Language teachers, particularly those employing the communicative approach, understand that language is central to our sense of self. They understand the pivotal role that interpersonal communication plays in identity formation and make pedagogical choices designed to produce deep, personal change, the kind of transformation characteristic of all successful signature pedagogies. Shulman (2005) describes "signature pedagogies" as *pedagogies of formation*, that is, as "pedagogies that can build identity and character, dispositions and values" (pp. 13–14). They "teach *habits of mind* . . . but . . . in a very deep sense they also teach *habits of the heart*, as well, because of the marriage of reason, interdependence and emotion" (Shulman, 2005, p. 14).[2] Although most students are unaware of it, they are engaging in a curriculum designed to produce the kind of deep transformation of "identity and character" and personal growth Shulman describes. As Guiora indicates, "second language learning in all of its aspects demands that the individual, to a certain extent, take on a new identity" (1972, p. 145). Language pedagogies are geared toward both cognitive and attitudinal change in students, who encounter new ways of thinking not just about communication and their place in the world but also about their unexamined values and roles as learners.

In part, in response to the rise of cultural studies and a heightened awareness of the role culture plays in identity formation, but also to the communicative method's focus on authentic contexts, most language programs have augmented traditional language instruction with a greater emphasis on culture. Although language students often develop ownership and affinities for the culture "their" language connects them to, they usually only start to identify deeply with the culture after they have had extended firsthand experience living immersed in the target language and culture, usually while studying abroad. Much like actors taking their cues from natives of that country, students abroad leave behind aspects of their own identities and appropriate new cultural behaviors and speech patterns, enacting, in effect what they believe "being" French, German, or Spanish means. As was the case in their classrooms back home, where native or near-native teachers and authentic materials were their primary cultural conduits, their locale abroad is a ludic, improvisational space, a theater where new identities are temporarily assumed and where constant linguistic and cultural bungling produce tragicomic effects. The moment they feel like imposters is also the moment they begin to develop a deeper understanding of the "foreign" and a profound sense of the perplexing interdependence and fluidity of their own identity.

By the time they graduate, these students will have become practiced in confronting uncertainty, learned to at least tolerate if not even enjoy their visibility, become adept in group communication dynamics, have developed mental discipline, gained a deep respect for otherness and a new sense of themselves. In addition to being able to converse intelligently, for example, in French, German, Italian, Japanese, or Spanish on a wider range of international issues, they will also, knowingly or not, have become thoroughly initiated into and accountable to these unique disciplinary expectations. Whereas they might have entered hoping to learn a few phrases in order to talk with their grandparents, they emerge as internationals able to speak (in either language) with confident authority and insight about a cultural reality far from their own. Taken seriously, mastering another language and becoming proficient in another culture is a process that not only fosters personal growth but also can transform individuals into global citizens, who are much better equipped to respond to the needs of the global society we now inhabit.

Current Issues in the Profession

Many national organizations play a vital role in supporting the language teaching profession, namely, the American Council on the Teaching of Foreign Languages (ACTFL) and language-specific teacher's organizations.[3] These organizations work toward bridging the gaps between foreign language education at the elementary, secondary, and tertiary levels and facilitating articulation and cooperation within and across courses, programs, and levels. One of ACTFL's major accomplishments in the 1990s was to develop national standards, which were initially intended to guide K–12 foreign language education in the United States but have slowly gained interest beyond K–12. The Standards present the "5 *Cs*" of foreign language education—communication, cultures, connections, comparisons, and communities—along with recommendations for their implementation. Although the ACTFL standards for foreign language learning "reflect the best instructional practice" they do not claim to "describe what is being attained by the majority of foreign language students" (ACTFL, p. 2). Furthermore, proficiency goals "will not be achieved overnight; rather, they provide a gauge against which to measure improvement in the years to come" (ACTFL, p. 2). A reminder that becoming proficient in a second language can be a slow process (at any level) is necessary more than ever in today's technologically advanced world. As early as 1994, before multitasking was commonly applied to human behavior, Critchfield likens Americans' unrealistic expectations for learning a foreign language to those of losing weight, namely, that the process will be "substantial, effortless, and immediate" (p. 14). Methods for learning a foreign language, she explains, typically claim to be "accelerated" and promote the learner's ability to "engage in other activities simultaneously, such as driving a car or washing the dishes, while effortlessly learning to speak in a foreign tongue" (pp. 14–15). Although Critchfield was most likely referring to nonclassroom instructional programs (i.e., books with audiocassette tapes or CDs), more high-tech methods available now (e.g., Rosetta Stone) still promise fun, easy, and fast results.

Partly as a consequence of such marketing, some students in university foreign language classes expect fluency after a few semesters of language study or even to sound like native speakers, a deeply ingrained yet unrealistic goal (and disciplinary "habit of mind") that is unachievable by most and questioned by applied linguists. As Cook (2010, section 2.0) points out, "Until recently it was simply taken for granted that the only reality in language was the native speaker, the only people that students would talk to would be native speakers and that in every aspect they should try to be native speakers: 'After all, the ultimate goal—perhaps unattainable for some—is, nonetheless, to "sound like a native speaker" in all aspects of the language.'" Kramsch (1993) suggests moving beyond the "linguistic development of a learner on an interlanguage continuum" that ends with the native speaker and daunts both students and nonnative teachers, to consider "language study as an initiation into a kind of social practice that is at the boundary of two or more cultures . . . a linguistic reality that is born from the L1 speech environment of the learners and the social environment of the L2 native speakers, but is a *third culture* [italics added] in its own right" (p. 9).

Other assumptions of language teaching remain thorny issues in the discipline. Most language departments provide a curriculum that is overall linear and cumulative, advancing students from basic functional knowledge of the language toward literacy and cultural proficiency. The curriculum for language learners is, however, not a seamless one. No sooner do students begin to master the rituals of the language classroom, than they are challenged and often surprised again in later courses by the shift in focus onto literature.[4] This "language-literature divide," a vestige traceable back to the humanistic gymnasia of 19th century Europe, although continually debated, is nonetheless a dichotomous and deep-seated disciplinary "habit of mind" that continues to persist in the discipline (Tucker, 2006). In 2007, a report by an ad hoc committee on foreign languages established by the Modern Language Association (MLA) called on language departments to do away with the simplistic two-track model that has led to a ubiquitous division in the field among so-called language and content courses—as if language classes were devoid of content and content courses did not engage students' language skills. The transformation envisioned in the MLA report claims to better enable language majors to produce "educated speakers who have deep translingual and transcultural competence" and to "attract students from other fields and students with interests beyond literary studies" (MLA, 2007). Questions pertaining to *what* should be covered in language classes and *how* languages should be taught and are best learned remain sources of much continued discussion and research among language professionals.

Transformations in the Pedagogical Landscape

The fields of language acquisition and language teaching methodology, in existence for more than a century, have already articulated many shifts in language theory and teaching practice. Indeed, as Shulman (2005) points out, even though signature pedagogies might "seem remarkably stable at any one point in time," they "are not eternal and unchanging," but rather shift over time in response to professional, historical, and economic changes "as conditions in the practice of the profession itself and in the institutions that provide professional service or care undergo larger societal change" (p. 5).

As foreign language education continues to evolve, so, too, must its signature pedagogies. In a recent essay, Schulz (2006) reevaluates the aim of postsecondary language requirement courses, examining, in particular, communicative competence. To go beyond "gaining survival competence" and communicative language proficiency, we need to prioritize new goals, such as "critical thinking; problem solving; acquiring knowledge of the world at large; developing cross-cultural awareness; developing cognition and metacognition about language and culture; and shaping attitudes essential for living in and contributing to a democratic society, particularly a society that plays the role of an economic, political, and military superpower with responsibilities not only within its own borders, but in the world at large" (p. 253). Although communicative approaches might achieve such outcomes, they exist largely as by-products and not as explicit goals of instruction (p. 253).

Similarly, Kramsch (2006) appeals to the profession to do away with a "tourist-like competence" (p. 251) that merely enables students to communicate with native speakers, calling instead for a greater appreciation for the importance of "form, genre, style, register, and a focus on social semiotics"

(p. 251). The "ecological approach" she and others advocate (e.g., Kern & Schultz, 2005; Walther, 2007) signals a fundamental and necessary change in foreign language education, for as Kramsch (2006) notes:

> Language learners are not just communicators and problem solvers, but whole persons with hearts, bodies, and minds, with memories, fantasies, loyalties, identities. Symbolic forms are not just items of vocabulary or communication strategies, but embodied experiences, emotional resonances, and moral imaginings. We could call the competence that collegiate students need nowadays a symbolic competence. Symbolic competence does not do away with the ability to express, interpret, and negotiate meanings in dialogue with others, but enriches it and embeds it into the ability to produce and exchange symbolic goods in the complex global context in which we live today. (p. 251)

Indeed, the future of communicative language teaching rests on its ability to adapt to the fluctuating "habits of heart and mind" of the field, to a "pedagogy that addresses students' subjectivity, not just the effectiveness of their information exchanges or their ability to satisfy the rules of grammar, play predetermined roles, or accomplish predesigned tasks" (Kramsch, 2009, p. 202). Kramsch (2009) suggests that this type of "pedagogy might not be characterized by any new kinds of tasks or activities, but it would be guided by special attention paid to crucial aspects of language learning as symbolic activity" (p. 202).

Research on Language Teaching and Learning

With its systematic inquiry into both instructional methods and learning, SoTL enables language practitioners with diverse backgrounds to explore, assess, and improve student learning in their own classes. Several interdisciplinary peer-reviewed journals, such as *MountainRise*, the *International Journal for the Scholarship of Teaching and Learning*, and the *Journal of the Scholarship of Teaching and Learning*, as well as national and international conferences are explicitly dedicated to advancing the field of SoTL. SoTL as a method of inquiry can be traced back to the early 1990s, when Boyer (1990) argued for broadening the scope of scholarship to include teaching and learning and Cross (1990) looked forward to the day when teachers would use their classrooms as laboratories to better understand student learning.

Research on classroom methods and their effect on learning foreign languages had actually begun decades earlier within two subdisciplines of applied linguistics, namely, foreign language pedagogy and second language acquisition (SLA), both of which provide important insights into the language learning process.[5] The study of foreign language pedagogy shares SoTL goals in seeking to improve language instruction through classroom-based research. SLA researchers, on the other hand, focus more specifically on hypotheses about how and why adult learners' proficiency in a target language differs from that of native speakers, but in general do not make pedagogical recommendations. In fact, Gass and Selinker (2001) point out that SLA research is "not about pedagogy unless the pedagogy affects the course of acquisition" (p. 2). Similarly, Cook (2008) notes that although "some SLA research is intended to be applied to teaching, most is either 'pure' study of second language acquisition for its own sake, or uses second language acquisition as a testing ground for linguistic theories" (p. 7). Applied linguists and language specialists have numerous professional organizations and outlets for presenting their work, and the discipline boasts a strong tradition of publishing research on language teaching and acquisition in numerous peer-reviewed journals[6] (two of the oldest, *PMLA* and *The Modern Language Journal,* first appeared in 1884 and 1916, respectively).

Research in applied linguistics already spans a continuum from experimental (interventionist) methods testing the relationship between independent and dependent variables to purely ethnographic (observational and noninterventionist) procedures, which is longitudinal and interpretive in nature (Nunan, 1992). The array of topics is too broad in scope to enumerate, but includes, for example, first language influence on second language acquisition, individual learner differences, language learning styles, bilingual and multilingual identity, testing and assessment, the efficacy of teaching methods, whether and how to teach grammar, technology-enhanced language learning and classroom discourse.

"Action" research, an important part of language research, involves practitioners initiating collaborative studies in order to investigate a classroom problem (Nunan, 1992). What is distinctive about classroom research projects as compared with many studies published in applied linguistics journals is their self-reflective nature, a core component of SoTL research. Like SoTL, language classroom research is recursive, leading to new questions and learning objectives, and providing educators, as Lui (2005) underscores, with opportunities to reflect on their pedagogy and evaluate its effectiveness.

Ciccone (2009) urges us to consider what the "pedagogical literature of the discipline suggest[s] are the optimal ways to teach material in that field—and verify that learning" (p. xvi). In reviewing the theoretical and empirical developments in research on language teaching and learning, we are confronted with conflicting and overwhelming outcomes. It seems that for every finding that supports a particular aspect of language instruction, another empirical study refutes it. With regard to attempts to define authenticity, Gilmore's (2007) position resonates with many instructors: "from the classroom teacher's perspective rather than chasing our tails in pointless debates we should focus instead on learning aims" (p. 98). As in the medical profession, where ongoing debates over the effects of consuming eggs, butter, coffee, or alcohol seek to perpetually improve health behaviors, controversies in language disciplines similarly continue to address all aspects of foreign language teaching and learning in a persistent quest for the "best" method. Signature pedagogies in the foreign language curriculum emerge from research findings, anecdotal evidence of what works, and instincts about the learning process. Although language teaching and learning are steeped in tradition, the discipline embraces its evolutionary nature and capacity to transform learners in profound ways.

Notes

1. According to Rodgers (2001), language teaching methodology can been seen as a threefold relationship among (a) theories of language and learning (in particular, theories of second language acquisition), (b) instructional design features, and (c) observed teaching practices.

2. Although Shulman uses the training of medical students to illustrate this concept, it also can be seen as characterizing aspects of the process of identity formation in second language learners.

3. For a list of links to professional language associations and ACTFL's business partners, funding agencies, and national, state, and regional language associations, see http://www.actfl.org/i4a/links/.

4. Ciccone (2009) commented on this shift in the introduction to *Exploring Signature Pedagogies: Approaches to Teaching Disciplinary Habits of Mind*: "If the beginning language class was a forced march through linguistic forms, the graduate seminar was more like a creative dance. Although both involved watching and listening to models, the former sought mastery through repetition whereas the latter encouraged understanding through elaboration" (p. xi).

5. SLA as a subdiscipline originated in the early 1980s; research on foreign language pedagogy, however, began decades earlier.

6. Some peer-reviewed periodicals include *Applied Language Learning, CALICO Journal, Canadian Modern Language Review, Computer Assisted Language Learning, Foreign Language Annals, International Review of Applied Linguistics, Journal of Applied Linguistics, Journal of Second Language Writing, Language Learning, Language Learning and Technology, Language Teaching Research, Linguistics and Education, The Modern Language Journal, PMLA, Reading in a Foreign Language, The Reading Matrix, Second Language Research, Studies in Second Language Acquisition, System: An International Journal of Educational Technology and Applied Linguistics, TESOL Quarterly,* and *Unterrichtspraxis/Teaching German.*

References

ACTFL Standards for foreign language learning: Executive summary. Retrieved August 17, 2010, from http://www.actfl.org/i4a/pages/index.cfm?pageid=3324

Allwright, D. (1983). Classroom-centered research on language teaching and learning: A brief historical overview. *TESOL Quarterly, 17*(2), 191–204.

Arendt, J. D., & Hallock, M. (1979). Windmills and dragons. In J. D. Arendt, D. L. Lange, & P. J. Myers (Eds.), *Foreign language learning, today and tomorrow: Essays in honor of Emma M. Birkmaier* (pp. 124–145). New York, NY: Pergamon Press.

Boyer, E. L. (1990). *Scholarship reconsidered: Priorities of the professoriate.* Princeton, NJ: The Carnegie Foundation for the Advancement of Teaching.

Ciccone, A. (2009). Foreword. In R. A. R. Gurung, N. L. Chick, & A. Haynie (Eds.), *Exploring signature pedagogies* (pp. xi–xvi). Sterling, VA: Stylus Publishing.

Cook, V. (2008). *Second language learning and language teaching* (4th ed.). London, UK: Hodder Arnold.

Cook, V. (2010). *Questioning traditional assumptions of language teaching.* Retrieved August 17, 2010, from http://homepage.ntlworld.com/vivian.c/Writings/Papers/TradAs sumptions.htm

Critchfield, A. L. (1994). A primer for teachers of German: Five lessons for the new millennium. *Die Unterrichtspraxis/Teaching German, 27*(1), 11–17.

Cross, K. P. (1990). Teachers as scholars. *AAHE Bulletin, 43*(4), 3–5.

Gass, S., & Selinker, L. (2001). *Second language acquisition: An introductory course* (2nd ed.). London, UK: Lawrence Erlbaum.

Gilmore, A. (2007). Authentic materials and authenticity in foreign language learning. *Language Teaching, 40*, 97–118.

Guiora, A. (1972). Construct validity and transpositional research: Toward an empirical study of psychoanalytic concepts. *Comprehensive Psychiatry, 13*, 139–150.

Horwitz, E. K. (2008). *Becoming a language teacher: A practical guide to second language learning and teaching.* Boston, MA: Allyn & Bacon.

Kern, R., & Schultz, J. M. (2005). Beyond orality: Investigating literacy and the literary in second and foreign language instruction. *The Modern Language Journal, 85*(3), 381–392.

Kramsch, C. (1993). *Context and culture in language teaching.* Oxford, UK: Oxford University Press.

Kramsch, C. (2006). From communicative competence to symbolic competence. *The Modern Language Journal, 90*(2), 249–252.

Kramsch, C. (2009). *The multilingual subject.* Oxford, UK: Oxford University Press.

Krashen, S. (1982). *Principles and practice in second language acquisition.* New York, NY: Pergamon.

Krashen, S. D., & Terrell, T. D. (1983). *The natural approach: Language acquisition in the classroom.* Hayward, CA: Alemany Press.

Larsen-Freeman, D. (2000). *Techniques and principles in language teaching.* Oxford, UK: Oxford University Press.

Lui, K. (2005, April). *The somethingness of learning plans: Self-directed learning.* Presented at OPID Spring Conference, Madison, WI.

Met, M., & Rhodes, N. (1990). Elementary school foreign language instruction: Priorities for the 1990s. *Foreign Language Annals, 23*(5), 433–443.

MLA. (2007). *Foreign languages and higher education: New structures for a changed world.* Retrieved August 27, 2010, from http://www.mla.org/flreport

Omaggio Hadley, A. (2001). *Teaching language in context* (3rd ed.). Boston, MA: Heinle & Heinle.

Nunan, D. (1992). *Research methods in language learning.* Cambridge, MA: Cambridge University Press.

Richards, J. C., & Rodgers, T. S. (2001). *Approaches and methods in language teaching* (2nd ed.). Cambridge, MA: Cambridge University Press.

Rodgers, T. S. (2001). *Language teaching methodology.* Center for Applied Linguistics Online Resources. Retrieved August 12, 2010, from http://www.cal.org/resources/digest/rodgers.html

Savignon, S. (1983). *Communicative competence: Theory and classroom practice.* Reading, MA: Addison Wesley.

Schulz, R. (2006). Reevaluating communicative competence as a major goal in postsecondary language requirement courses. *The Modern Language Journal, 90*(2), 252–255.

Shulman, L. (2005, February). *The signature pedagogies of the professions of law, medicine, engineering, and the clergy: Potential lessons for the education of teachers.* Math Science Partnerships Workshop, Irvine, CA. Retrieved August 15, 2010, from http://www.taylorprograms.com/images/Shulman_Signature_Pedagogies.pdf

Strasheim, L. (1976). What is a foreign language teacher today? *Canadian Modern Language Review, 33*, 39–48.

Tucker, H. (2006). Communicative collaboration: Language, literature, and communicative competence redefined. *The Modern Language Journal, 90*(2), 264–266.

Walther, I. (2007). Ecological perspectives on language and literacy: Implications for foreign language instruction at the collegiate level. *ADFL Bulletin, 38*(3)/*39*(1), 6–14.

4

COUNTERSIGNATURES IN COMMUNICATION PEDAGOGY

Dugald Williamson

Communication is a broad field that goes by various names, including *communication studies* and *media and communications*. Work in this field seeks to understand the multiple relations between communication and social and cultural life. It explores written and spoken communication, print, audio and visual media, and digital technologies, including the Internet and mobile communications. As technology changes, so do the roles that media play. As McQuail remarks (2010), "forms of communication infuse activities of leisure, work, conversation, and lifestyle" (p. 4). Mass media such as film, television, and the press provide important means of "cultural representation and expression," defining social realities and influencing modern formations of personal and cultural identity (p. 4) and significantly shaping the nature of political discourse. Media and communications also have important economic dimensions. (For instance, the film and television industries require structures of funding, production, and distribution, which in turn affect patterns of screen form and content.) As McQuail suggests, many topics arise in the communications field, which no "single set of methods" can handle (p. 5). Thus, communication is a multidisciplinary area of study, in which varying approaches—different media, culture, politics, economics, and others—interact. This chapter will outline theoretical developments in this field, highlighting values and ways of thinking that scholars share across these approaches. I then discuss common forms of pedagogy and offer a description of a signature pedagogy that provides students with opportunities to understand those values and ways of generating and applying knowledge within this field.

The present discussion refers to developments of communication studies in Western countries, such as Australia, Britain, Canada, New Zealand, and the United States, although there are certain similarities as well as necessary differences to recognize among these and numerous other national contexts (see Curran & Park, 2000). Historical developments of communication research and teaching vary considerably among, indeed within, those countries named. So, for instance, the longstanding tradition of speech education and rhetoric has been particularly influential in the United States; other approaches could be added to those mentioned here, including ethnographic studies of media practices and audiences.[1]

Multidisciplinary Developments and Scholarly Habits of Mind

Communication has expanded as a field, particularly since the 1960s. Accounts of its history generally emphasize two kinds of approaches: social science methodologies—coming from sociology and psychology, for instance—and humanities methodologies. These methodologies developed primarily in research projects at first but soon contributed to what McQuail (2002) calls a "first generation of post-war research and teaching" (p. 4). They cover questions ranging from how media systems and organizations operate to "detailed aspects of individual information sending and receiving" (p. 13). These approaches helped to establish "mass communication" theory, which initially related to the mass media of the press, cinema, radio, and television. Until relatively late in the 20th century, before the convergences of digital media, these forms were distinguished by their centralized and standardized industrial production and one-way transmission of content. Mass communication research has frequently used quantitative methods, such as surveys, social psychological experiments intended to measure psychological or behavioral effects of media, for instance, and statistical analysis. It also complemented political-economics studies of factors such as media ownership and concentration, national and international markets for media, and political support for, and regulation of, media and communications.

In recent decades, social science approaches have intersected increasingly with cultural theories, which incorporate traditions in the humanities, including linguistics, semiotics, rhetoric, feminism, philosophy, and literary and narrative theory. Cultural approaches are primarily qualitative, analyzing how media techniques of representation construct meaning. Often this inquiry has a critical edge, intended to reveal the ideological determinations of dominant meanings and definitions of identity supposedly embraced, unwittingly, at the surface level of media practice.

Added to this mix of theoretical approaches, the surrounding social practices of communication have affected the development of the academic field. These broader practices have been broadly distinguished as "normative," "operational," and "everyday" (McQuail, 2010, pp. 13–15). In normative practices, some work in communication studies analyzes conceptions of "how media ought to operate if certain social values are to be observed or attained" (p. 14). In democratic culture, these values relate to norms such as freedom of expression and social responsibility and are evident in communication policy, ethics, and public debate. Operational theory engages communication studies with the knowledge and methods that are relevant to working in professional or industrial contexts. Everyday, or "common-sense theory," enables people to make sense of the media as they read, watch, and use them in everyday life. Other writers have referred to these surrounding practices as "symbolic environments" (Dorland, 1996, p. xii) that shape understandings of "media, culture, communication and community" (Robinson, 2000). Scholars often combine forms of inquiry to examine these environments. So, for example, theoretical studies of the news might use qualitative methods of textual analysis to focus on how meaning is constructed by the use of techniques for selecting and arranging information and by conventions such as the narrative ordering of events. They might also connect this formal ordering of content with analysis of organizational factors, such as the impact of industrial routines on newsgathering and production. Or they might link textual analysis to professional habits, such as practitioners' application of news values, that is, criteria for deciding the newsworthiness of events.

From the multidisciplinary field sketched here, three dispositions of specialist work emerge, all of which are relevant to identifying a signature pedagogy. First is the theoretical commitment to developing analytical methods to explore how media and communication operate socially and mediate ideas of reality and identity. Second is an epistemological recognition that the scholarly production of knowledge depends on the use of particular concepts, ways of constructing arguments, and criteria for evaluating and arranging evidence. As McQuail (2010) observes, different theoretical approaches entail "different ways of defining . . . issues and problems" (p. 5). This point relates to what Corner (1995) has called a "knowledge problem": "what it is that academic inquiries seek to find out, and the kinds and quality of data and of explanatory relations which particular ideas and methods might be expected to produce" (p. 147). Responses to this problem are important in developing a signature pedagogy that equips students to negotiate disciplinary ideas. A third interest among experts is in building a common ground on which differences among approaches can play out constructively. This is the disposition to pursue greater understanding of communications and "the processes which construct us as subjects of a common culture" (Cunningham & Turner, 1997, p. 19). It reflects a pluralist ethic of respect for diverse approaches and the development of independent thinking through dialogue.

These three priorities find expression in professional organizations, as indicated in the film stream of the European Communication Research and Education Association:

> On a methodological level, we strive towards openness and multilevel approaches on the study of historical and contemporary cinema: film text, context, production, representation, and reception. Cultural studies perspectives, historical approaches, political economy, textual analysis, audience research all find their place within the section. We want to leave behind the institutional tensions between humanities and social sciences approaches. (European Communication Research and Education Association, n.d.)

Many scholarly publications share the desire stated here to transcend such intellectual dichotomies. For example, Curran and Morley (2006) argue for the need to bring together issues of political economy, including media control, with the cultural analysis of "issues of consumption, identity and taste" in a "catholic spirit" (p. 6). For many scholars, reflecting on teaching and learning as socially situated practices of communication is a priority, related to the dispositions outlined. The challenges of grasping theories, reflecting on knowledge production, and fostering a community of scholarship, all extend to communications pedagogy.

Pedagogical Literature on Media and Communications

Discussion of teaching and learning is part of what Sprague calls the "heritage" of the communication discipline (1993, p. 106). It is represented in journals such as, in the United States, *Communication Education*, sponsored by the National Communication Association (the journal and the association both originating in speech and rhetoric education), and *Journalism and Mass Communication Educator*, published on behalf of the Association for Education in Journalism and Mass Communication (Levine, 2009). The *Canadian Journal of Communication* has published reflections on teaching over time (e.g., Bruck, 1985; Straw, 1985). In Britain, the organization that began in the 1950s as the Society of Film Teachers produced journals (under different names but merging into *Screen*, now published by the John Logie Baird Centre at the University of Glasgow) that have included important work on media education as well as theory.

Some publications on communication pedagogy have connected explicitly with the scholarship of teaching and learning (SoTL) movement since the 1990s. Surveys of these publications include the study by McCroskey, Richmond, and McCroskey (2002) and an overview of literature on student participation in the college communication classroom by Rocca (2010). Soon after the publication of Boyer's influential work (1990) on the scholarship of teaching, Sprague (1993) argued for a "discipline-specific" pedagogy, in contrast to what she perceived as a growing reliance in communication education on "generic instructional models" of psychological and intellectual development (p. 109). Sprague detects a tendency in textbooks and teaching to create dependence on "received theories" and "assume that communication competence is a static goal that students can achieve through following certain prescriptions" (pp. 113, 116). In contrast, she indicates what one might see as the elements of an emerging signature pedagogy. This is a pedagogy that helps students to relate disciplinary concepts to the complexities of communication "in action" and achieve higher levels of understanding and skill by exploring particular roles and techniques of researching, speaking, listening, and writing in the immediate learning context (p. 116). Sprague says that although "we may write about organizations, the media, or politics, it is in our classrooms that we ourselves wield power and manipulate symbols with real consequences on other human lives" (p. 106). In other words, for a pedagogy that helps students enact the field's scholarly habits of mind, the same disciplinary insights that specialists apply and expect students to apply to communication and knowledge practices outside the classroom need to first be enacted within the classroom as a communication community in itself.

Other discipline specialists have presented similar arguments, either before the field discovered the SoTL literature or without direct reference to that literature. Significant discussion lines in this regard are indicated by Alvarado, Gutch, and Wollen (1987), Durant (1991), Corner (1995), Morgan (1996), and Schwarz (2006). This work shows how curriculum design and delivery, as well as pedagogic practice, play a vital part in what Schwarz (2006) calls the "complex of intellectual production" that constitutes a disciplinary field (p. 19). Schwarz cautions against the recycling of techniques derived from favorite theories, which results in classroom recipes. Such replication typically works by summarizing concepts from "the key authorities" and proceeding to demonstrate, for instance, how to deconstruct advertisements and popular media as ideological representations (pp. 20–21). It culminates perhaps in the sense of having "covered" the necessary theories and content of a subject. The issue that Schwarz raises about teaching according to a prepackaged methodology points toward a standard or default pedagogy that several writers consider has emerged in media and communication studies. What he values instead is "a mode of thought" that rejuvenates itself and allows students to share in exploring a variety of theoretical and practical approaches and the many "fractures and mediations" of communication (p. 27). In similar terms, Durant (1991) has emphasized the value of teaching approaches that allow students to place "inherited frameworks and vocabularies" of theory and criticism in "the history of their development," and reflect on a range of questions about media practices as they work in specific historical moments and cultural contexts, including their own (p. 422).

The Loose Professional Orientation of Communications Pedagogy

The signature pedagogy that emerges from the recent literature takes shape through factors beyond theoretical practice. These further factors include the institutional circumstances of media education and the nature of student constituencies, as well as the shifting relations of academic studies to other communicative and social practices. For instance, many university programs in media and communications have incorporated technical and vocational training related to industry and professional practice, including film and television production, and journalism.[2] The relation of academic studies to wider media and communication practices creates challenges for both curriculum design and pedagogy. Durant (1991) observes that "a vocational aspiration and sense of identificatory pleasure underpin much . . . student interest" in media studies (p. 414). Equally, however, many students have not decided on their career objectives or might be taking media and communication courses because they are interested in generalist education for personal and intellectual development. Questions of how to balance academic and vocationally relevant work or how to make purposeful links between critical-theoretical and practical study do not have one-size-fits-all answers. They need to be negotiated in particular institutional contexts and branches of media and communications.

Importantly, the multidisciplinary communications field has not developed—and is unlikely to develop—a signature pedagogy of the type that belongs, as Shulman (2005) argues, to those disciplines that "must measure up to the standards not just of the academy, but also of the particular professions" and thereby provide an "early socialization" into a specific field (pp. 53, 59). Communication pedagogy does not trace the modes of knowledge, roles, and procedures of thinking and performing that belong to any single profession in a specialized way. Instead, it relates potentially to diverse usages of media and communications in rapidly changing workplace and community contexts. Graduates might transfer the knowledge and skills they gain in communication courses to many areas of cultural practice, business, and creative industries other than the traditional media industries such as cinema and broadcasting (cf., Flew, 2002, pp. 114–138, 162–182). Where educators recognize the relatively loose nature of these educative affiliations of media and communication studies with industry and professional domains, the impulse toward signature pedagogy is not to rely on a single, canonical theory or model of practice. Rather, from various approaches there is a cosigning, or countersigning, of pedagogic initiatives to help students explore processes of thinking, researching, and analyzing the forms of theory and practice.

Examples of Signature Pedagogies

The following examples illustrate various communication pedagogies that enact disciplinary ways of thinking and performing. They indicate strategies for fostering independent learning by relating communication theories to classroom practices of interactive communication. These strategies involve designing and organizing activities that help students to familiarize themselves with disciplinary habits of mind and practice, and see them as relevant to their own needs, by building on what they already know.

The principle of guided development toward self-motivated learning operates in a program based on a series of learning activities (Murray, 2006). In the course that Murray describes, staff provide an overview of key concepts and purposes, after which students present their own critical evaluation of theoretical readings in seminars with their peers, summarizing arguments and relating them to a media example. In small-group discussions, students apply key questions, arising from the initial analyses, to new examples. Then, in "whole-class debate," they take more lead in directing discussion of familiar "real world" products (p. 98). By applying and working through a range of approaches, students can illuminate the "implicit theoretical investments" operating in everyday media usage. Assessment strategies support the transition toward self-directed learning. In an early essay, students identify "strengths and weaknesses" in one or more theoretical methods. In a longer essay, they can customize a topic according to their interests, but also extend their analysis of approaches for understanding the issues that the topic raises. Contrasting with the predetermined application of favored theories mentioned previously, this testing of approaches calls for more than "uncritical allegiance to a specific methodology as the 'obvious' way of constructing a research project" (p. 100).

Murray refers to teaching in an Australian Honors program, a transitional year to postgraduate research, but the pedagogic approach that she describes is pertinent at the undergraduate level. An example is a subject on "research and writing" in which I have been involved (Williamson, 2010). A disciplinary concern of this subject is how media discourse can contribute to democratic debate on contested and divisive topics—a concern central to the normative and everyday communication theories mentioned before. In the Australian context for this subject, topics include controversies over government policies on asylum seekers or indigenous affairs. To familiarize students with scholarly approaches relevant to examining and potentially participating in the media, learning and assessment activities focus on how to construct a manageable research question and embed it in a research proposal. The latter includes an aim, rationale, and initial sources and thread of inquiry, to develop later into a researched essay or article. Students often encounter the need to write an original question and proposal only in higher levels of study, or in workplace communications, with the undergraduate focus being on answering set questions. To help students think about the process of opening up new questions, staff provide examples for dividing a topic into smaller issues and for presenting reasons why a selected issue would matter to readers as well as the writer. Support for this process comes from the fact that the subject is designed in partnership with the university library, and the arts librarian helps students to apply information-retrieval techniques in a way that relates directly to communications. Academic and library staff have designed an online trial, showing how to use keywords, including truncations and synonyms, to open up but also delimit searches on a broad topic, through relevant databases (for accessing newspapers, television, press releases, and expert and community responses). Experimenting independently with keywords then helps students to focus the terms of their question, while comparing arguments in sources that they locate. By weighing claims and evidence, students begin to construct their own analysis of media and public discourses, including questions of who speaks, to or for whom, and how others have listened or responded. Proposals and final projects are assessed progressively, not by success with isolated procedures, but on a range of evidence that students have sought to understand the disciplinary processes involved in studying the media within their learning context.

Another way of familiarizing students with disciplinary ways of thinking is represented in work on intercultural communication. Dillon (2008) describes a course in which the scholarly ideas and values include the formation of diverse understandings of communication in different cultural contexts and the intercultural competence that depends on awareness of one's own communication. To assist students to engage with those ideas and values through communication in action, assignment work includes a structured opportunity for them to talk about "their early experiences and realizations of culture, communication, and difference" (p. 44). The teaching situation becomes an occasion for interpersonal storytelling and listening, providing students with a "common ground" on which to explore disciplinary themes and values of intercultural communications.

A final example from journalism education extends pedagogic strategies to create a conversation for students between academic and industry contexts. Here a closer alignment of academic study with a particular professional field appears than in some other areas of media and communication studies. However, insofar as journalism education has become interrelated in many contexts with academic disciplines, particularly in the humanities, it, too, has some features of generalist communication. Acknowledging differing views among discipline specialists on how and why academic theory and research are relevant to journalism, Meadows (1997) illustrates the construction of a work environment in which students can explore the relations of theory, research, and journalistic practices in a sustained way. Students participate in projects in which they have responsibility for framing a problem for investigation, rather than working on a given topic. The pedagogic method foregrounds a "processing framework," which provides questions and prompts that encourage students to work out how to find the information they need to learn about a problem, refine questions, and plan group roles in order to share information and present material (p. 103). The structured development of practical work creates spaces for students to reflect on the immediate and wider social and cultural context of their work, their responsibilities in using sources, and their use of style and modes of address in relation to a chosen audience. Assessment materials include the journalistic productions and students' reflective writing on the practical methods by which they produce knowledge. The pedagogic strategy situates skills valued by communication specialists, such as problem solving and intellectual and ethical judgment, in a concrete learning environment with a view to enabling students to use them in self-directed ways.

Similar disciplinary priorities and associated pedagogies have developed more broadly in journalism and mass communication contexts over decades (e.g, Adam, 1988; Carey, 1980). New digital media are now transforming journalism and redefining traditional roles of journalists. The need continues for pedagogic approaches that integrate technological skills with the ability to think in new and independent ways about how journalism and related communication practices can contribute to public knowledge and social understanding (Quinn, 2010).

Conclusion

The previous examples suggest how applying theoretical categories in structured learning situations helps students to understand the complexities of communication, both in academic and further cultural contexts. In proposing ways in which we could think about the formation of a communication signature pedagogy, the aim is not to unify diverse educational practices.

Rather, it is to explore dispositions of scholarly work in the project of communications and how these might be formed and consolidated in the processes of teaching and learning. These dispositions include concerns to develop approaches for understanding diverse forms and practices of communication, to reflect on how knowledge is produced, and to work in ways that foster communities of practice and learning. Teaching is not an add-on to research in advancing knowledge. The renewal of a multidisciplinary field, in a changing world of communications, depends on giving students imaginative reasons to engage in its practices.

Notes

1. On national developments, see, among others, Maras (2006) on Australia; Corner (1995) and Durant (1991) on Britain; Robinson (2000) and Tate, Osler, Fouts, and Siegel (2000) on Canada; Craig and Carlone (1998) on the Unites States; and McQuail (2010) on North America and Europe.

2. Practical and vocational training has grown unevenly in university education across different national contexts, with varying degrees of acceptance and support (Durant, 1991; Meadows, 1997; Robinson, 2000).

References

Adam, G. (1988, July–August). Thinking journalism. *Content*, 4–11.

Alvarado, M., Gutch, R., & Wollen, T. (Eds.). (1987). *Learning the media: An introduction to media teaching*. London, UK: Macmillan.

Boyer, E. (1990). *Scholarship reconsidered: Priorities of the professoriate*. Lawrenceville, NJ: Carnegie Foundation for the Advancement of Teaching.

Bruck, P. (1985). Communication teaching: Labour in silence and critique. *Canadian Journal of Communication, 11*(1), 1–4.

Carey, J. (1980). The university tradition in journalism education. *Carleton Journalism Review, 2*(6), 3–7.

Corner, J. (1995). Media studies and the "knowledge problem." *Screen, 36*(2), 147–155.

Craig, R., & Carlone, D. (1998). Growth and transformation of communication studies in U.S. higher education: Towards reinterpretation. *Communication Education, 47*(1), 67–81. Retrieved July 31, 2010, from http://dx.doi.org/10.1080/03634529809379111

Cunningham, S., & Turner, G. (1997). The media in Australia today. In S. Cunningham & G. Turner (Eds.), *The media in Australia: Industries, texts, audiences* (pp. 1–19). Sydney, Australia: Allen & Unwin.

Curran, J., & Morley, D. (2006). Editors' introduction. In J. Curran & D. Morley (Eds.), *Media and cultural theory* (pp. 1–13). London, UK: Routledge.

Curran, J., & Park, M-J. (Eds.). (2000). *De-Westernizing media studies*. London, UK: Routledge.

Dillon, R. (2008). How alumni narratives of intercultural competence can inform the scholarship of teaching and learning of intercultural communication. *Journal of the Scholarship of Teaching and Learning, 8*(3), 36–49. Retrieved July 31, 2010, from https://www.iupui.edu/~josotl/archive/vol_8/no_3/v8n3dillon.pdf

Dorland, M. (Ed.). (1996). *The cultural industries in Canada: Problems, policies and prospects*. Toronto, Canada: James Lorimer.

Durant, A. (1991). Noises offscreen: Could a crisis of confidence be good for media studies? *Screen, 32*(4), 407–428.

European Communication Research and Education Association. (n.d.). *Thematic sections: Film studies*. Retrieved September 6, 2010, from http://www.ecrea.eu/divisions/section/id/6

Flew, T. (2002). *New media: An introduction*. Melbourne, Australia: Oxford University Press.

Levine, T. R. (2009). Rankings and trends in citation patterns of communication journals. *Communication Education, 59*(1), 41–51. Retrieved September 13, 2010, from http://dx.doi.org/10.1080/03634520903296825

Maras, S. (2006). The emergence of communication studies in Australia as a "curriculum idea." *Australian Journal of Communication, 33*(2, 3), 43–62.

McCroskey, L., Richmond, V., & McCroskey, J. (2002). The scholarship of teaching and learning: Contributions from the discipline of communication. *Communication Education, 59*(4), 383–391. Retrieved July 31, 2010, from http://dx.doi.org/10.1080/03634520216521

McQuail, D. (2002). General introduction. In D. McQuail (Ed.), *McQuail's reader in mass communication theory* (pp. 3–20). London, UK: Sage.

McQuail, D. (2010). *McQuail's mass communication theory*. London, UK: Sage.

Meadows, M. (1997). Taking a problem-based learning approach to journalism education. *Asia Pacific Media Educator*, (3), 89–107, Retrieved September 6, 2010, from http:/http://ro.uow.edu.au/apme/vol1/iss3/6/

Morgan, R. (1996). Pan textualism, everyday life and media education. *Continuum 9*(2), 13–34.

Murray, S. (2006). Designing communication Honours curricula: Theory and practice in Australian higher education. *Australian Journal of Communication, 33*(1), 91–104.

Quinn, S. (2010). Opportunities for journalism education in an online entrepreneurial world. *Asia Pacific Media Educator*, (20), 69–80. Retrieved February 15, 2011, from http://ro.uow.edu.au/apme/vol1/iss20/7

Robinson, G. (2000). Remembering our past: Reconstructing the field of Canadian communication studies. *Canadian Journal of Communication, 25*(1). Retrieved September 18, 2010, from http://www.cjc-online.ca/index.php/journal/article/viewArticle/1145/1064

Rocca, K. (2010). Student participation in the college classroom: An extended multidisciplinary literature review. *Communication Education, 59*(2), 185–213. Retrieved September 13, 2010, from http://dx.doi.org/10.1080/03634520903505936

Schwarz, B. (2006). The "poetics" of communication. In J. Curran & D. Morley (Eds.), *Media and cultural theory* (pp. 19–29). London, UK: Routledge.

Shulman, L. (2005). Signature pedagogies in the professions. *Dædalus, 134*, 52–59.

Sprague, J. (1993). Retrieving the research agenda for communication education: Asking the pedagogical questions that are "embarrassments to theory." *Communication Education, 42*, 106–122. Retrieved July 31, 2010, from http://www.csus.edu/indiv/s/stonerm/Sprague-RetrievingTheResearchAgenda.pdf

Straw, W. (1985). Teaching critical media analysis. *Canadian Journal of Communication, 11*(1), 5–16.

Tate, E., Osler, A., Fouts, G., & Siegel, A. (2000). The beginnings of communication studies in Canada: Remembering and narrating the past. *Canadian Journal of Communication, 20*(1). Retrieved September 18, 2010, from http://www.cjc-online.ca/index.php/journal/article/view/1139

Williamson, D. (2010). Media and civics: A pedagogic strategy for integrating Internet research and writing. *Refereed Proceedings of the Australian and New Zealand Communication Association Annual Conference*. Retrieved January 8, 2011, from http://www.proceedings.anzca10.org

5

SIGNATURE PEDAGOGIES IN ART AND DESIGN

Ellen Sims and Alison Shreeve

Art and design is a broad discipline area encompassing many different professional spheres and subjects, such as design in graphics, textiles, fashion, product, theater and interiors, and fine art and time-based media. Combined, they comprise what is referred to in the United Kingdom (UK) as the creative industries, many arising out of recently developed technologies and media. However, they all require skilled working and thinking in visual and material ways and the ability to create two- and three-dimensional objects or performances. For these reasons, we will use the generic term *art and design* to encompass these disciplines.

Because of their close association with specific professional practices, pedagogies within art and design might differ because of media and context. For example, graphic designers might use collaborative digital communication in their teaching to mirror the professional technology environment. Art and design as a whole, however, has many commonalities. An awareness of the audience and the social context underlie both fine art *and* design pedagogies, because the outputs are destined for the public domain (Sims, 2008). Creativity, visual, and material outcomes are what link these subdisciplines together. We will base this chapter on research indicating that signature pedagogies exist to support the general requirements of creative practice in the arts (Shreeve, Sims, & Trowler, 2010).

We begin this chapter with a very brief history of art and design education in the UK, in order to trace the aspects of current pedagogies that are remnants of earlier traditions. We conclude this section with a description of activities in art and design, which constitute our understanding of signature pedagogies today. We will then provide an outline of scholarship of teaching and learning (SoTL) in art and design before going on to discuss signature pedagogies for art and design in more depth.

History

Art and design pedagogy began with the practices of the atelier, or artist's studio, where pupils learned from watching the master artist, progressively undertaking more complex tasks. In applied arts they were apprenticed to a master craftsman in the guild system for seven years. This kind of learning has been characterized as "sitting by Nellie" (Swann, 2002), where learning was achieved through a slow process of engagement in the practice. These models remained largely in place in the UK until the 19th century, when government schools of art and design were created in order to improve manufacturing output. Professional teachers were engaged who were also practitioners, for example, W. R. Lethaby at Central School of Art in London. Courses of study were created including evening classes for tradesmen in silversmithing and furniture making, servicing nearby industries with classes in drawing, design, and technical skills (Swift, 1988). As the curriculum became more defined, specific exercises were undertaken to structure learning, and the study of artifacts in museums added a cultural and historic dimension. Although funded by central government, these art schools remained relatively independent until the last quarter of the 20th century, when they began to be incorporated into universities and polytechnics.

In the 1960s, distinctions were drawn between technical or vocational education and degree-level education, creating an emphasis on theoretical and contextual studies of art and design within degree curricula. This introduced written and text-based "academic" educational practices to the materially focused art and design curriculum. Subsequently, art and design were awarded Bachelor of Arts–degree status alongside other discipline areas.

Currently the Bachelor and Master of Arts degrees are the accepted standards for academic and professional practice in art and design. Elkins (2009) suggests the PhD will become more widely accepted as the terminal degree for academic study of the practice of art and design, but this is not yet widely accepted. In this chapter we draw mainly on research into pedagogies in undergraduate education.

Art and Design Pedagogies Today

The most significant issue for undergraduates in art and design is the need to cope with uncertainty, ambiguity, and the unknown. Creative practice requires working toward new and adapted solutions to complex problems or creating original artifacts. This need to investigate and propose appropriate responses means that teachers do not hold all the answers before they begin to teach; they need to help students come up with original outcomes. The underlying principle is that students learn through doing; they practice the procedures of their discipline in a studio environment with additional workshops in technical skills. The studio mirrors practices outside the academy as found in the artist's or designer's studio (Schön, 1985), wherein there is no given position for the teacher to hold forth, or lecture (Smith Taylor, 2009). Instead, teachers move around and engage in dialogue with their students. The studio is therefore not simply a place but a contributor to signature pedagogies, because it helps to structure learning and teaching and prepares students for professional studio activities. Research underpins students' creative practices; they are required to explore potential outcomes in their sketchbooks where they record and develop ideas visually and produce material artifacts, all of which are sites of discussion between teacher and student. These conversations often deal with indeterminate and unknown creative outcomes: pedagogies of ambiguity (Austerlitz et al., 2008) or uncertainty (Shulman, 2005). The critique, or "crit," is a significant aspect of these disciplines, as identified by Klebesadel and Kornetsky (2009). We argue that all the activities just described, embedded in studio interactions, are signature pedagogies in art and design.

Before we examine signature pedagogies in more depth we will look at the existing scholarship of teaching and learning in creative arts disciplines. As Klebesadel and Kornetsky (2009) suggested, this is a relatively under-researched area in higher education.

SoTL in Art and Design

Academics are generally under pressure to undertake research into their discipline areas rather than researching, teaching, and learning. In the UK, SoTL activities have increased owing to national initiatives and concerns about the quality of the student experience. In the past decade, substantial government funding has been directed at the professionalization of university teaching, leading to the creation of the Higher Education Academy in 2004 and Centres for Excellence in Learning and Teaching (CELTs) that operated from 2005 to 2010. These initiatives have helped to raise the profile of pedagogic research while building research networks and communities enabling teachers in higher education to undertake SoTL. Most outputs tend to be based on action research, where the teacher identifies an issue in their teaching, develops an intervention to improve it, and evaluates its impact. The academic culture and experience of art and design instructors, including the predominance of visual rather than text-based communication modes, might be one reason for restricted dissemination of art and design SoTL (Klebesadel & Kornetsky, 2009; de la Harpe & Peterson, 2008).

Nonetheless, there are publications such as *Art, Design and Communication in Higher Education*, *International Journal of Art & Design Education* and *Arts and Humanities in Higher Education* that provide forums for scholarly debate on art and design pedagogy. In their study of SoTL publications by academics in art, design, and architecture, de la Harpe and Peterson (2008) identified only 118 journal articles in peer-reviewed journals in these disciplines over a decade. These articles focused on studio reform (including studio practice), teaching methods, art and design thinking, or the industry-education nexus. The nature of learning in the subjects is frequently addressed, although often through a philosophical approach rather than empirically. These debates include arguments about the relationship between practice and theory (Danvers, 2003), what to include in the curriculum (Corner, 2005), and the nature of creativity and assessment (Cunliffe, 2005). The issue of the identity of artists as they become teachers is also noted in the literature (Adams, 2007; Shreeve, 2009) and highlights the relationship between the outside world of practice and learning in institutional settings. For many practitioners taking on the role of teacher changes their identity, often with conflict or a sense of loss. Instructors' feelings about these changes can impact their students' learning experiences (Shreeve, 2010, 2011).

The seminal work of Marton and Saljo (1976a, 1976b) examined qualitative differences in approaches to learning, where some students read a text in order to remember the content (surface approaches) and others seek to understand the meaning (deep approaches). Further research has explored disciplinary-specific approaches to learning (Drew, Bailey, & Shreeve, 2002; Shreeve, Bailey, & Drew, 2003). These studies also suggest that art and design students approached their studies with different intentions, which broadly aligned with deep and surface approaches, but also included a procedural dimension not identified in text-based studies. This process dimension is critical to the pedagogies used, thus helping to create the habits of mind associated with professional practice. Drew (2004) identifies a "community of practice" (Wenger, 1998) intention when teaching art and design. This research suggests that teachers are helping their students to become part of the professional world of artists and designers through using signature pedagogies relevant to the community of practice.

Disciplinary Ways of Knowing

Any discussion about pedagogy must necessarily include a consideration of the nature and range of knowledge within that discipline. For art and design, knowledge is a problematic concept. Most of the knowledge is procedural, *knowing how* (Ryle, 1949) or *knowing in action* (Schön, 1983). It is a much more fluid kind of knowing that includes diverse and sometimes complex skills, processes, understanding about cultural practices, and current aesthetic notions, all of which involve much more than written facts. Knowledge and disciplinary "habits" are therefore both accumulated and built upon. This entails knowing through embodied, sensory, and emotional ways (Austerlitz & Aravot, 2002), as well as knowing about people, art and design histories, and some theories that illuminate practices. Such knowledge is often elusive and hard to articulate (Dormer, 1994; Eraut, 2000); therefore, art and design pedagogies have been described as "pedagogies of ambiguity" (Austerlitz et al., 2008). Teachers find it hard to provide precise answers and direct instructions because the creative process sets out to respond to complex challenges entering unknown territory. The outcome is unique to the person creating the work, and the teacher is trying to bring this creativity forth from the student, enabling rather than instructing. Working with uncertainty and unclear outcomes is characteristic of both the professional practice and the learning environment. Teachers encourage individual experimentation with materials and processes and expect students to question and evaluate their own activities in order to make judgments for themselves. The signature pedagogies of art and design are those that help students develop as artists and designers. In the next section we discuss in more detail what we believe these pedagogies to be.

Signature Pedagogies

The Studio

An artist or designer traditionally practices in a studio, the place she or he creates. A studio might be the sole province of the artist, whereas in design they are more likely to house a team of people working on one or many projects. The studio is not only a location, but also an environment filled with the accoutrements of creation. Images, objects, and works in progress are often situated here. Conversations, criticism, evaluation, and the generation of ideas are key activities. Hence, the studio in education mirrors the practice of the profession and helps to create the habits of mind associated with the profession.

The studio is the subject of a seminal study by Schön (1985), who identifies a studio culture, a physical space, a mode of teaching, a program of activity. Smith Taylor (2009) claims that the studio structures teaching toward student-centered approaches. In contrast, others view the studio as leading to "studio cruising," in which teachers act as "the expert," passing judgment on students' work, an approach that is entirely teacher-centered (Trigwell & Prosser, 1999). However, an extensive and more recent study by de la Harpe and Peterson (2008) identifies predominant "teaching methods" in the studio as case-based instruction, problem-based learning and practices, including critique, experimentation, and making. Here there are opportunities for dialogue between peers, teachers, and students, the essential dialogic component, a signature pedagogy of art and design. Notable and distinctive is that visible and material artifacts often form the basis for discussion (Cunliffe, 2005), as they would in a professional studio.

The Brief

Students are usually provided with a brief, much like a professional designer or a commissioned artist would receive from a client. This structures learning activities and sets out the parameters for creating a particular product. As students engage in work required by the brief, they engage in discussions and get informal feedback from the teacher, who checks their progress, probes students about their thinking, and makes suggestions about alternative routes to follow. Teachers will rarely tell a student what to do when addressing complex design briefs entailing problems that are not easily resolved. Rather, they will suggest alternatives to try or role models to examine and question why a particular route has been followed. They encourage the student to critically evaluate their own work and judge for themselves whether it meets the criteria for fulfilling the brief and developing an individual, creative response. The "live project" (i.e., one in which industry practitioners have proposed a "problem" or situation) is characteristic of design teaching, and we would argue that this use of a "real-world" project is also a signature pedagogy. Fine arts students similarly are required to organize public exhibitions of their work.

Along with the brief, which guides learning activities, the studio is also the site of the critique (Blair, 2007; Percy 2004). As Klebesadel and Kornetsky (2009) state, this is a signature pedagogy and essential to developing a self-critical habit of mind, inculcating current value systems in art and design (p. 111), and enabling students to position themselves within professional practice.

Critique

Critiques can be conducted in different ways, for example, by evaluating works in progress or completed works, including those conducted by visiting artists or critics, where students may or may not be allowed to speak. Focus is sometimes on teacher feedback and at other times on encouraging feedback and discussion among students. Elkins (2001) suggests that, "Critiques are different enough from one another so that it is not possible to sort out all the things that can happen" (p. 112).

However, a common aim of the crit is for students to become practiced in articulating their critical and contextual awareness and judgments, ideally with decreasing intervention from the teacher. However, the power relationship inherent in the crit does not always support a student-centered process. When they work well, critiques are a good opportunity for students to receive a range of views, providing both supportive criticism and validation of the direction of a student's endeavors and preparing them for the public judgment of their work, whether through artworks in an exhibition or through designed products.

Blair (2006, 2007) studied the critique in a variety of settings, analyzing both teacher and student interviews about the crit. The findings indicate that many positive conditions for learning might be absent, particularly in large groups (25 or more). She found these crits were less effective in engaging students in deep approaches to learning and posed challenges to both teachers and students. In addition, the relevance of the crit to the professional environment has been called into question, challenging its potential as a signature pedagogy for art and design, because the crit actually rarely happens in the professional context. In Blair's study (2006) students and teachers described critiques as "scary" and "nerve-wracking" experiences. To be successful, the crit must be a dialogue, "and if there's no dialogue, there's no learning" (Sara & Parnell, 2004, p. 59). A UK study building on Blair's research, "Critiquing the Critique" (Blythman, Orr, & Blair, 2007) sought to systematically examine the critique from both learning and teaching perspectives. The study found that the crit could be studied as a means of group work, peer learning, and collaboration.

Abrams (in Elkins, 2001, p. 119) suggests that possible orientations and themes pervade crits, which are not always made explicit and can result in *disordered conversations* (p. 121). Students learn to understand that there is an appropriate critical discourse, although they might be reluctant to be critical of each other's work, fearing public ridicule if their views are not in line with the teacher's. Thus the intention of the crit to develop students' critical abilities, and professional confidence is not always realized in practice.

These views suggest that signature pedagogies in themselves can produce variable learning experiences, even though they exist in order to enable students to become professionals. The teacher's underlying intentions might subvert the purpose of the crit from developing students' critical abilities, instead providing an opportunity for the teacher's judgment to be demonstrated. Expanding on Klebesadel and Kornetsky (2009), who explored the critique as a signature pedagogy in fine art and performance, we maintain that there are additional signature pedagogies that characterize art and design disciplines, which we will now go on to discuss.

The Sketchbook

Documenting one's thought processes visually is a requirement in most art and design teaching situations, and is most often produced as a sketchbook. Here students explore ideas, thinking visually about a range of problems. They collect inspirational material, adapt, modify, and play with shape and form. Teachers expect sketchbooks to be available in tutorials and assessment, because this provides a material object on which to base discussion and helps to explain students' thinking process. The emphasis on this process of learning in art and design rather than the end product, is culturally different to art and design education in Asia, for example, where technical skill evidenced in the end product might be more important (Sovic, 2008). The sketchbook is a form of visual thinking and an important part of the research process that practicing artists and designers undertake before they can produce finished artworks or designs.

Research

Teachers expect students to undertake research. It is a vital component of undergraduate study in the arts because it underpins all professional creative practices. However, research in art and design differs from conceptions of research (Brew, 2001) in other disciplines. For example, design students are expected to select source materials, to find out about the context of their design, and determine their market or end user. If they are fine artists they develop questions about living in the world to which they will respond through creative activities. A study by Shreeve, Bailey, and Drew (2003) on textiles and fashion indicated that there were four possible ways that students approached the research component of their studies: focusing on visual images, reproducing certain elements in the finished product, understanding the subject they were researching in order to demonstrate this knowledge in the finished product, and, finally, conducting research in order to construct their own response through conceptual and emotional abstraction conveyed through the designed product. Research, therefore, has variable meanings, but is present and expected by teachers as part of the process of learning in the arts. Barrett (2007) describes it thus:

> Creative arts research is often motivated by emotional, personal and subjective concerns, it operates not only on the basis of explicit and exact knowledge, but also on that of tacit and experiential knowledge . . . creative arts practice as research is an intensification of everyday experiences from which new knowledge or knowing emerges. (p. 115)

Research is fundamental because of the enquiry-based learning approach in the discipline, and there is a close relationship between academic research, the creative process, and professional activity (Wareham & Trowler, 2007), which prepares students by developing disciplinary ways of thinking in art and design.

Dialogue and Discussion

Fundamental in the signature pedagogies we have proposed is the dialogue and discussion that takes place between students and teachers around sketchbooks, artifacts, and research processes. Dialogue in art and design takes place formally and informally, in structured one-to-one tutorials in which progress is assessed and next directions are confirmed or suggested, and in brief and regular interactions conducted in the studio. Teachers and students build an interaction that is "*fluid . . . conversational . . . less passive*" (Sims, 2008). Others overhear these interchanges in the studio, and students sometimes gather together for impromptu discussion. These dialogues help develop the ways of thinking that professional artists and designers employ; dialogic signature pedagogies make visible artists' and designers' ways of thinking and doing.

Concluding Remarks

Teachers, who are often simultaneously practitioners, show students professional ways of thinking and doing. Although this might create tensions for some teachers, many are able to draw on their experiences of working in the creative industries to teach students what it means to be a creative practitioner. Through learning activities involving project briefs and learning environments that mirror practice situations, dialogic interactions in the studio make visible professional ways of thinking and acting.

The signature pedagogies we have described in this chapter are the outcomes of unique disciplinary practices and the nature of knowledge in the creative arts. In universities today these disciplines are coming under attack as the economic pressures on higher education lead to increased student numbers and reduced resources (Clarke & Budge, 2010). The studio is frequently seen as a luxury that can no longer be afforded. Higher education managers might not understand the importance of dialogue and material spaces for learning in creative arts subjects, and these signature pedagogies might be forced to change with time. These pressures and innovations in technology might alter the range of signature pedagogies currently employed in these creative subjects.

References

Adams, J. (2007). Artists becoming teachers: Expressions of identity transformation in a virtual forum. *Journal of Art and Design Education, 26*(3), 264–273.

Austerlitz, N., & Aravot, I. (2002). Emotions in the design studio. In A. Davies (Ed.), *Enhancing curricula: Exploring effective curriculum practices in design and communication in higher education* (pp. 84–101). Proceedings of 1st International conference. London, UK: Centre for Learning & Teaching in Art & Design.

Austerlitz, N., Blythman, M., Grove-White, A., Jones, B. A., Jones, C. A., Morgan, S., Orr, S., Shreeve, A., & Vaughan, S. (2008). Mind the gap: Expectations, ambiguity and pedagogy within art and design higher education. In L. Drew (Ed.), *The student experience in art and design higher education: Drivers for change* (pp. 125–148). Cambridge: JRA Publishing.

Barrett, E. (2007). Experiential learning in practice as research: Context, method knowledge. *Journal of Visual Art Practice, 6*(2), 115–124.

Blair, B. (2006). Does the studio crit still have a role to play in 21st century design education and student learning? In A. Davies (Ed.), *Enhancing curricula: Contributing to the future—meeting the challenges of the 21st century in the disciplines of art, design and communication* (pp. 107–120). Proceedings of the 3rd International Conference. London, UK: Centre for Learning & Teaching in Art & Design.

Blair, B. (2007). At the end of a huge crit in the summer, it was crap—I'd worked really hard but all she said was "Fine" and I was gutted. *Art, Design and Communication in Higher Education, 5*(2), 83–95.

Blythman, M., Orr, S., & Blair, B. (2007). *The strengths and weaknesses of the crit—A discussion paper.* Retrieved September 29, 2010, from http://www.adm.heacademy.ac.uk/projects/adm-hea-projects/learning-and-teaching-projects/critiquing-the-crit

Brew, A. (2001). Conceptions of research: A phenomenographic study. *Studies in Higher Education, 26*(3), 271–285.

Clarke, A., & Budge, K. (2010). Listening for creative voices amid the cacophony of fiscal complaint about art and design education. *International Journal of Art & Design Education, 29*(2), 153–162.

Corner, F. (2005). Identifying the core in the subject of fine art. *International Journal of Art & Design Education, 24*(3), 334–342.

Cunliffe, L. (2005). Forms of knowledge in art education and the corollary of authenticity in the teaching and assessment of such forms of knowledge. *International Journal of Art & Design Education, 24*(2), 199–208.

Danvers, J. (2003). Towards a radical pedagogy: Provisional notes on learning and teaching in art and design. *International Journal of Art & Design Education, 22*(1), 47–57.

de la Harpe, B., & Peterson, F. (2008). Through the looking glass: What do academics in art, design and architecture publish about most? *Art, Design and Communication in Higher Education, 7*(3), 135–154.

Dormer, P. (1994). *The art of the maker.* London, UK: Thames and Hudson.

Drew, L. (2004). The experience of teaching creative practices: Conceptions and approaches to teaching in the community of practice dimension. In A. Davies (Ed.), *Enhancing the curricula: Towards the scholarship of teaching in art, design and communication* (pp. 106–123). Proceedings of the 2nd International Conference. London, UK: Centre for Learning & Teaching in Art & Design.

Drew, L., Bailey, S., & Shreeve, A. (2002). Fashion variations: Student approaches to learning in fashion design. In A. Davies (Ed.), *Exploring effective curriculum practices in design and communication in higher education* (pp. 179–198). Proceedings of 1st International Conference. London, UK: Centre for Learning & Teaching in Art & Design.

Elkins, J. (2001). *Why art cannot be taught: A handbook for art students.* Urbana: University of Illinois Press.

Elkins, J. (Ed.). (2009). *Artists with PhDs: On the new doctoral degree in studio art.* Washington, DC: New Academia Publishing.

Eraut, M. (2000). Non-formal learning and tacit knowledge in professional work. *Journal of Educational Psychology, 70*(1), 113–136.

Klebesadel, H., & Kornetsky, L. (2009). Critique as signature pedagogy in the arts. In R. A. R. Gurung, N. L. Chick, & A. Haynie (Eds.), *Exploring signature pedagogies: Approaches to teaching disciplinary habits of mind.* Sterling, VA: Stylus.

Marton, F., & Saljo, R. (1976a). On qualitative difference in learning 1: Outcome and process. *British Journal of Educational Psychology, 46*(1), 4–11.

Marton, F., & Saljo, R. (1976b). On qualitative difference in learning 2: Outcome as a function of the learner's conception of the task. *British Journal of Educational Psychology, 46*(2), 115–127.

Percy, C. (2004). Critical absence versus critical engagement: Problematics of the crit in design learning and teaching. *Art, Design and Communication in Higher Education, 2*(3), 143–154.

Ryle, G. (1949). *The concept of mind.* London, UK: Hutchinson.

Sara, R., & Parnell, R. (2004). The review process. *CEBE Transactions, Briefing Guide Series, 1*(2), 56–69.

Schön, D. A. (1983). *The reflective practitioner.* New York, NY: Basic Books.

Schön, D. A. (1985). *The design studio: An exploration of its traditions and potentials.* London, UK: RIBA Publications Ltd.

Shreeve, A. (2009). I'd rather be seen as a practitioner, come in to teach my subject: Identity work in part-time art and design tutors. *International Journal of Art & Design Education, 28*(2), 151–159.

Shreeve, A. (2010). A phenomenographic study of the relationship between professional practice and teaching your practice to others. *Studies in Higher Education, 35*(6), 691–703.

Shreeve, A. (2011). Being in two camps: Conflicting experiences for practice-based academics. *Studies in Continuing Education, 33*(1), 79–91.

Shreeve, A., Bailey, S., & Drew, L. (2003). Students' approaches to the "research" component in the fashion design project. *Art, Design and Communication in Higher Education, 2*(3), 113–130.

Shreeve, A., Sims, E., & Trowler, P. (2010). A kind of exchange: Learning from art and design teaching. *Higher Education Research and Development, 29*(2), 125–138.

Shulman, L. S. (2005). Pedagogies of uncertainty. *Liberal Education, 91*, 18–25.

Sims, E. (2008). *Teaching landscapes in creative arts subjects.* Report on the CLIP CETL funded UAL research project. Retrieved September 29, 2010, from http://www.arts.ac.uk/docs/Landscapes-final-report.pdf

Smith Taylor, S. (2009). Effects of studio space on teaching and learning: Preliminary findings from two case studies. *Innovative Higher Education, 33*(4), 217–228.

Sovic, S. (2008). Coping with stress: The perspective of international students. *Art design and communication in higher education, 6*(3), 145–158.

Swann, C. (2002). Nellie is dead. *Art, Design and Communication in Higher Education, 1*(1), 50–58.

Swift, J. (1988). Birmingham and its art school: Changing views 1800–1921. *International Journal of Art & Design Education, 7*(1), 5–29.

Trigwell, K., & Prosser, M. (1999). *Understanding learning and teaching.* Buckingham: SRHE/Open University Press.

Wareham, T., & Trowler, P. (2007, August). *Deconstructing and reconstructing 'The Teaching-Research Nexus': Lessons from art and design.* Presented at All Ireland Society for Higher Education Conference, National University Ireland, Maynooth.

Wenger, E. (1998). *Communities of practice. Learning meaning and identity.* Cambridge: Cambridge University Press.

6

THE ENTERPRISING ARTIST AND THE ARTS ENTREPRENEUR

Emergent Pedagogies for New Disciplinary Habits of Mind

Christina Hong, Linda Essig, and Ruth Bridgstock

Traditional pedagogies in the arts in higher education focus largely on the studio experience in which a novice artist studies under one or more master teachers (e.g., Don, Garvey, & Sadeghpour, 2009). In more recent times, however, a shift in higher education curriculum and pedagogy in the arts has expanded this traditional conservatory model of training to include, among other components, career self-management and enterprise creation—in a word, entrepreneurship.

This chapter examines the developing field of arts enterprise and arts entrepreneurship in higher education in a multinational context. The field is contextualized within the broader landscape of the creative industries and the consequential development of knowledge, skills, and the habits of mind necessary for artistic venture creation, sustainability, and success. Whereas the discourse about learning and teaching for business entrepreneurship is well established (e.g., Fiet, 2001), equivalent conversations about arts enterprise and entrepreneurship have only recently begun (Beckman, 2007, 2011; Essig, 2009). This chapter will address the contested definitions of key terms and concepts and also the question of how arts educators, although mindful of the pedagogic traditions of the arts school, are also drawing on the pedagogies of business entrepreneurship and cognitive theories of entrepreneurship to create innovative new transdisciplinary signature pedagogies for creative enterprise and entrepreneurship education in the arts.

Defining the signature pedagogies (Shulman, 2005, p. 52) for the important practices of arts enterprise and entrepreneurship is particularly challenging, given that the field in question is an emergent one and the subject of some controversy within and among schools of the arts. As a result, a singular and agreed-upon definition of what the terms *art enterprise* and *entrepreneurship* mean remains contested, making consideration of its signature pedagogy similarly emergent.

There are also differences in definition by country (Breen, 2004). In Europe and Australia, the terms *enterprise education* and *entrepreneurship education* are often used interchangeably (Hytti & O'Gorman, 2004). In the United States, the term *enterprise education* is rarely used, and *entrepreneurship education* refers to education for new venture creation, employability aims, and more abstract concepts such as opportunity recognition and self-actualization, all fueled by creativity. However, some authors in Europe, the United States, and Australia have suggested a differentiation between entrepreneurship and enterprise: Entrepreneurship denotes new venture creation, and enterprise denotes employability (e.g., Bridge, O'Neill, & Cromie, 2003) and self-management.

Although the interchangeability and conflation of the two terms in the literature is apparent, it is also apparent that entrepreneurship education and enterprise education, generally speaking, are associated with two broad educational aims. Individual education programs tend to adopt one or a combination of both aims. The first broad aim (more generally linked to entrepreneurship education) is focused on the development of skills and knowledge for business start-up and new venture creation and management. The second broad aim (more generally linked to enterprise education and closely related to the notion of employability [Yorke, 2004]) is focused on the development of skills and knowledge necessary to engage proactively and effectively in the process of career self-management and to add value through work (Hearn & Bridgstock, 2010). Other authors (e.g., Beckman & Cherwitz, 2009) reject the narrow new venture creation orientation of business school entrepreneurship education while retaining some of its nomenclature.

For the purposes of this chapter, the term *arts entrepreneurship education* will be used to refer broadly to the essential activities of business start-up and new venture creation (both for profit and nonprofit) inclusive of the acquisition and development of enterprising skills, abilities, behaviors, and habits of mind that will advantage and sustain personal growth and portfolio careers in the arts over time.

In Australia, as in the United Kingdom and Europe, emphasis on the economic importance of the arts has led policy makers to cluster many disciplines where creativity is important into a collective entity known as the creative industries, defined as "those activities which have their origin in individual creativity, skill and talent, and have the potential to create wealth and jobs through the generation and exploitation of intellectual property" (Department for Culture Media and Sport, 1998, p. 3). Therefore, the creative industries encompass what is defined traditionally as "the arts" but extends to include fields such as film, television, radio, advertising, games and interactive content, publishing, architecture, and design. In the United States, the creative industries discourse has not been taken up widely, although there (as elsewhere) much scrutiny has been devoted in recent times to the economic impact of the arts (e.g., Americans for the Arts, 2007) and how best to educate arts workers for their careers and roles in the national and global creative economy.

In all advanced economies, the arts labor force shows a profile that is quite distinctive. In contrast with more conventional industries such as financial services or manufacturing, the commercial arts sector is dominated by networked clusters of small-to-medium enterprises, sole-traders, and micro-businesses (Creigh-Tyte & Thomas, 2001). Larger-scale arts organizations across the globe, such as theater companies and museums, are often partially or fully funded by government program grants. Although there is some variation by discipline, in general an arts practitioner can expect to engage in a "portfolio" career comprising a patchwork of individually navigated opportunities (Bridgstock, 2005), which could be a mixture of grant-based (i.e., publicly subsidized) and commercial projects, sometimes supported by parallel concurrent work activities, or "day jobs."

Because of the nature of the work in the arts sector, entrepreneurship (and by implication education programs in arts entrepreneurship) would therefore support lifelong success in the arts. Several features of arts entrepreneurship can be identified that distinguish it from entrepreneurship in traditional business sectors. One distinctive feature is that the value derived from an arts product or service might be commercial, social, cultural, or some combination of these. A second distinctive feature is that in addition to a variety of instrumental reasons for, and benefits arising out of, arts practice, there is often a very high degree of intrinsic motivation in arts work. A strong link between the arts practitioner's personal identity and their practice is common, to the extent that many performing artists literally "embody" their practices, for example, dancers and performance artists. A third distinctive feature of arts entrepreneurship arises from the nature of the working world that arts practitioners must navigate, as described earlier. These distinctive features therefore mean that particular entrepreneurship skills, habits of mind, and teaching approaches (that is, signature pedagogies) are required for arts entrepreneurship.

Arts Entrepreneurship Skills and Habits of Mind

The relatively narrowly focused entrepreneurial skill components of early business entrepreneurship programs (e.g., Jamieson, 1984) have been broadened more recently by a greater focus on innovation and creativity as the engine of entrepreneurship (Drucker, 1985) and newer notions of venture creation that are the result of ideation, collaboration, and communication. Habits of mind such as entrepreneurial drive, competitiveness, persistent optimism, a propensity for risk-taking, comfort with change, resilience, and visionary leadership have also been observed repeatedly to be important to entrepreneurial behavior and enterprise success in multiple fields (e.g., Jacobowitz & Vidler, 1982).

Taking this emphasis on entrepreneurial habits of mind further, engineering entrepreneurship educator Thomas Duening (2010) recently adapted Howard Gardner's (2006) *Five Minds for the Future* into "Five Minds for the Entrepreneurial Future": the Opportunity Recognizing Mind, the Designing Mind, the Risk-Managing Mind, the Resilient Mind, and the Effectuating Mind. Duening suggests that recent research into the cognitive skills possessed by entrepreneurs can guide the development of entrepreneurship curriculum and pedagogy. For example, to employ this concept in an arts entrepreneurship context, one might teach budding arts entrepreneurs to be risk managers through lectures on financial management strategy combined with experiential learning situations where students undertake limited, but real, risk.

Arts entrepreneurship educators (e.g., Beckman, 2011) argue that a broad understanding of the cultural contexts of the arts is also needed for the development of an entrepreneurial mind-set for artists. Others focus on self-actualization and the "cultivation of independence" (Kuuskoski, 2011, p. 99). Kuuskoski, writing from the perspective of tertiary music program, views mentorship as a key pedagogic technique for developing said independence and self-efficacy *if* the advanced student remains wary of adherence to "curricular standards without first acquiring a unique set of personal, career, and artistic goals" (p. 99).

Thus, these shifts in mind-sets and skills are reliant on the development of flexible and adaptive practitioner professional identities that meet the needs of the individual and the market place concurrently. Recent literature (e.g., Bridgstock, 2009, 2011; Hearn & Bridgstock, 2010) yields some insights into what constitutes a capable, employable, and entrepreneurial arts professional for the creative economy. Creativity and disciplinary technical expertise are highly desirable skill sets and knowledge capabilities in arts fields, and it has also been suggested that graduate arts professionals should possess the abilities necessary to self-manage their careers, such that they can recurrently obtain or create suitable work.

Emerging Signature Pedagogies for Arts Entrepreneurship: Business and Beyond

To foster the distinctive skills and habits of mind required of enterprising artists and arts entrepreneurs, signature pedagogies for arts entrepreneurship are evolving. The signature pedagogies in the field of business entrepreneurship education are being adopted and adapted for arts entrepreneurship education. Faculty lecture, case studies delivered by guest entrepreneurs, business plan development, and internship are four signature pedagogies of business entrepreneurship, with business plan development and guest entrepreneurs being the most popular (Solomon, 2007) in the traditional new venture creation model of entrepreneurship education found in business schools.

Lectures on entrepreneurship, in the new venture creation sense of the word, often focus on topics such as management, financing, and the start-up structure (e.g., Timmons & Spinelli, 2007). In the arts enterprise classroom, finance topics will include not only venture finance, but also personal finance to help the student artist maintain personal solvency while building an enterprise infrastructure, thus supporting preparation for the portfolio career of an artist. Additionally, because many arts-based ventures are organized on a nonprofit basis, grant writing is another topic in the arts entrepreneurship lecture hall not generally found in the business school curriculum. By introducing students to grant writing requirements, including the structure of project narratives and selection of work samples, in the lecture hall, they are better equipped to develop such proposals upon entry into the professional realm.

For the student of business entrepreneurship, opportunity recognition is itself considered a creative act (DeTienne & Chandler, 2004, Solomon, 2007). For a student in arts and creative industries, *recognizing* an opportunity might not be sufficient; the student arts entrepreneur might need to *create* his or her own opportunities. Opportunity recognition can be construed as a form of pattern recognition (Baron, 2004, 2006), a cognitive process of conceptual combining (Ward, 2004). The lecture hall is a venue, but not the only one, for introducing this concept.

Although lectures are a useful pedagogy for introducing the concept of opportunity recognition, case studies are also employed on a comparative basis to exercise the student's ability to recognize patterns and make connections that can lead to the creation of new opportunities. Because a written body of case studies in arts entrepreneurship is not yet available, arts venture case studies are often delivered by the entrepreneurs themselves via visits to the classroom, supplemented by student research. Some educators (e.g., Thomas, 2011) adapt business case studies for use in teaching arts entrepreneurship.

Fiet (2000) notes that unless these guests are brought into the classroom to illustrate theory that will help students understand the consequences of entrepreneurial decision making, case studies teach only failure. Others (Pittaway & Cope, 2007; Solomon, 2007) underscore the impact that interaction with actual entrepreneurs, successful or not, have on entrepreneurship education. First-person narratives by guest entrepreneurs who have failed as well as succeeded support the training of a resilient mind-set. Arts leaders are also widely employed in the arts entrepreneurship classroom to discuss the entrepreneurial process, or specific topics such as grant writing or business management. Such visits are most effective if students are given the opportunity to question the visiting entrepreneur and subsequently analyze the successes and failures of the venture.

The business plan competition is a mainstay of the traditional entrepreneurship curriculum (Solomon, 2007), considered by a majority of U.S. universities to be the most important feature of entrepreneurship education (Matlay, 2008). Many business plan competitions award winners a small amount of seed money to launch their venture. Although some universities open their competitions to arts and creative industries entrepreneurs, business plan competitions are not yet a critical component of arts entrepreneurship/enterprise education, perhaps because such competitions require supplemental funding. Seemingly, Arizona State University, Eastman School of Music, and Beloit College are the only U.S. higher education institutions that hold arts venture enterprise competitions at the time of this writing, resulting in seed grants of $500 and $5,000. These competitions have resulted in the launch of several arts-based ventures, both for profit and nonprofit. As in business school competitions, winners receive one-on-one mentorship in addition to cash awards. The very act of applying—and reapplying, if rejected—supports the development of persistence. Gustafson (2011) notes, "*Doing* is the best way to learn how creativity and entrepreneurial practice are unified" (p. 73). Incubators provide a structure within which students learn by "doing" entrepreneurship in a far more directly experiential way than an internship opportunity can provide. Students who launch an enterprise have the opportunity to undertake actual entrepreneurship under the guidance of faculty and guest mentors.

Because working in heterogeneous groups has been shown to increase the generation of unique ideas (e.g., Paulus & Nijstad, 2003), exercises that spur collaboration (sometimes between arts and business students) are used to incite and excite cognitive creative processes. Group exercises might include brainstorming, collaborative research, and project development. Exercises in missioning and visioning, often conducted in small workgroups, encourage students to focus and clarify their artistic and personal goals, while spurring creativity. A typical brainstorming activity might involve students in groups of four listing as many arts venture ideas as possible in a fixed time period (e.g., ten minutes) and then finding the confluences between the ideas within their group and across groups in a discussion facilitated by the instructor. An exercise such as this teaches students to collaborate, to make cognitive connections, and ultimately might lead them to ideas that can be developed beyond the classroom.

Many business schools adhere to McMullan and Long's (1987) call to provide students with hands-on experience by administrating internship programs. Similarly, and perhaps most commonly, experiential learning through internship programs is a feature of entrepreneurship pedagogy as well as arts entrepreneurship education. Although arts entrepreneurship programs might also include internships, the unique mission of arts programs and therefore a unique factor of arts entrepreneurship education and a defining aspect of its signature pedagogy (as discussed in the next section) is the practice of making art work in and for the real world. Given that only a certain amount of text-based learning will allow advancement in the field of arts entrepreneurship, the focus of signature pedagogies in arts entrepreneurship therefore resides in the enactment of pedagogies that facilitate real-world experiential learning. Interactive and problem-based learning, often involving real-world multidisciplinary projects, which also facilitate the engagement of the learner as reflective practitioners (Schön, 1987), lie at the heart of the signature pedagogies of arts entrepreneurship.

It is not uncommon to see student-run theater companies or art galleries on university campuses that can provide experiential real-world learning opportunities within the safety net of the higher education institution. These might be start-up or stand-alone entities or might be institutionalized through a formal class structure. Students engaged in such activities learn both personnel and financial management, problem-solving, marketing, and communication skills that can be applied to their own arts-based ventures upon graduation. More importantly, they have the opportunity to practice the enterprising habits of mind necessary to sustain their creative practices and their careers.

Whereas the adoption of the signature pedagogies from business that incorporate the integration of experiential learning and skill building is evident, other developing features of emerging signature pedagogies for arts entrepreneurship are worthy of specific mention. One very important feature is that of mind-set shifting. Because entrepreneurship and enterprise relate to a mind-set as well as a skill set, arts entrepreneurship education need not take place only in discreet classes with those words in their course titles. Rather, arts entrepreneurship can be suffused throughout the appropriate disciplinary curriculum (Essig, 2009) and enterprising behaviors rewarded. Even as early as a freshman orientation or first-year seminar course, faculty can and should shift student mind-sets away from the traditional arts mind-set of dependency on funding and introduce students to the concept of opportunity creation and the risk–reward relationship inherent therein. As students progress through their program of study, and especially as they near completion, they can be exposed—within their disciplinary coursework—to techniques for managing and marketing their work, including portfolio development and audition techniques.

Another key feature of pedagogical practices in arts entrepreneurship is the extensive use made of digital tools and multimedia technology both as teaching tools and as distribution channels for bringing emerging artists and their products to the online market. As the distinction between the role of producers and users of content has dissolved, so the realm of cultural production and distribution has undergone significant change with more fluid roles of users and contributors within Web 2.0 social media environments. This emergence of user-led content generation has enabled artists, writers, dancers, musicians, video makers, and other content creators access to multiple portals, through which to post their creative work and build an audience base (Hong, Caldwell, Ashley, & Alpert, 2009). Arts entrepreneurship pedagogies therefore leverage the use of technologies to enhance the capability and capacity of students to adopt and engage with new media and in particular information and communications technologies to further venture creation.

The implications of these emergent signature pedagogies are significant for the ongoing sustainability and development of the arts in higher education. As the pressure to rationalize the resource-hungry studio-based practices in traditional arts programs increases concurrent with the more general demand for university graduates with a propensity toward ideation and new venture creation, the impetus toward reconceptualizing curriculum design, teacher professional development, and stakeholder partnerships that embrace more enterprising and entrepreneurial endeavors in the arts will increase.

Developing a broader framework for arts entrepreneurship education that also takes into account disciplinary distinctiveness in each of the art forms is necessary to more deeply embed entrepreneurial learning from the outset and throughout programs of study. At present, there is a tendency to "bolt on" this activity, rather than integrate it throughout, and in so doing enable a richer and more nuanced set of outcomes. As a corollary, curriculum models for arts entrepreneurship education will require further expansion and investigation. The challenge will be to resist the temptation to import standardized prepackaged curricula in favor of curricula that require facilitators with creative and enterprising capacities who can develop courses of study that, although mindful of global themes, remain contextualized to local and national content and case-study scenarios.

Teachers of arts entrepreneurship are active as facilitators, networkers, and moderators rather than as lecturers in the more traditional vein of higher education teaching. Teachers of arts who wish to embed enterprising habits of mind and entrepreneurial activity within their teaching must themselves be entrepreneurial in thought and action as they collaborate with various stakeholders to create learning environments and problem-based scenarios for their students. The interactive and applied nature of arts entrepreneurship pedagogies requires a facilitative teaching style that is significantly different in both approach and application from the "sage on the stage" model of traditional teaching. Moreover, arts-based mentoring toward the development of an entrepreneurial mind-set is also more holistic and is based in the "reciprocal nature of forging mutual respect" (Kuuskoski, 2011 p. 98). Bidirectional mentoring leads to the "cultivation of independence" (p. 99), a trait that supports entrepreneurship as an action and employability as a characteristic.

Arts entrepreneurship and the signature pedagogies that are emerging provide opportunities for greater engagement and establishment of stronger links among academia, the business community, and the community at large. There are significant opportunities to undertake qualitative and quantitative research into arts entrepreneurship education and its impact on the creative industries and professions. The role for the institution of higher education, as chief purveyor of professional skills and knowledge for many emerging arts practitioners, is a complex one. In addition to engendering high levels of disciplinary expertise, usually via learning processes involving resource-intensive studio practice, higher education is also tasked with preparing nascent arts practitioners to self-navigate the fluid, diverse, and multifaceted world of arts.

As mentioned at the beginning of this chapter, the field of arts entrepreneurship education is, as yet, conceptually undeveloped. There is considerable debate surrounding what it encompasses, what its aims are, and what might be achieved through it. Some arts educators have questioned the value of entrepreneurship education programs. Detractors have suggested that many arts practitioners have little natural propensity for, or interest in, *entrepreneurship* in the Steve Jobs or Richard Branson sense of the word (Richards, 2005). It is important to note that arts entrepreneurship is often conducted for social or cultural ends, but even when art is commercial in nature, it does not need to involve compromising artistic objectives. Thus, arts entrepreneurship education programs should ideally be built on a foundational shift in thinking from "money ruins art" to "money enables art." Indeed, arts entrepreneurship can serve to preserve aesthetic tradition as well as to create new and innovative outcomes (Beckman, 2007).

Conversations around arts curricula for the 21st century and the signature pedagogies that instruct our emerging arts practitioners to think, engage, and act entrepreneurially in the creative industries and professions must continue to be examined and articulated. The territory is a largely uncharted one that challenges arts educators to rethink their pedagogical assumptions—to teach so as to enable the *enterprising artist* and the *arts entrepreneur*, not just in the heroic few but as a set of skills, knowledge, and habits of mind that every student in the arts should acquire.

References

Americans for the Arts. (2007). *Arts and economic prosperity III: National report.* Retrieved from http://www.artsusa.org/

Baron, R. A. (2004). Opportunity recognition: A cognitive perspective. *Academy of Management Best Conference Paper.* Retrieved from http://faculty.insead.edu/andersonp/VOBM_MAYJUN2005

Baron, R. A. (2006). Opportunity recognition as pattern recognition: How entrepreneurs "connect the dots" to identify new business opportunities. *Academy of Management Perspectives, 20*(1), 104–119.

Beckman, G. D. (2007). "Adventuring" arts entrepreneurship curricula in higher education: An examination of present efforts, obstacles, and best practices. *The Journal of Arts Management, Law, and Society, 37*(2), 87–112.

Beckman, G. D. (2011). Disciplining arts entrepreneurship education: A call to action. In G. Beckman (Ed.), *Disciplining the arts: Teaching entrepreneurship in context* (pp. 1–12). Plymouth, UK: Rowman & Littlefield Education.

Beckman, G. D., & Cherwitz, R. A. (2009). Intellectual entrepreneurships: An authentic foundation for higher education reform. *Planning for Higher Education, 37*(4), 27–36.

Breen, J. (2004). Enterprise, entrepreneurship and small business: Where are the boundaries? *International Journal of Entrepreneurship and Small Business, 1*(1), 21–34.

Bridge, S., O'Neill, K., & Cromie, S. (2003). *Understanding enterprise, entrepreneurship and small business.* New York, NY: Palgrave Macmillan.

Bridgstock, R. (2005). Australian artists, starving and well-nourished: What can we learn from the prototypical protean career? *Australian Journal of Career Development, 14*(3), 40–48.

Bridgstock, R. (2009). The graduate attributes we've overlooked: Enhancing graduate employability through career management skills. *Higher Education Research and Development, 28*(1), 27–39.

Bridgstock, R. (2011). Skills for creative industries graduate success. *Education & Training, 53*(1), 9–26.

Creigh-Tyte, A., & Thomas, B. (2001). Employment. In S. Selwood (Ed.), *The UK cultural sector: Profile and policy issues* (pp. 250–279). London, UK: Policy Studies Institute.

Department for Culture, Media, and Sport. (1998). *Creative Industries Mapping Document 1998.* London, UK: Department for Culture, Media and Sport.

DeTienne, D. R., & Chandler, G. N. (2004). Opportunity identification and its role in the entrepreneurship classroom: A pedagogical approach and empirical test. *Academy of Management Learning and Education, 3*(3), 242–257.

Don, G., Garvey, C., & Sadeghpour, M. (2009). Signature pedagogies in music theory and performance. In R. A. R. Gurung, N. Chick, & A. Haynie (Eds.), *Exploring signature pedagogies: Approaches to teaching disciplinary habits of mind* (pp. 81–98). Sterling, VA: Stylus Publishing.

Drucker, P. F (1985). *Innovation and entrepreneurship: Practice and principles.* New York, NY: Harper & Row.

Duening, T. N. (2010). Five minds for the entrepreneurial future: Cognitive skills as the intellectual foundation for next generation entrepreneurship curricula. *Journal of Entrepreneurship, 19*(1), 1–22.

Essig, L. (2009). Suffusing entrepreneurship education throughout the theatre curriculum. *Theatre Topics, 19*(2), 117–124.

Fiet, J. O. (2000). The theoretical side of teaching entrepreneurship. *Journal of Business Venturing, 16*, 1–24.

Fiet, J. O. (2001). The pedagogical side of entrepreneurship theory. *Journal of Business Venturing, 16*, 101–117.

Gardner, H. (2006). *Five minds for the future.* Cambridge, MA: Harvard Business Press.

Gustafson, J. (2011). Teaching entrepreneurship by conservatory methods. In G. Beckman (Ed.), *Disciplining the arts: Teaching entrepreneurship in context* (pp. 69–81). Plymouth, UK: Rowman & Littlefield Education.

Hearn, G., & Bridgstock, R. S. (2010). Education for the creative economy: Innovation, transdisciplinarity and networks. In M. Peters & D. Araya (Eds.), *Education in the creative economy* (pp. 93–116). New York, NY: Peter Lang.

Hong, C., Caldwell, L., Ashley, T., & Alpert, V. (2009, July). Transcultural perspectives on digital practices and the arts in higher education. In C. Stock (Ed.), *Dance dialogues: Conversations across cultures, artforms and practices.* Proceedings of the 2008 World Dance Alliance Global Summit, Brisbane. Online publication, QUT Creative Industries and Ausdance, http://www.ausdance.org.au/resources/publications/dance-dialogues.html

Hytti, U., & O'Gorman, C. (2004). What is "enterprise education?" An analysis of the objectives and methods of enterprise education programmes in four European countries. *Education + Training, 46*(1), 11–23.

Jacobowitz, A., & Vidler, D. C. (1982). Characteristics of entrepreneurs: Implications for vocational guidance. *Vocational Guidance Quarterly, 30*(3), 252–257.

Jamieson, I. (1984). Education for enterprise. In A. Watts & P. Moran (Eds.), *CRAC* (pp. 19–27). Cambridge: Ballinger.

Kuuskoski, J. (2011). The complete pianist: Leveraging entrepreneurial mentorship to foster a renewed vision of piano pedagogy. In G. Beckman (Ed.), *Disciplining the arts: Teaching entrepreneurship in context* (pp. 95–116). Plymouth, UK: Rowman & Littlefield Education.

Matlay, H. (2008). The impact of entrepreneurship education on entrepreneurial outcomes. *Journal of Small Business and Enterprise Development, 15*(2), 382–396.

McMullan, W. E., & Long, W. A. (1987). Entrepreneurship education in the nineties. *Journal of Business Venturing, 2*, 261–275.

Paulus, P. B., & Nijstad, B. A. (2003). Group creativity: An introduction. In P. B. Paulus & B. A. Nijstad (Eds.), *Group creativity* (pp. 3–11). Oxford, UK: Oxford University Press.

Pittaway, L., & Cope, J. (2007). Entrepreneurship education: A systematic review of the evidence. *International Small Business Journal, 25*(5), 479–510.

Richards, G. (2005). *Development for the creative industries: The role of higher and further education media and sport.* London, UK: Skills and Entrepreneurship Task Group.

Schön, D. (1987). *Educating the reflective practitioner.* San Francisco, CA: Jossey-Bass.

Shulman, L. (2005). Signature pedagogies in the professions. *Daedalus, 134*(3), 52–59.

Solomon, G. (2007). An examination of entrepreneurship education in the United States. *Journal of Small Business and Enterprise Development, 14*(2), 168–182.

Thomas, K. (2011). The importance of case studies in arts entrepreneurship curricula. In G. Beckman (Ed.), *Disciplining the arts: Teaching entrepreneurship in context* (pp. 161–165). Plymouth, UK: Rowman & Littlefield Education.

Timmons, J. A., & Spinelli, S. (2007). *New venture creation: Entrepreneurship for the 21st century* (7th ed.) New York, NY: McGraw Hill.

Ward, T. B. (2004). Cognition, creativity and entrepreneurship. *Journal of Small Business Venturing, 19*, 173–188.

Yorke, M. (2004). *Employability in higher education: What it is—what it is not.* York, UK: The Higher Education Academy.

PART TWO

SOCIAL AND NATURAL SCIENCES

7

SIGNATURE PEDAGOGIES IN POLITICAL SCIENCE

Teaching Students How Political Actors Behave

Jeffrey L. Bernstein

Signature Pedagogies and the Disciplines

One of the most significant contributions of the scholarship of teaching and learning (SoTL) to higher education pedagogy has been the notion that good teaching looks different across academic disciplines (Gurung, Chick, & Haynie, 2009; Huber & Morreale, 2002). Clearly, aspects of effective teaching are shared throughout the academy; all good teachers need the abilities to plan a lesson, to present material in a clear and engaging manner, and to engage students. But SoTL shows a laudable respect for the disciplines. Good teaching in chemistry, it is argued, looks different than good teaching in English, which is different than good teaching in medicine. A combination of the content, the instructional setting, and the goals of the program in which the course is embedded matter; although the effective teacher in any discipline does things common to all other teachers, she also undoubtedly does things unique to her course, discipline, and instructional context.

I argue here that a significant component of effective disciplinary teaching is also its signature pedagogy: It requires that we help students see how disciplinary experts approach a task and then help students build the skills to do this on their own. Just as chemists perform experiments in the laboratory, effective chemical pedagogy puts the students in the lab for the same kind of inquiry-based tasks. And, just as historians immerse themselves in the time period and context in which they study, history students ought to do the same. Because students often struggle to do this (Wineburg, 2001), effective history pedagogy finds ways to put students in the position of historical figures so that they can understand historical acts in their temporal context.

To apply this to political science, one common analytical approach in the discipline is to examine the goals of political actors and then predict how they will behave in order to maximize their utility in a particular situation (Downs [1957] was the forerunner of this approach). Rational actor models might be used to explain the position-taking behaviors of candidates for office, or the decisions of political parties to enter coalitions, or the presence or absence of military moves by a country in a border dispute. Evaluating the predictive power of these models allows us to determine when they work and when we must modify our models. In such analyses, it is critical to evaluate the behavior of each actor from that actor's perspective—candidates, parties, and nation-states are assumed to pursue *their own* conceptions of their interests, not the interests that outsiders would ascribe to them. Thus, one component of a signature pedagogy in political science ideally fosters students' abilities to predict and explain behavior through the perspectives of others.

Political Science and the Scholarship of Teaching and Learning

Later in this chapter, I will discuss further the idea of signature pedagogies in political science. Before that, however, I want to summarize recent SoTL trends in political science. As a discipline, political science is increasingly embracing the principles of the SoTL movement—specifically, moving toward evidence-based practice in teaching and learning, as well as going public with the results of our inquiries into student learning.

Studying teaching and learning in this manner seems particularly apt for political science for two reasons. First, the study of political learning is part of political science. Studying political learning in the home, the schools, between peers, through the media, and in other ways was an established practice of political scientists from the 1950s through the 1970s. This subfield of political socialization no longer has the cache that it once did, but remains a valid political science subfield. Thus, a political scientist who adds the study of teaching and learning in her classes to her research agenda need not completely turn her back on disciplinary research.

Second, the diversity of methodological tools used in political science, both quantitative and qualitative, provides a wide range of ways to understand student learning. This analysis can use pre- and postclass survey data, with all possible statistical bells and whistles, or close textual analysis of student papers and exams, or interviews with students, or other means of assessing and describing learning. When the scholarship of teaching and learning suggests that we transition from anecdotal accounts of student learning to rigorous, evidence-based reports, political science is poised to do so.

Political scientists who wish to make the scholarship of teaching and learning part of their professional agenda face many of the same challenges faced by colleagues across the academy, which are beyond the scope of this chapter to address. But some positive changes have occurred in the discipline. Within the last decade, the American Political Science Association has inaugurated an annual Teaching and Learning Conference. This has helped to build community for more teaching-oriented political scientists and provided a forum for sharing work on teaching and learning (both descriptive work on teaching innovations as well as more empirical work studying its effects on student learning). In addition, the *Journal of Political Science Education* began publishing in 2005. John Ishiyama, the founding editor, was a political scientist with a background in SoTL, forged through his year as a Carnegie Scholar at the Carnegie Foundation for the Advancement of Teaching. The journal provides a peer-reviewed outlet for high-quality, evidence-based work on teaching and learning in political science. These forums make it easier for political scientists to engage in SoTL.

What has this scholarship of teaching and learning in political science taught us? To this point, the bulk of SoTL in political science has consisted of course-based studies, examinations of the effectiveness of particular pedagogical techniques such as simulations, experiential learning, or discussions in online classes (e.g., Bernstein, 2008; Bernstein & Meizlish, 2003; Gershtenson, Rainey, & Rainey, 2010; Hamann, Pollock, & Wilson, 2009b; Shaw, 2004; van Assendelft, 2008). Taken as a whole, these studies document that, simply speaking, active learning works. Students who engage in innovative political science pedagogy emerge more highly engaged in the subject matter, with a richer understanding of the course material, and with a stronger sense of their ability to understand the discipline and to participate in politics when they are moved to do so. It appears, then, that pedagogies that engage students and that connect what they are learning to the real world are high-impact activities.

To be sure, not all SoTL in political science looks at individual classes. Thornton (2010), for example, examines students' informational literacy, an important area to study in the ever-changing political media environment. Hamann, Pollock, and Wilson (2009a) offer one of the few political science SoTL studies that attempts to "go meta" and examine the movement in the field as a whole. They determine, not surprisingly, that scholars engaging in SoTL tend to be younger, more often are female, and are teaching disproportionately at bachelor's or master's institutions (as opposed to doctoral-granting schools). Overall, though, SoTL in political science has focused on examining the results of active-learning pedagogies, revealing the successes and limitations of these methods.

Signature Pedagogies in Political Science

With this background on SoTL in political science in place, I turn now to a discussion of signature pedagogies. Articulated first by Shulman (2005), signature pedagogies were defined by their ability to encourage students "to think, to perform and to act with integrity" in the discipline; it was, in short, a form of socialization (p. 52). Calder (2006) echoes this point in noting that signature pedagogies encourage students "to do, think and value what practitioners in the field are doing, thinking and valuing" (p. 1361). Signature pedagogies can lead disciplines to identify themselves through a pedagogical perspective: They force the disciplines to define the content, skills, and values most important to the discipline and then lead experts to discern how best to teach these content, skills, and values to novices. As I have argued, signature pedagogies in political science should ideally lead students to be able to consider and evaluate the behaviors of goal-seeking actors in political science.

Signature pedagogies involve both empirical and normative dimensions. On the one hand, the phrase *signature pedagogy* can be used to explain what the signature pedagogy *is* within a particular discipline. We know, for example, that the Socratic method is commonly used in law school, grand rounds in medical school, and the design studio in many areas of engineering. We must ask, however, whether these pedagogies are, in fact, the most appropriate pedagogies for their disciplines. This suggests a normative perspective: In addition to asking what the signature pedagogy *is* in a particular discipline, an additional question might be, "What *should* the signature pedagogy be in this discipline?" I focus on this normative question in the remainder of this chapter: I suggest that political science is moving toward a more normatively desirable signature pedagogy, with a greater possibility of using our classes to help our students develop the skills and dispositions our students ought to have.

It is difficult to come to grips with the notion of a signature pedagogy in political science for a couple of reasons. First, signature pedagogies in other fields suggest uniformity in how that subject area is taught. As noted previously, law and medicine, to take the two most obvious examples in the professions, have signature pedagogies that are widely practiced in their disciplines; even the casual observer can recognize the Socratic method as portrayed in films like *The Paper Chase* or medical rounds as portrayed on the television show *Scrubs* as "authentic" portrayals of a legal or medical education, respectively. We expect that legal or medical education will look this way and are surprised when it does not. No such dominant pedagogy exists in political science.

A second challenge to the search for political science's signature pedagogy (related to the first) is the diversity of the discipline. Like many other disciplines, the types of courses we teach in political science vary a great deal. Some, such as political theory courses, look more like philosophy or literature courses, in which classic texts are dissected in great depth. Research methods courses, on the other hand, frequently resemble statistics courses, in which students learn quantitative techniques and apply them to large data sets (e.g., Bos & Schneider, 2009; Thies & Hogan, 2005). In between these two extremes, we see a range of courses in subdisciplines and a range of dominant methodologies. In some subfields (e.g., American political behavior), research is almost entirely quantitative; in others, such as in courses on the developing world, research is often descriptive and case-based. This diversity in subject matter often leads to diversity in method: One might teach research methods courses or public opinion courses in a computer lab but would never do that in a political theory course. This range of courses and methodologies ideally shapes a broadly trained political scientist by the time students complete the major.

An additional reason that defining our signature pedagogy is difficult is that political science, like many disciplines in the liberal arts, does not lead to a professional degree. Signature pedagogies are traditionally associated with professional degree programs, such as law and medicine, in which all graduates are expected to emerge with a body of knowledge and a commitment to the standards of professional practice in that field. Law schools turn out lawyers, medical schools turn out doctors. We cannot say with any precision that political science programs turn out "political scientists." Although we hope that our students emerge as competent, capable thinkers about politics and have internalized the epistemological norms of the discipline, a precious few will pursue graduate studies in the field. Instead, we are simultaneously turning out future law students, civil servants, lobbyists, teachers, diplomats, and so on. The lack of uniformity in where our students are going perhaps contributes to a lack of uniformity in how we get them there.

Is there a default pedagogy (Gurung, Chick, & Haynie, 2009) in political science, one that de facto dominates teaching in the discipline? Although reliable data are hard to come by, a strong anecdotal sense suggests that lecture is the most common form of instruction within political science. Virtually every professor teaching political science uses lecture in teaching; furthermore, because the large introductory classes are where we see the most students, and where lecture is most commonly practiced, it is fair to say that the vast majority of students who take political science at the college or university level experience it as predominantly a lecture-oriented field. This is not to say all political science teaching is lecture-based. As will be discussed in what follows, some more active-learning techniques (particularly simulations and service-learning) are increasingly being practiced in political science. In graduate programs, as well as in advanced undergraduate classes, the seminar is the dominant form of instruction; sometimes it is done well, other times, less so. Of course, neither lecture nor the seminar are uniquely practiced in political science, nor is their practice especially different in political science than in other disciplines.

A Normative Perspective on Signature Pedagogies in Political Science

Lecture, the likely default signature pedagogy in political science, has some well-known limitations. The decision to use lecture is often made because of inertia or contextual factors (such as a large lecture class) that accompany its use; lecture also represents the most efficient way to convey material from the instructor to the students. Although it might have empirical support as the most ubiquitous approach, *should* it be the signature pedagogy in political science? The answer to that is a resounding no; there are many better approaches, more appropriate to teaching the unique content of political science as well as the disciplinary skills we want students to acquire (see, for example, Bernstein & Meizlish's [2003] experimental and control group study comparing classes that had an extended simulation with similar classes that did not).

What *should* political science's signature pedagogy be? My earlier discussion suggests that an understanding of politics requires that we consider how the actors in a given situation gather information and make decisions. Thus, if we are using signature pedagogies as a way to get our students to think like political actors, the role-playing simulation becomes a logical candidate. Simulations have a long history in political science as a way to achieve higher-order educational goals (Boocock & Schild, 1968; Dewey, 1938; Heitzmann, 1974; Walcott, 1980). They have proven to be an effective way to put students in the role of a political actor, get them to consider the goals of the actor and the means by which goals can be achieved, and the possible moves by others in the situation. Ideally, they help students understand how decisions get made, as well as the consequences of these decisions.

In recent years, the depth and range of political science simulations has grown exponentially. In U.S. politics, for example, simulations have been used to teach issues such as legislative politics (Bernstein & Meizlish, 2003; Sands & Shelton, 2010), public policy making and iron triangles (Endersby & Webber, 1995), constitutional law and judicial decision making (Hardy, Rackaway, & Sonnier, 2005; Hensley, 1993), elections and voting (Endersby & Shaw, 2009), citizen assemblies (Gershtenson, Rainey, & Rainey, 2010), and as a tool to help students form their own political attitudes (Bernstein, 2008). The foregoing are just examples drawn from a large literature of games and simulations for use in the classroom.

Outside of U.S. politics, simulations seem even more popular; more than half of the simulation-related articles published in "The Teacher" section of *PS: Political Science and Politics*, for example, have dealt with simulations of international relations. (This section of *PS* has historically been the most common place to find teaching-related articles; as such, it is a reasonable bellwether of the profession. This journal is also included as part of the membership package for members of the American Political Science Association.) One can find simulations of the United Nations (McIntosh, 2001), energy policy (Garrison, Redd, & Carter, 2010), peacekeeping (Shaw, 2004), free trade (Switky & Avilés, 2007), the European Union (Galatas, 2006), terrorism (Franke, 2006; Siegel & Young, 2009), arms control (Kelle, 2008), and the Middle East (Raymond & Sorensen, 2008). Again, these examples are just samples of the extensive literature out there on simulations in political science.

The totality of the literature on simulations (including many pieces not cited here) reveals that simulations are an effective way to engage students in the course material: Students learn the material better when they are actively participating rather than passively listening to lectures. More importantly, from a political science perspective, simulations help students to interpret current issues through a different lens, a disciplinary lens. By allowing themselves to stand in the shoes of different actors in a political system, students gain the perspective they need to interpret strategic choices made by different actors. Furthermore, simulations allow students to learn how the actions of one actor might influence or constrain the actions of subsequent actors; often, political figures will act strategically in making their moves, hoping to constrain the choices available to their opponents. Professors could talk about this in class and offer examples of these strategic interactions (Allison's [1971] work on the Cuban Missile Crisis being a classic example that is still used in classes). We might even be able to do it well. But allowing students to participate in this process themselves and make the decisions that constrain others (or to be constrained by the decisions of others) is a far superior way to help students understand the nature of political decision making.

An additional simulation-based pedagogical enhancement in political science has been the use of large-scale, extracurricular learning activities. Moving outside the classroom, increasing numbers of schools have successful programs such as Model United Nations, or Mock Trial. In these programs, students learn about international affairs or courtroom procedures by acting as nations in the UN, or as attorneys or witnesses in simulated trials. This activity can sometimes be connected to a class, but other times it is purely extracurricular. Students then compete against other schools in regional and national tournaments. In Mock Trial, later rounds of the tournaments are conducted in federal courtrooms, with federal judges playing the judicial role in the trial. The Model United Nations program has an annual competition in New York, at the site of the UN. Like the in-class simulations, the enhanced discipline-based learning opportunities offered through these methods are quite impressive. Mock Trial and Model United Nations have the advantage of involving students for far more hours, and in more social ways, in this disciplinary activity than any in-class simulation could ever hope to.

In addition to simulations, an increasingly popular form of pedagogy in political science (and across the academy) has been academic service-learning. Academic service-learning takes students into the community to perform community service; it is different from volunteer work in that the service work is connected to the learning aims of the course. Having students volunteer in a soup kitchen is community service; when students do this as part of a public policy class, for example, and use the experience to help them do research on poverty, it becomes service-learning. An even higher form of service-learning might occur if students can provide something more long lasting for the soup kitchen, such as a plan to help them serve people in the community more effectively.

Political science is well-positioned to take advantage of service-learning as a pedagogy (Battistoni & Hudson, 1997). For one thing, it offers our students the opportunity to connect what they are doing to the real world—to *do* political science. Students should also be learning skills in their classes that might be valuable to local agencies: Classes might, for example, be able to perform surveys on local policy matters for city governments that cannot afford to contract out for this service (Bernstein, Ohren, & Shue, 2003). Students get enhanced disciplinary learning in their courses, and the local communities obtain a valuable project that they otherwise could not get. Service-learning is most often practiced at the local level (Redlawsk, Rice, & Associates, 2009; van Assendelft, 2008), but is increasingly being used in a wider variety of contexts (Tan, 2009).

Although simulations and service-learning are becoming ever more popular and are being used in a wider variety of classes, they still do not predominate nearly enough to have become the signature pedagogy of political science. Their increasing use does, however, serve to push the discipline to more sustained thinking about the knowledge, attitudes, and skills with which we wish our students to leave our classes (and our major). As more and more political scientists use simulations and service-learning and see the benefit of each approach, they will be led to consider further what we really want our students to learn. In this way, political science can move closer to developing a true signature pedagogy (or pedagogies), by which experts in the discipline will help novices uncover the habits of mind that characterize political science as a discipline.

Conclusion

Lecture has persisted as the empirically most common pedagogy in political science for many reasons, including inertia. As more faculty begin to explore different pedagogies (such as simulations and service-learning), opportunities for meaningful disciplinary learning increase dramatically. These pedagogies emphasize some of the important theoretical considerations in the discipline of political science, such as the need to understand the nature of goal-driven actions by self-interested political actors, and the need to understand how actions encourage or constrain other actions. Thus, normatively, they are more appropriate signature pedagogies for the discipline. As these pedagogies proliferate, the field has also created more opportunities to rigorously explore their effectiveness, in ways that are appropriate to the epistemology of political science. In an ideal world, more rigorous evaluation of these burgeoning signature pedagogies will help other political scientists see their value. When that happens, the revolution toward better pedagogy in political science will have taken a dramatic leap forward.

References

Allison, G. T. (1971). *Essence of decision: Explaining the Cuban Missile Crisis.* Boston, MA: Little Brown.

Battistoni, R. M., & Hudson, W. E. (1997). *Experiencing citizenship: Concepts and models for service-learning in political science.* Washington, DC: American Association for Higher Education.

Bernstein, J. L. (2008). Cultivating civic competence: Simulations and skill-building in an introductory government class. *Journal of Political Science Education, 4*, 1–20.

Bernstein, J. L., & Meizlish, D. S. (2003). Becoming Congress: A longitudinal study of the civic engagement implications of a classroom simulation. *Simulation & Gaming, 34*, 198–219.

Bernstein, J. L., Ohren, J., & Shue, L. (2003). A collaborative teaching approach to linking classes and community. *Journal of Public Affairs Education, 9*, 117–127.

Boocock, S. S., & Schild, E. O. (1968). *Simulation games in learning.* Beverly Hills, CA: Sage.

Bos, A. L., & Schneider, M. C. (2009). Stepping around the brick wall: Overcoming student obstacles in methods courses. *PS: Political Science & Politics, 42*, 375–383.

Calder, L. (2006). Uncoverage: Toward a signature pedagogy for the history survey. *Journal of American History, 92*, 1359–1369.

Dewey, J. (1938). *Education and experience.* New York, NY: Touchstone.

Downs, A. (1957). *An economic theory of democracy.* New York, NY: Harper.

Endersby, J. W., & Shaw, K. B. (2009). Strategic voting in plurality elections: A simulation of Duverger's law. *PS: Political Science and Politics, 42*, 393–399.

Endersby, J. W., & Webber, D. M. (1995). Iron triangle simulation: A role-playing game for undergraduates in Congress, interest groups, and public policy classes. *PS: Political Science and Politics, 28*, 520–523.

Franke, V. (2006). The Meyerhoff incident: Simulating bioterrorism in a national security class. *PS: Political Science and Politics, 39*, 153–156.

Galatas, S. E. (2006). A simulation of the Council of the European Union: Assessment of the impact on student learning. *PS: Political Science and Politics, 39*, 147–151.

Garrison, J. A., Redd, S. B., & Carter, R. G. (2010). Energy security under conditions of uncertainty: Simulating a comparative bureaucratic politics approach. *Journal of Political Science Education, 6*, 19–48.

Gershtenson, J., Rainey, G. W., Jr., & Rainey, J. G. (2010). Creating better citizens? Effects of a model citizens' assembly on student political attitudes and behavior. *Journal of Political Science Education, 6*, 95–116.

Gurung, R. A. R., Chick, N. L., & Haynie, A. (2009). *Exploring signature pedagogies: Approaches to teaching disciplinary habits of mind.* Sterling, VA: Stylus.

Hamann, K., Pollock, P. H., & Wilson, B. W. (2009a). Who SoTLs where? Publishing the scholarship of teaching and learning in political science. *PS: Political Science & Politics, 42*, 729–735.

Hamann, K., Pollock, P. H., & Wilson, B. W. (2009b). Learning from "listening" to peers in online political science classes. *Journal of Political Science Education, 5*, 1–11.

Hardy, R. J., Rackaway, C., & Sonnier, L. E. (2005). In the Supreme Court justices' shoes: Critical thinking through the use of hypothetical case law analysis and interactive simulations. *PS: Political Science and Politics, 38*, 411–414.

Heitzmann, W. R. (1974). *Educational games and simulations:* Washington, DC: National Science Teachers Association.

Hensley, T. R. (1993). Come to the edge: Role playing activities in a constitutional law class. *PS: Political Science and Politics, 26,* 64–68.

Huber, M. T., & Morreale, S. T. (2002). *Disciplinary styles in the scholarship of teaching and learning: Exploring common ground.* Washington, DC: American Association for Higher Education and the Carnegie Foundation for the Advancement of Teaching.

Kelle, A. (2008). Experiential learning in an arms control simulation. *PS: Political Science and Politics, 41,* 379–385.

McIntosh, D. (2001). The uses and limits of the Model United Nations in an international relations classroom. *International Studies Perspectives, 2*(3), 269–280.

Raymond, C., & Sorensen, K. (2008). The use of a Middle East crisis simulation in an international relations course. *PS: Political Science and Politics, 41,* 179–182.

Redlawsk, D. P., Rice, T., & Associates. (2009). *Civic service: Service learning with state and local government partners.* San Francisco, CA: Jossey-Bass.

Sands, E. C., & Shelton, Allison. (2010). Learning by doing: A simulation for teaching how Congress works. *PS: Political Science and Politics, 43,* 133–138.

Shaw, C. (2004). Using role-play scenarios in the IR classroom: An examination of exercises on peacekeeping operations and foreign policy decision making. *International Studies Perspectives, 5,* 1–22.

Shulman, L. S. (2005). Signature pedagogies in the professions. *Daedalus, 134,* 52–59.

Siegel, D. A., & Young, J. K. (2009). Simulating terrorism: Credible commitment, costly signaling, and strategic behavior. *PS: Political Science and Politics, 42,* 765–771.

Switky, B., & Avilés, W. (2007). Simulating the free trade area of the Americas. *PS: Political Science and Politics, 40,* 399–405.

Tan, K. P. (2009). Service learning outside the U.S.: Initial experiences in Singapore's higher education. *PS: Political Science and Politics, 42,* 549–557.

Thies, C. G., & Hogan, R. E. (2005). The state of undergraduate research methods training in political science. *PS: Political Science & Politics, 38,* 293–297.

Thornton, S. (2010). From "scuba-diving" to "jet-skiing": Information behavior, political science, and the Google generation. *Journal of Political Science Education, 6,* 353–368.

van Assendelft, L. (2008). City council meetings are cool: Increasing student civic engagement through service learning. *Journal of Political Science Education, 4,* 86–97.

Walcott, C. (1980). *Simple simulations.* Washington, DC: American Political Science Association.

Wineburg, S. (2001). *Historical thinking and other unnatural acts: Charting the future of teaching the past.* Philadelphia, PA: Temple University Press.

8

IS THERE A SIGNATURE PEDAGOGY IN ECONOMICS?

Mark H. Maier, KimMarie McGoldrick, and Scott P. Simkins

On the surface, economic education appears relatively static: The same material has been taught in the same way for decades. As in many disciplines, lecture remains the dominant teaching practice, but alternatives to traditional approaches that actively involve students in the learning process are beginning to emerge. Some of these pedagogical innovations are tied to discipline-based research (e.g., classroom-based economic experiments that mimic research-based experiments in behavioral economics), others are linked to pedagogical research in other disciplines or the scholarship of teaching and learning more generally (e.g., see the pedagogical practices highlighted in the *Starting Point: Teaching and Learning Economics* project)[1], and still others result from changes in the way that economists "do economics" (e.g., service-learning activities prompted by attempts to understand the financial crisis).

Although new pedagogic practices have been slow to take hold in the discipline, there is a growing unease about whether current teaching methods will adequately prepare the next generation of economists for the unstructured and interdisciplinary societal challenges they are likely to face as business leaders, policy makers, politicians, and teachers. Ultimately, if economic education and its signature pedagogies aim to teach students to "think like an economist," as most economists would argue, then the critical question becomes: What teaching practices, content, and skills are best suited to reach that goal? There is a lack of disciplinary consensus on the answer to this question. As a result, we argue here that there is currently no "signature pedagogy" in economics.

In this chapter we lay out influences that have shaped content and teaching practices in economics courses, as well as the focus of economic education research. We begin by providing background on who takes economics, what they study, and how it is taught, and then focus on why economists adapt an expedient, rather than signature pedagogy, in the classroom. Next, we summarize historical influences on the practice and research of economic education, along with recent calls for change. Finally, we describe a major stumbling block to developing a signature pedagogy and emerging influences on economic education and their implications for a potential signature pedagogy in economics.

Default Teaching in Economics: An Expedient, Not Signature, Pedagogy

Although only 2% of undergraduates choose economics as their major, estimates suggest that between 40 and 60% of all college students (roughly 1.5 million) take at least one introductory economics course (Bosshardt & Watts, 2008; Siegfried, 2000). What is taught in these introductory courses? For the most part, the structure and topics covered in these courses closely mimic those outlined in traditional economics textbooks, which have changed little since Samuelson's pathbreaking *Economics* (Samuelson, 1997a) was published in 1948 (Colander, 2005, 2006; Wirtz, 1998). Although a number of economic educators across political and ideological spectrums have argued that the introductory curriculum outlined in modern principles textbooks is out of date, overly abstract, and too encyclopedic in nature (Becker, 2007; Colander, 2006; Nelson, 2006, 2009; Samuelson, 1997b; Skousen, 1997), there is no universal agreement on what should replace it. A commonly proposed alternative focuses on fewer core concepts in a one-semester survey course, but economists have yet to agree on a common set of key disciplinary concepts. Some have advocated for a small set of mainstream concepts (Hansen, Salemi, & Siegfried, 2002), whereas others have favored a focus on Nobel Prize–winning research (Becker & Greene, 2005), the contested political underpinnings of economic theory (Knoedler & Underwood, 2003; Schneider & Shackelford, 2001), a social issues approach (Grimes,

2009), or an emphasis on "big think" questions that invite students to investigate topics across courses and disciplines (Colander & McGoldrick, 2009).

How is undergraduate economics taught? In 1995, 2000, and 2005, Becker and Watts (Becker & Watts, 1996, 2001;Watts & Becker, 2008) surveyed U.S. academic economists, documenting how economics is taught in four different types of undergraduate courses (introductory, intermediate, econometrics/statistics, and electives). Their work reveals a "status quo of students as passive receptors of textbook driven knowledge" (McGoldrick & Peterson, in press, p. 5). Specifically, economics instructors rely on "lecturing and writing or drawing on the chalkboard/whiteboard" as the overwhelmingly dominant pedagogical classroom practice, regardless of course or institutional classification (Watts & Becker, 2008, p. 274). These surveys indicate that there has been remarkably little change in pedagogic practice in the field over the past 15 years, with only small increases in the use of classroom experiments in introductory courses. Although the surveys point to relatively high use of discussion in a variety of economics courses, much of this practice employs instructor–student discussion rather than student–student discussion (e.g., cooperative learning) (Watts & Becker, 2008, p. 283). Some may argue that demands on faculty time drive this reliance on lecture-based methods, yet Becker and Watts (2000) suggest current practices are "established by convenience, custom and inertia rather than efficiency or, especially, by what represents effective teaching practices in today's undergraduate curriculum" (p. 4).

Clearly, economics is not alone in its reliance on the lecture approach, although there is some evidence that lectures are even more predominant in economics than in other disciplines (Allgood, Bosshardt, van der Klaauw, & Watts, 2004, p. 263). However, the typical structure of economics lectures makes the discipline somewhat unique among the social sciences. Most economics instruction follows a sequence beginning with the presentation of an abstract model, typically in graphical form, which is then used to predict economic behavior under various conditions and evaluate the economic impacts of alternative policies. In a very limited sense, this pedagogy models how economists "do economics." Economists rely heavily on deductive reasoning, beginning with assumptions about human behavior—sometimes explicit, sometimes not (Cohn 2007; Keen, 2001; Klamer, McCloskey, & Ziliak, 2010; Nelson, 2006)—rather than insights gathered inductively based on history, case studies, or observations, as is common in other social sciences.

Because of the reliance on abstract analytical models to teach economic concepts and principles, typical classroom instruction imparts a sense of unwarranted certainty to economics, in stark contrast to the reality observed as one follows the news and debates among economists. In particular, this approach neglects hypothesis testing, a key component of what economists do as professionals (Colander, 2005). For the most part, economics students do not reenact the procedures that professional economists use, testing models with data and sophisticated statistical techniques, especially in introductory courses where students get their first (and often last) exposure to economics.[2] Instead, economics instructors typically assert a model and then explore its ramifications; students are rarely asked to compare their own economic experience with that predicted by the models they are taught.

For the college principles of economics course, this narrow implementation of what it means to think like an economist, in conjunction with the encyclopedic nature of textbooks, creates an "expedient pedagogy" (Ciccone, 2009, p. xiii) that relies primarily on one-way transmission of ideas and information, rather than providing students with the opportunity to relate economic ideas to their own lives, consider alternative models of economic behavior, or discuss normative issues of equity or values. It is one in which instructors race to cover the economics "canon"—often with increasing mathematical and analytical precision, but with little connection to complex, interdisciplinary, and global challenges that students will face after they graduate.

As Ciccone (2009, p. xiii) cautions, we should not confuse a widespread, traditional, or expedient pedagogy with a signature pedagogy. He notes that in many disciplines, the "usual pedagogy may be at odds with, or at least unsupportive of" the desired habits of mind that distinguish one discipline from another. The same is true in economics, raising the question as to whether there is currently a signature pedagogy in the discipline, in the sense that Shulman (2005) defined it: "the types of teaching that organize the fundamental ways in which future practitioners are educated for their new profession" (p. 52). Pedagogical practice in economics appears to be driven by "convenience, custom and inertia" rather than by an intentional connection to how economics students will use economics concepts or ways of thinking in their future lives.

The Practice and Research of Economic Education

Despite the lack of change in economics instruction or the structure of introductory economics courses over time, there is a long history of support within the discipline for both the teaching of economics and research on economic education (Saunders, in press) by the primary professional association in economics, the American Economic Association (AEA), as well as the Council for Economic Education.[3] Since its founding in 1885, the AEA has demonstrated support for improving economics education at all levels, with interest increasing after the publication of "The Teaching of Undergraduate Economics" (Taylor, 1950), a study undertaken in 1944 by the newly formed Committee on Undergraduate Teaching of Economics and Training of Economists. The AEA's Committee on Economic Education (AEA–CEE) was formed in 1955 and was later charged with "improving the quality of economic education at all levels, from precollege to college, adult and general economic education" (Hinshaw & Siegfried, 1991, p. 378). Since 1967, the AEA–CEE has arranged at least one session on economic education at the AEA annual meeting, with the proceedings of this session published in the flagship *American Economic Review* (Saunders, in press). Over the last decade, the AEA–CEE has increased the number of sessions on economics education at the annual meeting and since 2000 has sponsored a poster session focused on teaching innovations in economics.[4]

Until the mid-1940s "the teaching of economics was regularly a central topic for discussion and debate *among the leaders* of the association" (Hinshaw & Siegfried, 1991, p. 379). However, although well-known economists remain involved in the textbook market, economic education research is now conducted by a wider, if less prominent, group. Broader disciplinary interest in economic education grew significantly in the 1970s, from eight studies available in this field in 1969 to 179 research articles and books in 1979 (Hinshaw & Siegfried, 1991, p. 379). Expansion of economic education research during the 1970s is closely correlated with the establishment of the premier journal in the field, the *Journal of Economic Education* (*JEE*), which originated in 1969. The journal classifies publications into research in economic education, economic content, economic instruction, features, and information and also includes an online section. Over the last 20 years, the *JEE* has published more articles in the area of economic instruction (innovations in pedagogy, materials, methods, and the way economics is taught)—33% of all articles over this period—than in any of the other areas.

Despite significant research on pedagogical practice in economics, there has been relatively little actual change in classroom teaching. One reason is that there are few identifiable long-term research projects—experimental economics is an exception, as described later—and few efforts focused on identifying and addressing student learning gaps in economics. As a result, although the methods of economic education research are clearly established (quantitative studies comparing control and intervention groups), the outcomes are narrowly defined or limited to single, small sample studies. By contrast, support for discipline-based educational research in some fields, such as physics, comes in the form of research groups focusing on understanding how students learn, or fail to learn, disciplinary concepts. Researchers in these fields have developed a cumulative knowledge base on this topic by systematically identifying student learning gaps, creating innovative teaching practices and curricular materials that intentionally address those gaps, and assessing the efficacy of these efforts in a variety of ways (Maier & Simkins, in press). Unfortunately, similar efforts in economics are hard to find. Moreover, fewer economists are currently being trained in the economic education research-specific statistical and empirical tools necessary to advance knowledge in this field, and fewer graduate programs recommend economic education as a specialized field.[5]

Paralleling the overall rise in economic education research over the past 40 years has been a series of national teacher-training workshops in economics, first offered in research universities (the biggest producers of economics instructors) and later more broadly (Goodman, Maier, & Moore, 2003; Salemi, Saunders, & Walstad, 1996). The most recent program, the *Teaching Innovations Program* (2005–2009), included both a traditional (three-day) workshop focused on interactive teaching strategies and a follow-up Web-based tutorial aimed at promoting on-campus implementation of interactive teaching methods, along with opportunities for presenting and publishing classroom-based research on these methods (Salemi & Walstad, 2010).

Additionally, economics educators have benefited from extensive National Science Foundation research support for new and effective teaching methods in economics; since 1999 the National Science Foundation has awarded 23 grants for economic education research and training, totaling more than $5.7 million. Of that, approximately half ($2.81 million) has been awarded to nine projects supporting classroom or online economics experiments, with another $1.7 million divided among six projects developing economic simulations, online trading markets, and adaptations of pedagogies developed in other fields. The National Science Foundation recently awarded $1.17 million for two comprehensive projects introducing economists to a wide variety of innovative pedagogical practices—the *Teaching Innovations Project* described previously and the Web-based *Starting Point: Teaching and Learning Economics* pedagogic portal (http://serc.carleton.edu/econ/index.html) described later in this chapter.

Although disciplinary organizations in economics have provided support for pedagogical innovation and economic education research for more than 60 years, these efforts have been diffuse in nature and disciplinary consensus on their overall goals has been largely absent. As a result, despite decades of support for pedagogical change in the discipline, there has been surprisingly little change in teaching practices in the field.

Training Students to "Think Like Economists"

Perhaps the central reason why economics continues to be dominated by an expedient pedagogy of lecture-based teaching focused on abstract (and increasingly mathematical) models, rather than a signature pedagogy aimed at helping students "think like economists," is the growing dichotomy between the way future economic educators are taught in graduate school and the broad economic thinking skills that many economists view as the defining characteristic of the discipline. Siegfried et al. (1991), in the first major report on the purpose and structure of the undergraduate economics major, viewed thinking like an economist in a broad sense, focusing not only on deductive reasoning processes and abstract models, but also on creative skills such as the following:

> identifying economic issues and problems, framing them in ways other people do not see, devising novel policy proposals for dealing with problems, analyzing both the intended and unintended effects of policies, and devising innovative methods to estimate the magnitude of these effects. (p. 21)

This conception of "thinking like an economist" stands in stark contrast to the way that most economists are currently taught in graduate school, a system that rewards technical analysis of narrow topics where one can make a significant contribution to the discipline rather than attempts to tackle messy, interdisciplinary "big think" questions that remain resistant to easy solutions. As a result, "graduate economics training has become more technical, more and more reliant on mathematics and statistics," a trend mirroring the discipline as a whole (Colander & McGoldrick, 2009, p. 16). Graduate students in economics today are trained to be researchers, not teachers. Newly minted PhDs, although well-versed in highly technical skills, are ill prepared to teach introductory courses, relying heavily on encyclopedic textbooks to organize topics and adopting an expedient, lecture-based teaching approach in order to cover as much content as possible—while also preserving valuable time for research activity, which dominates annual reviews and tenure decisions.

Siegfried's vision for economic education hints at the possibility of a signature pedagogy in economics, one that provides students with not only technical mathematical and statistical skills, but also the ability to think broadly, creatively, and analytically about a wide range of social problems. In order to develop this type of shared pedagogical foundation, however, economists will need to close the gap between the way economics is taught to future economic educators in graduate school and the broader educational aim of helping undergraduate students think like economists. Until then, economics education will continue to be dominated by an expedient, rather than signature, pedagogy.

Shifting Ground: New Influences on Economic Education Practice and Research

Despite economists' longstanding reliance on lecture methods, we sense a nascent disciplinary interest in pedagogical innovation that provides us with hope that the pace of pedagogical change might accelerate in the future. The sources of this interest are quite disparate, but together might provide enough force to effect broad change in economics classrooms. We briefly describe the influences that have, in our opinion, the most promise for the development of a signature pedagogy that supports the goal of teaching students to think like an economist.

Incorporating Ideas From Experimental and Behavioral Economics

The most extensive change in undergraduate teaching is grounded in expanding interest in economics experiments and behavioral economics as a research field, elevated by the awarding of the 2002 Nobel Memorial Prize in Economic Sciences to Vernon Smith and Daniel Kahneman. Classroom experiments are now supported by an extensive set of resources for economics instructors and have been the focus of multiple National Science Foundation grants in recent years.[6] Economic experiments are being used in an increasing number of courses to make concepts more relevant to students and engage them more actively in the learning process.

Classroom experiments in economics differ from traditional science laboratory experiments in that all data derives from student activity in simulated markets carried out during a classroom (or online) session. As a result, students are both the experimenter, analyzing the results, as well as the subject of investigation. For example, in the most commonly used economics experiment (Hazlett & Emerson, in press; Holt & McDaniel, 1998), the interaction of buyers and sellers in an auction market (similar to floor trading on the New York Stock Exchange) demonstrates the emergence of an equilibrium price and the impact of variations such as a price ceiling or asymmetric information between buyers and sellers. Research on this new pedagogic practice suggests increased student learning, greater interest in the discipline, and enhanced course enjoyment (Durham, McKinnon, & Schulman, 2007). If there is a single pedagogical innovation that has begun to move economics instruction away from an expedient pedagogy toward a signature pedagogy, classroom experiments would be it, because students perform economic analysis in ways that mimic what economists actually do and therefore develop skills consistent with thinking like an economist. Nevertheless, as the surveys of Watts and Becker (2008; Becker & Watts, 1996, 2001) indicate, classroom experiments are still used in only a small fraction of economics courses.

Changing the Nature of Graduate Education

Perhaps the most direct influence on undergraduate economics emerges from educational experiences of instructors. As noted previously, graduate training of economics instructors has become more specialized, technical, and quantitatively oriented. As a result, new college instructors are unlikely to teach in a way that develops the kind of broad "economic thinking" skills envisioned by Siegfried et al. (1991). However, disciplinary initiatives designed to expand graduate students' training are under way, including a pilot project designed to provide supplemental training through a "Creativity Boot Camp." Developers of this program hope to complement conventional graduate training by exposing students to an educational process that invites questions addressing broad-based, interdisciplinary social problems. The program is intended to extend graduate students' views about what it means to think like economists and ultimately begin to change undergraduate teaching as new professors enter the academic market.

Responding to Recent Economic Events

As a result of the recent financial crisis and associated worldwide recession, leaders in the discipline of economics are increasingly interested in the purpose and practice of economic education and its relevance to real-world economic issues. The recent economic crisis has engaged leading economists to "be more open about the limitations in economic research when teaching economics and to incorporate emerging insights and methods from the research into the classroom" (McGoldrick & Peterson, in press, p. 5). As this shift takes hold, instructors are more likely to provide students with opportunities to address messy, ill-structured, and interdisciplinary problems that are resistant to simple abstract modeling, mirroring the processes that economists face as analysts, policy makers, and business leaders.

Learning From Interdisciplinary Exchange

Our own work (Maier, McGoldrick, & Simkins, 2009) on the *Starting Point: Pedagogical Resources for Teaching and Learning Economics* pedagogic portal is another attempt to expand economists' pedagogical practice by creating and sharing Web-based pedagogical modules that provide economic educators with comprehensive resources on research-based pedagogical innovations developed in economics and adapted from other disciplines. *Starting Point* provides instructors with resources that support a shift away from an expedient pedagogy, a necessary complement to training undergraduates to think like economists. The site contains 16 online modules, each including a general description of a specific pedagogical method, theory, and evidence supporting effective use of the method, classroom implementation guides, and a library of economics-based examples that illustrate use of the teaching method. Modules were authored by interdisciplinary teams, and several explicitly adapt pedagogies successfully developed in other disciplines, such as context-rich problems, just-in-time teaching, and interactive lecture demonstrations. The portal also provides a location for economists to contribute examples associated with each pedagogic practice, contributing to a cumulative knowledge base on effective teaching practices. In short, *Starting Point* is helping to reduce barriers for implementing pedagogical innovation and develop a cumulative knowledge base covering both practice and implementation. Although the primary purpose of the *Starting Point* project is to increase the effectiveness of pedagogical practice in economics, the modules provide extensive examples of how to more fully engage students in the practice of *doing* economics (in a broad sense), the central issue at the heart of developing a signature pedagogy in the field.

Conclusion

Although teaching practices in economics have been slow to change, recent influences in economics education hint at the possibility of a signature pedagogy that more closely aligns how economics is taught with what economists do and how they think. However, major challenges will need to be overcome before this becomes a reality. For example, graduate students in economics are so narrowly trained to develop technical research skills that they are ill prepared to teach the broader "economic thinking" skills needed to address complex interdisciplinary problems facing the world economy. In addition, economists with an interest in research on effective teaching practices are often not trained in the requisite statistical and empirical tools necessary to carry out high-quality research in this area. Further, the development of a cumulative knowledge base on how best to teach economics to undergraduates to develop their "economic thinking" skills is inhibited by the dearth of leaders dedicated to economic education as their primary field of research.

Despite these challenges, the growing use of classroom-based economic experiments in undergraduate education, new initiatives to expand the nature of graduate education in economics, and the development of broad-based Web resources supporting pedagogical innovation provide hope for change. Over time, we envision movement away from the current expedient, model-oriented, analytical, and lecture-based teaching approach, toward a pedagogy that more fully engages students to think like economists. Only then will students be able to address the multifaceted, interdisciplinary, and global challenges they are likely to face in their lifetimes. And only then will economics make headway toward defining and employing a signature pedagogy.

Notes

1. See *Starting Point: Pedagogical Resources for Teaching and Learning Economics* at http://serc.carleton.edu/econ/index.html

2. The exception occurs in economic statistics and econometrics classes, in which hypothesis testing is standard curricular content. These courses are typically problem-oriented and focus on building statistical skills, much like mathematics courses that focus on developing mathematical problem-solving skills. However, such courses are not always required of students in the major.

3. The Council for Economic Education was incorporated with an explicit mission to focus on K–12 education. Their projects include the development of materials for the K–12 curriculum, educational programs for students, national assessment, and teacher training programs.

4. The AEA is not the only sponsor of economic education sessions at the national meetings. The National Association of Economic Educators and the Council for Economic Education typically cosponsor three sessions. Economic education sessions are also not relegated solely to the national meetings, as many sessions are organized annually at each of the four regional economic association meetings.

5. For one effort to train economic educators in statistical methods, see http://www.aeaweb.org/home/committees/AEACEE/Econometrics_Handbook/index.php

6. See Bergstrom & Miller (2000), the journal *Experimental Economics*, the teaching method "Classroom Experiments" at *Starting Point: Teaching and Learning Economics*, VECONLAB, EconPort, and Aplia for a wide variety of supporting materials.

References

Allgood, S., Bosshardt, W., van der Klaauw, W., & Watts, M. (2004). What students remember and say about college economics years later. *American Economic Review*, *94*(2), 259–265.

Becker, W. E. (2007). Quit lying and address the controversies: There are no dogmata, laws, rules or standards in the science of economics. *American Economist*, *51*(1), 3–14.

Becker, W. E., & Greene, W. H. (2005). Using the Nobel laureates in economics to teach quantitative methods. *Journal of Economic Education*, *36*(3), 261–277.

Becker, W. E., & Watts, M. (1996). Chalk and talk: A national survey on teaching undergraduate economics. *American Economic Review*, *86*(2), 448–453.

Becker, W. E., & Watts, M. (2000). Teaching economics: What it was, is and could be. In W. E. Becker & M. Watts (Eds.), *Teaching economics to undergraduates: Alternatives to chalk and talk* (pp. 1–10). Northampton, MA: Edward Elgar.

Becker, W. E., & Watts, M. (2001). Teaching methods in U.S. undergraduate economics courses. *Journal of Economic Education*, *32*(3), 269–279.

Bergstrom, T. C., & Miller, J. H. (2000). *Experiments with economic principles.* New York, NY: McGraw Hill.

Bosshardt, W., & Watts, M. (2008). Undergraduate students' coursework in economics. *Journal of Economic Education, 39*(2), 198–205.

Ciccone, A. A. (2009). Forward. In R. A. R. Gurung, N. L. Chick, & A. Haynie (Eds.), *Exploring signature pedagogies: Approaches to teaching disciplinary habits* (pp. xi–xvi). Sterling, VA: Stylus.

Cohn, S. M. (2007). *Reintroducing macroeconomics: A critical approach.* Armonk, NY: M. E. Sharpe.

Colander, D. (2005). What economists teach and what economists do. *Journal of Economic Education, 36*(3), 249–260.

Colander, D. (2006). Caveat lector: Living with the 15% rule. In D. Colander (Ed.), *The stories economists tell: Essays on the art of teaching economics* (pp. 33–43). New York, NY: McGraw-Hill.

Colander, D., & McGoldrick, K. (2009). The Teagle Foundation report: The economics major as part of a liberal education. In D. Colander & K. McGoldrick (Eds.), *Educating Economists: The Teagle Discussion on Re-evaluating the Undergraduate Economics Major* (pp. 3–39). Northampton, MA: Edward Elgar.

Durham, Y., McKinnon, T., & Schulman, C. (2007). Classroom experiments: Not just fun and games. *Economic Inquiry, 45*, 162–178.

Ferber, M. A. (1999). Guidelines for pre-college economic education: A critique. *Feminist Economics, 5*(3), 135–142.

Goodman, R. J. B., Maier, M., & Moore, R. L. (2003). Regional workshops to improve the teaching skills of economics faculty. *American Economic Review, 93*(2), 460–462.

Grimes, P. W. (2009). Reflections on introductory course structures. In D. Colander & K. McGoldrick (Eds.), *Educating economists: The Teagle Discussion on re-evaluating the undergraduate economics major* (pp. 95–98). Northampton, MA: Edward Elgar.

Hansen, W. L., Salemi, M. K., & Siegfried, J. J. (2002). Use it or lose it: Teaching literacy in the economics principles course. *American Economic Review, 92*(2), 463–472.

Hazlett, D., & Emerson, T. (in press). Experiments. In K. McGoldrick & G. Hoyt (Eds.), *The international handbook on teaching and learning economics.* Northampton, MA: Edward Elgar.

Hinshaw, C. E., & Siegfried, J. J. (1991). The role of the American Economic Association in economic education: A brief history. *The Journal of Economic Education, 22*(4), 373–381.

Holt, C. A., & McDaniel, T. (1998). Experimental economics in the classroom. In W. B. Walstad & P. Saunders (Eds.), *Teaching undergraduate economics* (pp. 257–268). Boston, MA: Irwin-McGraw-Hill.

Keen, S. (2001). *Debunking economics: The naked emperor of the social sciences.* Australia: Pluto Press.

Klamer, A., McCloskey, D., & Ziliak, S. (2010). *The economic conversation.* Retrieved from http://www.theeconomicconversation.com/

Knoedler, J. T., & Underwood, D. A. (2003). Teaching the principles of economics: A proposal for a multi-paradigmatic approach. *Journal of Economic Issues, 37*(3), 697–724.

Maier, M., McGoldrick, K., & Simkins, S. (2009). *Starting point: Pedagogical resources for teaching and learning economics.* Working paper. Retrieved from http://serc.carleton.edu/files/econ/project/working_paper_starting_point.pdf

Maier, M., & Simkins, S. (in press). Learning from physics education research: Lessons for economics education. In K. McGoldrick & G. Hoyt (Eds.), *The international handbook on teaching and learning economics.* Northampton, MA: Edward Elgar.

McGoldrick, K., & Peterson, J. (in press). Significant learning and civic education: Frameworks for teaching and learning about the financial crisis. *Journal of Social Science Education.*

Nelson, J. (2006). *Economics for humans.* Chicago, IL: University of Chicago Press.

Nelson, J. (2009). The principles course. In J. Reardon (Ed.), *The handbook for pluralist economics education* (pp. 57–68). London, UK: Routledge.

Salemi, M. K., Saunders, P., & Walstad, W. B. (1996). Teacher training programs in economics: Past, present, and future. *American Economic Review, 86*(2), 460–464.

Salemi, M. K., & Walstad, W. B. (Eds.). (2010). *Teaching innovations in economics: Strategies and applications for interactive instruction.* Northampton, MA: Edward Elgar.

Samuelson, P. A. (1997a). *Economics: The Original 1948 Edition.* New York, NY: McGraw-Hill/Irwin.

Samuelson, P. A. (1997b). Credo of a lucky textbook author. *The Journal of Economic Perspectives, 11*(2), 153–161.

Saunders, P. (in press). The history of economic education. In G. Hoyt & K. McGoldrick (Eds.), *The international handbook on teaching and learning economics.* Northampton, MA: Edward Elgar.

Schneider, G., & Shackelford, J. (2001). Economic standards and lists: Proposed antidotes for feminist economists. *Feminist Economics, 7*(2), 77–89.

Shulman, L. S. (2005). Signature pedagogies in the disciplines. *Daedalus, 134*(3), 52–59.

Siegfried, J. (2000). How many college students are exposed to economics? *Journal of Economic Education, 31*(2), 202–204.

Siegfried, J. J., Bartlett, R. L., Hansen, W. L., Kelley, A. C., McCloskey, D. N., & Tietenberg, T. H. (1991). The economics major: Can and should we do better than a B–? *American Economic Review, 81*(2), 20–25.

Skousen, M. (1997). The perseverance of Paul Samuelson's economics. *The Journal of Economic Perspectives, 11*(2), 137–152.

Taylor, H. (Ed.). (1950). The teaching of undergraduate economics: Report of the committee on the undergraduate teaching of economics and the training of economists. *American Economic Review, 40*(5) Part 2, i–226.

Watts, M., & Becker, W. (2008). A little more than chalk and talk: Results from a third national survey of teaching methods in undergraduate economics courses. *Journal of Economic Education, 39*(3), 273–286.

Wirtz, R. A. (1998). Econ 101: Is this the best way to teach economics? *The Region* (Federal Reserve Bank of Minneapolis), 54–57, 61–62.

9

SIGNATURE PEDAGOGIES IN CHEMISTRY

Steven Gravelle and Matthew A. Fisher

Similar to many other disciplines in science, technology, engineering, and mathematics (STEM), chemistry holds laboratory-based undergraduate research in particularly high regard. The American Chemical Society Committee on Professional Training (CPT, 2008) states:

> Undergraduate research allows students to integrate and reinforce chemistry knowledge from their formal course work, develop their scientific and professional skills, and create new scientific knowledge. A vigorous research program is also an effective means of keeping faculty current in their fields and provides a basis for acquiring modern instrumentation. Original research culminating in a comprehensive written report provides an effective means for integrating undergraduate learning experiences, and allows students to participate directly in the process of science. (p. 13)

Undergraduate research in a chemistry laboratory can be viewed as the signature pedagogy of chemistry, so chemical educators have explored pedagogies to provide similar experiences for students earlier in the curriculum or for those without ready access to such opportunities. But how do some of these pedagogies align with important characteristics of undergraduate research? This chapter examines undergraduate research and some of these pedagogies, including how students develop the habits that characterize the discipline of chemistry.

Thinking, Knowing, and Doing in Chemistry

What ways of thinking and knowing characterize chemistry as a discipline? CPT, in the same program guidelines quoted earlier, states that although chemistry increasingly overlaps with other sciences, "unchanged, however, is the molecular perspective which is at the heart of chemistry. Chemistry programs have the responsibility to communicate this molecular outlook to their students and to teach the skills necessary for their students to apply this perspective" (p. 1). Elsewhere, CPT clearly states that chemistry is an experimental science in which substantial laboratory work is essential: "[T]he ultimate goal of chemistry education is to provide students with the tools to solve problems" (p. 14). These tools include the ability to define a problem, develop an appropriate hypothesis amenable to testing, design and carry out experiments that are appropriate for the problem and hypothesis, analyze data using statistical methods, and draw appropriate conclusions, all while applying their knowledge of all chemistry subdisciplines, laboratory skills, and appropriate instrumentation.

This language, although helpful, strikes us as an incomplete answer to the question of how chemists think, know, and do. Additional insight can be gained by looking at the National Research Council Report *Beyond the Molecular Frontier* (2003), which describes chemists as scientists who seek to relate the properties of substances to their chemical composition and atomic level structure. Those properties could include physical properties (solid, liquid, or gas, the energy contained in the substance) and chemical properties (if a substance can be transformed into another substance by heating, exposure to light, or reaction with something else). Chemists seek to understand the mechanisms and speed by which these transformations and interactions occur, using that knowledge to develop predictive models of reaction sequences. Ultimately, this understanding of how the properties of substances are related to chemical composition and atomic structure can be used for both discovery (for already existing substances and living cells) and creation (for designing new molecules with desired properties).

There is one more significant aspect of how chemists think, know, and do. Johnstone (1993, 2000) has described the new chemical perspective as involving three corners of a triangle. In one corner is what Johnstone calls the "macroscopic": what can be seen, touched, smelled, or eaten. A second corner is the "submicroscopic": molecules, atoms, ions, and structures defined in these same terms. Finally, the third corner involves "representation": symbols, formulas, equations, stoichiometry, mathematical representations, and graphs. Johnstone emphasizes that professional chemists don't function in just one corner or along one edge but are ultimately called to function in the middle of the triangle, where they must move from one perspective to another without hesitation.

When seeking signature pedagogies in chemistry, the previous descriptions are still too broad. More detailed insight can be gained by looking more closely at *what* chemists do. A particularly effective approach is a model initially developed to better understand the characteristics of scientific inquiry. Reiff and colleagues (2002) surveyed more than 50 research scientists from 9 departments in a large research university about their conception of scientific inquiry. Although expecting to receive discipline-specific responses, they instead found commonality among scientists' responses regarding the characteristics of a scientific investigator and a scientific investigation. Scientific investigation should be fueled by questions posed by the investigator, a process focusing on the investigation and not the end result; that is, the investigator must be willing to be wrong and to be open to unexpected results, like good problem solvers. The single characteristic most frequently mentioned is the ability to make connections among ideas and among disciplines.

Based on their findings, Harwood (2004) developed a conceptual model called the "activity model" to describe scientific inquiry more authentically. This model consists of 10 activities, 9 of which surround the central theme of asking testable and meaningful questions (Harwood, Reiff, & Phillipson, 2002). One scientist confirms, "Even if students aren't designing a new question, they still should understand that information is the result of an inquiry-based kind of process," and another cautions that "the hardest thing to teach is the ability to ask the right question" (Reiff et al., 2002, p. 570). The other 9 activities include items such as defining the problem, examining the results, reflecting on the findings, and communicating with others. The activities are not in a prescribed order, nor are they the only ones that can be derived from their study, but they serve as a set of interconnected characteristics in a broad range of scientific investigations and, in our experience, mirror the experiences of chemists.

Undergraduate Chemical Research as a Signature Pedagogy of Chemistry

Undergraduate laboratory research, described by the Council on Undergraduate Research as "an inquiry or investigation conducted by an undergraduate student that makes an original, intellectual, or creative contribution to the discipline" (in Elrod, Husic, & Kinzie, 2010, p. 4), has been viewed as a signature pedagogy for any STEM field for several decades (Narum, 1991). If signature pedagogies are, in Shulman's words (2005), pedagogies that instruct novices in "critical aspects of the three fundamental aspects of professional work—to think, to perform, and to act with integrity" (p. 52), then it is hard to imagine a pedagogy that would come closer to the process of doing chemistry than undergraduate research in a chemistry lab. We propose that undergraduate chemical research in the laboratory is a signature pedagogy for chemistry because it situates student learning in the most authentic environment (Lave & Wenger, 1991)—laboratory research—and engages students in what chemists do.

The research on what students learn from undergraduate research is still young, but a good summary can be found in Crowe and Brakke (2008). Of particular interest are several publications (Hunter, Laursen, & Seymour, 2007; Lopatto, 2010; Seymour, Hunter, Laursen, & DeAntoni, 2004) focusing on students doing undergraduate research in STEM fields, including chemistry. These students showed significant gains in intellectual skills such as reading the primary literature, analysis, communication, and teamwork. Seymour and coworkers (Hunter et al., 2007; Seymour et al., 2004) also found that students showed significant gains in their confidence in their ability to work as scientists, a much more effective dimension of learning. At the same time, these studies do not shed much light on the extent to which students are engaged in a "cognitive apprenticeship" (Brown, Collins, & Duguid, 1989) in doing chemistry. More SoTL remains to be done for us to understand the full extent to which undergraduate laboratory research engages students in how chemists think and know.

Scholarship of Teaching and Learning in Chemistry

Chemistry as a discipline has a long tradition of focusing attention on education (Coppola & Jacobs, 2001). The American Chemical Society's Division of Chemical Education is more than 75 years old, makes major contributions to the technical program of each semiannual national meeting, sponsors a Biennial Conference on Chemical Education, and has published the *Journal of Chemical Education* since 1923. Other journals not published by the American Chemical Society, such as the *Journal of College Science Teaching* and the *Chemical Educator*, also serve as venues for SoTL. The scope of the *Journal of Chemical Education* is very broad: Chemical content, activities, laboratory experiments, instructional methods, and pedagogies are addressed through a variety of articles. Historically, published chemical education research has been based on learning theories, tested by experiments, and corroborated by data, whereas many of the other articles—teaching tips and methods, demonstrations, laboratory experiments—did not include evidence directly related to student learning. The situation in chemistry is quite similar to what Bauer-Dantoin (2009) describes for SoTL in biology.

The question of how chemists think, know, and do appears to be noticeably absent from attention within the *Journal of Chemical Education.* Almost all the articles focused on content and principles are from the perspective of chemistry teachers, much closer to pedagogical content knowledge (Shulman, 1986). In our conversations with chemistry colleagues, we find time and again that undergraduate research as the premier way to engage in the situated learning and cognitive apprenticeship of chemistry is intuitively obvious to chemists, which might have inadvertently hindered scholarly examination of how chemists think, know, and do, and how that relates to the experience of undergraduate research. We would argue that the same scholarly attention and investigation that chemistry teachers have recently given to the development of innovative pedagogies needs to be directed at the question of the disciplinary habits of mind most important to chemistry and its signature pedagogies.

Other Pedagogies With Potential to Prepare Students for Research

Although many sources assert the importance of undergraduate research, there are real constraints on how many students have these experiences. It can be costly and demanding of personnel time, both of which serve as barriers to the majority of undergraduate chemistry majors getting this experience. Elrod, Husic, and Kinzie (2010, p. 7) state that "understanding the essence of what makes undergraduate research such a valuable experience and then applying these principles more widely in courses and programs across the curriculum, we can provide opportunities for more undergraduates to experience similar benefits." Their recommendation is in accord with statements from Project Kaleidoscope's *What Works: Building Natural Science Communities* (Narum, 1991):

> Investigation should be invoked throughout a science curriculum. . . . A lean curriculum provides students and faculty with the time and resources to have a lab-rich curriculum which personalizes lessons and connects ideas to the investigative process. Laboratories are essential to such experiences. . . . "Lab-rich" refers to the property of a curriculum that provides experience in the subject matter, and many settings can do this. (p. 52)

In a 2010 article, Lopatto considers how students might benefit from "research-like" experiences embedded within courses, such as when students engage in research activities where the outcome is not known in advance to either students or the instructor, and students have input into both the topic and the approach used in the research. Lopatto points out that students in high research-like courses report learning gains similar to those reported by participants in dedicated summer research programs and higher than gains reported by students in more traditional lecture and lab courses.

Several pedagogies have the potential to bring the characteristics of undergraduate research to other places in the curriculum, increasing how many research-like courses students encounter in their undergraduate education. These pedagogies are characterized by what Svoboda and Passmore (2010) refer to as "heuristics for productive disciplinary engagement," such as role-modeling by mentors, opportunities for students to try on various roles, holding students accountable to disciplinary norms, making tasks problematic, granting authority and ownership to students, and providing relevant resources such as access to equipment or primary literature. Three such pedagogies that we will examine more closely in this chapter are discovery/inquiry/project-based laboratory experiments, the Science Writing Heuristic (SWH), and Process-Oriented Guided Inquiry Learning (POGIL).

Discovery/Inquiry/Project-Based Laboratory Experiments

In her chapter on signature pedagogies in biology, Bauer-Dantoin (2009) describes the traditional biology lab experience as a "cookbook experiment," where students get precise directions and the outcome is known in advance to both instructor and student. The traditional pedagogy in chemistry laboratory courses has been the same type of verification or "cookbook" experiment. The limitations Bauer-Dantoin points out for using this approach in biology education have also been voiced in the chemical education literature since the late 1970s. In response, new frameworks for designing laboratory experiments have been developed. Horowitz (2007) provides a useful taxonomy for these different frameworks. The most frequently used framework for pedagogical reform of laboratory experiments is the so-called discovery or puzzle experiment, where students are not told in advance the experimental outcomes, so they are put in a position where they can only determine the outcome of their reaction by solving several puzzles. However, the details of the methodology are provided by the instructor.

A second category is what Horowitz calls inquiry labs. These are more open-ended and typically require that students design some part of the procedure. The instructor often sets the overarching goal of the experiment but allows students some freedom to decide what aspect they will focus on. Inquiry labs are becoming more widely used in general chemistry, but Horowitz points out that designing laboratory procedures in more advanced courses often requires more experience and knowledge from students.

The third category is project-based labs in which students work on a multi-week experiment where they might need to modify one or more parts of the procedure to accomplish a specified goal more effectively. These experiments can vary in how broad their focus is, ranging from situations where students are free to pursue a question of their own to ones where students are given projects that often relate to a faculty member's research. A common characteristic of this approach is that the outcome is not known in advance to either the students or instructor, so they are a simplified and more defined research activity involving many of the disciplinary habits of mind that characterize chemistry. Project-based labs are more commonly used than inquiry labs in upper-level chemistry laboratory courses, but they also involve some significant limitations, such as costliness and the risk of student frustration if the project does not work out.

The June through October 2010 issues of the *Journal of Chemical Education* contain one to two experiments in each issue that would be viewed as discovery, guided inquiry, or project-based laboratory experiments. Unfortunately, the majority of evidence of the effect of these labs on student learning was limited to reports of student reaction to these experiments (like/dislike) along with selective reporting of student comments. The extent to which discovery labs engage students in how chemists think, act, and enact certain aspects of chemistry's signature pedagogy requires further investigation.

Science Writing Heuristic

Another approach for moving away from the verification type of laboratory experience is the Science Writing Heuristic (SWH; Burke, Greenbowe, & Hand, 2006; Poock, Burke, Greenbowe, & Hand, 2007; Rudd, Greenbowe, & Hand, 2007), an approach that's been used successfully at both the undergraduate and the secondary levels. In a conventional ("verification") laboratory, the instructor begins with a set of instructions regarding the theory underlying the experiment as well as the specific steps for the students to follow. In contrast, the SWH actively engages the students in selecting the beginning questions to address as well as the procedure for investigating those questions. Prior to each laboratory period, the students are given a scenario and some background material from which they develop their beginning questions, and which they write on the board so that the class as a whole can discuss which ones to address. This pre-lab discussion engages students in a key aspect of scientific research: the development of meaningful and testable questions. Then, the students select a procedure that will give them the data to answer those questions, so students must negotiate ideas for the class to arrive at an efficient plan. In the activity model (Harwood, 2004; Harwood et al., 2002; Reiff et al., 2002; Robinson, 2004), asking good questions is central to scientific inquiry and research.

The SWH not only affects what is done in the lab but also provides a structure for the laboratory reports. Harwood et al. (2002) have also identified communicating ideas as essential to scientific inquiry. The SWH laboratory report follows a structure that requires the students to think critically about their results and reflect on what they mean, preferably through all three perspectives identified by Johnstone (1993). The report begins, like the experimental portion of the laboratory, with the beginning questions and the chosen procedure, followed by reporting the data and observations they obtained during the experiment. The students must then provide claims (answers to the beginning questions) justified by evidence they've drawn from their data and observations. In a conventional verification lab, the students would typically report their data, compare that data to the expected results, and provide reasons (sometimes in an apologetic manner) for any differences between their results and what was expected. In the SWH format, students are required to take ownership of their data and results and present what actually happened, not merely what they (or the instructor) expected to happen. In the final section of an SWH report, the students reflect on their findings and relate them to a larger context by reading relevant external sources to allow students to examine how their ideas have changed after conducting the experiment.

In summary, this process of asking directly testable questions, providing evidenced-based claims drawn from direct experimentation, and reflecting on the underlying meaning behind their findings parallels what a chemist does (Harwood et al., 2002). There has been considerable research on the effectiveness of the SWH (Poock et al., 2007; Rudd et al., 2007), especially with regard to students' ability to understand the underlying concepts, but there appears to be little research on whether using the SWH in teaching laboratories prepares students for conducting chemistry research more effectively than using a conventional lab structure.

Process-Oriented Guided Inquiry Learning

Another guided inquiry technique that shares some of the characteristics of the SWH is Process-Oriented Guided Inquiry Learning (Moog & Spencer, 2008a), in which students form self-managed teams that engage in guided-inquiry activities selected or designed by the instructor, who guides students through the activities rather than lectures to them. Analogous to the SWH, students remain engaged in the subject matter, develop metacognitive skills, and take greater responsibility for their own learning than in the standard lecture class. In addition to the self-managed teams, an essential component of POGIL is the learning cycle, which consists of three stages—exploration, concept invention, and application (Moog & Spencer, 2008b)—that correspond roughly to the first three stages on Bloom's taxonomy—knowledge, comprehension, and application. Such guided inquiry methods provide students with a deeper learning experience and greater retention of information than straight lecture does (Lewis & Lewis, 2005).

POGIL is used in the laboratory as well as in the "lecture" class and is similar in many ways to the SWH. In both, an emphasis is placed on asking meaningful beginning questions, but in the POGIL laboratory, the instructor provides a "question of the day," whereas in the SWH laboratory, the students enter with their own set of beginning questions. As in SWH, students in the POGIL laboratory must develop evidenced-based claims from their data and observations; the learning cycle (exploration, concept invention, and application) is equally emphasized in both POGIL laboratories and classrooms. The major departure for the two methods is that the SWH provides a specific structure for the laboratory report. A critical common feature of both of these guided inquiry methods is that they strive to provide the students with an active learning environment where they learn the material more deeply. The purpose of these guided inquiry methods is to develop many of the same skills as would be expected for a research scientist.

Relationship Between Inquiry Pedagogies and Undergraduate Research

The inquiry pedagogies just described are not comprehensive of all the active learning strategies tried in chemistry labs. Rather, they represent a sample of ways faculty have endeavored to incorporate authentic scientific practice into their laboratory courses. To understand the relationship between these inquiry pedagogies and the signature pedagogy of undergraduate research, we first compare the characteristics of scientific research with the components of the SWH.

Many parallels can be drawn between the SWH guided-inquiry model and the activity model of scientific inquiry. Although Harwood and colleagues distinguish between scientific inquiry as practiced by researchers and inquiry methods used by teachers, they state, "Both aspects of inquiry are necessary for teachers to see that inquiry teaching methods provide the skills and building blocks to help their own students conduct inquiries" (Harwood et al., 2002, p. 1075). This suggests that inquiry activities in the classroom might provide students with tools needed to conduct scientific research: In both the SWH and the activity model, the centrality and challenge of asking meaningful and testable questions is obvious. In the SWH, particular attention is paid to training both students and instructors in crafting productive beginning questions (Burke, Hand, Poock, & Greenbowe, 2005).

Other parallels between the SWH model and the activity model further illustrate how the SWH can provide a research-like experience in a teaching laboratory. For example, in the SWH model students make evidence-based claims based on the results they obtained in the laboratory, not on speculation or theory. Similarly, the activity model includes an examination of results in which a researcher ensures the validity of his or her data. Experiments with an unacceptable degree of uncertainty must be repeated. In the teaching lab, if students do not have sufficient time to recheck questionable results, they must report what they explicitly know separately from any speculations about results that are not definitive. Another parallel between the two models is the importance for the student and the researcher to reflect on their findings. In both cases, it is critical to determine what the results mean and connect those results to what is known about the specific area of study. Another resemblance between the two models is the attention paid to communicating ideas. For the SWH, the communication is critical throughout the process, as the "report provides a format to guide student discussions, thinking, and writing via beginning questions, claims and evidence, and reflections" (Burke et al., 2006, p. 1035). Similarly, the activity model promotes good communication: "Scientists rarely work in isolation, so you shouldn't either. Throughout the course of an inquiry, scientists communicate with peers in their lab and colleagues elsewhere. Many inquiries involve collaborative efforts of several scientists. Good communication among them is an essential feature of inquiry" (Harwood, 2004, p. 31).

In summary, we find the parallels between guided inquiry methods in the laboratory (as exemplified by the SWH) and the characteristics of scientific inquiry (as described by the activity model) to be compelling. If the practices in the guided inquiry laboratory carry over to the undergraduate research experience, then one would expect that students would be able to think and to perform like chemists. Unfortunately, we do not find any studies that investigate the link between the SWH laboratory structure and undergraduate research, making the connection between guided inquiry (in the classroom or lab) and scientific inquiry (in the research laboratory) a fruitful investigation.

There have been some efforts to link guided inquiry practices in the laboratory with chemistry research. Hollenbeck and colleagues (2006) describe a course that strives to prepare students for their undergraduate research experience through project-based laboratory experiments and a peer-review of their laboratory report. In an effort to study the possible effects of inquiry-style teaching on disciplinary research, Spronken-Smith and Walker (2010) have made detailed studies of three courses that use differing levels of inquiry techniques. Their findings indicate that more open-ended inquiry strategies prepare students best for undergraduate research, but the courses involved were not chemistry, so it is difficult to say.

Conclusion

Because undergraduate research in a chemistry lab encompasses the activities that chemists do more than any other experience, it serves as a signature pedagogy. However, by providing experiences that put students in the position of thinking and acting like chemists, the inquiry methods described herein—project-based laboratories, the Science Writing Heuristic, and Process-Oriented Guided Inquiry Learning—should serve to engage students earlier in the disciplinary habits of mind that characterize chemistry and prepare students for their capstone experience. We have outlined ways that these inquiry methodologies *should* prepare students for the experience of doing chemistry through undergraduate research, but it is clear that more research is needed to demonstrate the relationship between inquiry teaching methods and the disciplinary habits that characterize what chemists know, do, and think.

References

American Chemical Society. (2008). *Undergraduate professional training in chemistry: ACS guidelines and evaluation procedures for bachelor's degree programs.* Washington, DC: Committee on Professional Training

Bauer-Dantoin, A. (2009). The evolution of scientific teaching within the biological sciences. In R. A. R. Gurung, N. L. Chick, & A. Haynie (Eds.), *Exploring signature pedagogies: Approaches to teaching disciplinary habits of mind* (pp. 224–243). Sterling, VA: Stylus.

Brown, J. S., Collins, A., & Duguid, P. (1989). Situated cognition and the culture of learning. *Educational Researcher, 18*(1), 32–41. doi: 10.2307/1176008

Burke, K. A., Greenbowe, T. J., & Hand, B. M. (2006). Implementing the science writing heuristic in the chemistry laboratory. *Journal of Chemical Education, 83,* 1032–1038. doi: 10.1021/ed083p1032

Burke, K. A., Hand, B. M., Poock, J. R., & Greenbowe, T. J. (2005). Using the science writing heuristic: Training chemistry teaching assistants. *Journal of College Science Teaching, 35*(1), 36–41.

Coppola, B. P., & Jacobs, D. (2001). Is the scholarship of teaching and learning new to chemistry? In M. T. Huber & S. Morreale (Eds.), *Disciplinary styles in the scholarship of teaching and learning* (pp. 197–216). Washington DC: American Association of Higher Education and The Carnegie Foundation for the Advancement of Teaching.

Crowe, M., & Brakke, D. (2008). Assessing the impact of undergraduate research experiences on students: An overview of current literature. *Council of Undergraduate Research Quarterly, 28*(4):43–50

Elrod, S., Husic, D., & Kinzie, J. (2010). Research and discovery across the curriculum. *Peer Review, 12,* 4–8.

Harwood, W. S. (2004). A new model for inquiry: Is the scientific method dead? *Journal of College Science Teaching, 33*(7), 29–33.

Harwood, W. S., Reiff, R., & Phillipson, T. (2002). Scientists conception of scientific inquiry: Voices from the front. *Proceedings of the 2002 Annual International Conference of the Association for the Education of Teachers in Science,* 1074–1104.

Hollenbeck, J. J., Wixson, E. N., Geske, G. D., Dodge, M. W., Tseng, T. A., Clauss, A. D., & Blackwell, H. E. (2006). A new model for transitioning students from the undergraduate teaching laboratory to the research laboratory: The evolution of an intermediate organic synthesis laboratory course. *Journal of Chemical Education, 83,* 1835–1843. doi: 10.1021/ed083p1835

Horowitz, G. (2007). The state of organic teaching labs. *Journal of Chemical Education, 84,* 346–353. doi: 10.1021/ed084p346

Hunter A. B., Laursen S. L., & Seymour E. (2007). Becoming a scientist: The role of undergraduate research in students' cognitive, personal, and professional development. *Science Education, 91*(1):36–74. doi: 10.1002/sce.20173

Johnstone, A. H. (1993). The development of chemistry teaching. *Journal of Chemical Education, 70,* 701–705. doi: 10.1021/ed070p701

Johnstone, A. H. (2000). Teaching of chemistry—logical or psychological? *Chemistry Education: Research and Practice in Europe, 1,* 9–15.

Journal of Chemical Education. (n.d.). *About the Journal.* Retrieved from http://pubs.acs.org/page/jceda8/about.html

Lave, J., & Wenger, E. (1991). *Situated cognition: Legitimate peripheral participation.* Cambridge, UK: Cambridge University Press.

Lewis, S. E., & Lewis, J. E. (2005). Departing from lectures: An evaluation of a peer-led guided inquiry alternative. *Journal of Chemical Education, 82,* 135–139. doi: 10.1021/ed082p135

Lopatto, D. (2010). Undergraduate research as a high-impact student experience. *Peer Review, 12*(2), 27–30.

Moog, R. S., & Spencer, J. N. (2008a). POGIL: An overview. In R. S. Moog & J. N. Spencer (Eds.). (2008). *Process-oriented guided inquiry learning: ACS symposium series 994* (pp. 1–13). Washington, DC: American Chemical Society. doi: 10.1021/bk-2008-0994.ch001

Moog, R. S., & Spencer, J. N. (Eds.). (2008b). *Process-oriented guided inquiry learning: ACS Symposium Series 994*. Washington, DC: American Chemical Society. doi: 10.1021/bk-2008-0994

Narum, J. L. (Ed.). (1991). *What works: Building natural science communities.* Washington, DC: Project Kaleidoscope.

National Research Council. (2003). *Beyond the molecular frontier: Challenges for chemistry and chemical engineering.* Washington, DC: National Academies Press.

Poock, J. R., Burke, K. A., Greenbowe, T. J., & Hand, B. M. (2007). Using the science writing heuristic in the general chemistry laboratory to improve students' academic performance. *Journal of Chemical Education, 84,* 1371–1379. doi: 10.1021/ed084p1371

Reiff, R., Harwood, W. S., & Phillipson, T. (2002). A scientific method based upon research scientists' conception of scientific inquiry. *Proceedings of the 2002 Annual International Conference of the Association for the Education of Teachers in Science,* 559–582.

Robinson, W. R. (2004). The inquiry wheel, an alternative to the scientific method: A view of the science education research literature. *Journal of Chemical Education, 81,* 791–792. doi: 10.1021/ed081p791

Rudd, J. R., Greenbowe, T. J., & Hand, B. M. (2007). Implementing the science writing heuristic in the chemistry laboratory. *Journal of Chemical Education, 84,* 2007–2011. doi: 10.1021/ed084p2007

Seymour, E., Hunter, A., Laursen, S., & DeAntoni, T. (2004). Establishing the benefits of research experiences for undergraduates: First findings from a three-year study. *Science Education, 88,* 493–534. doi: 10.1002/sce.10131

Shulman, L. S. (1986). Those who understand: Knowledge growth in teaching. *Educational Researcher, 15*(2), 4–14. doi: 10.2307/1175860

Shulman, L. S. (2005). Signature pedagogies in the professions. *Daedalus 134*(3), 52–59. doi:10.1162/0011526054622015

Spronken-Smith, R., & Walker, R. (2010). Can inquiry-based learning strengthen the links between teaching and disciplinary research? *Studies in Higher Education, 35,* 723–740. doi: 10.1080/03075070903315502

Svoboda, J., & Passmore, C. (2010). Evaluating a modeling curriculum by using heuristics for productive disciplinary engagement. *CBE Life Science Education, 9,* 266–276. doi: 10.1187/cbe.10-03-0037

PART THREE

INTERDISCIPLINARY FIELDS AND PROGRAMS

10

REFLECTION IN ACTION

A Signature Ignatian Pedagogy for the 21st Century

Rebecca S. Nowacek and Susan M. Mountin

What distinguishes a Jesuit education from the education provided at other colleges and universities? Many of the aims of Jesuit education—intellectual excellence, development of moral as well as intellectual capacities, a commitment to social justice—are shared by many institutions of higher education, whether religiously affiliated or secular. Is there, then, a distinctively Jesuit means toward those ends—one with deep roots in Jesuit tradition? We believe there is: a cycle of experience, reflection, action, and evaluation that can be traced back to the *Spiritual Exercises* of St. Ignatius.

To be clear from the start, we write together as two individuals with very different relationships to Catholicism: Susan is a practicing Catholic; Rebecca is not. What we share is a respect for the Jesuit mission of our university and a desire to understand better how it might catalyze student learning in distinctive ways. Although the signature pedagogy we describe is not one of a discipline or a profession, our exploration of Ignatian pedagogy has significance beyond the campuses of the 28 Jesuit institutions of higher education in the United States. Certainly the scope of Jesuit education is large: These colleges and universities serve more than 183,000 students through 260 undergraduate, graduate, and professional programs and have more than a million living alumni (Jesuit Conference, 2007). In addition, many instructors at non-Jesuit institutions might welcome a pedagogy committed to character formation, ethics, and global awareness as well as a commitment to dialogue (especially interfaith dialogue)—issues addressed by the Association of American Colleges and Universities (AAC&U), the Carnegie Foundation, and others. The five-century tradition of Jesuit education places it on the nexus between the ivory tower of higher education and the increasingly complex needs of a world with shrinking resources and conflict.

If we seek the foundation of a distinctively Ignatian pedagogy for the 21st century, we must grapple with the fact that it must be grounded in the Jesuit commitment to a life centered in God. In the words of the "First Principle and Foundation" of St. Ignatius's *Spiritual Exercises*, "our only desire and our one choice should be this: I want and I choose what better leads to the deepening of God's life in me" (Mullan, 1914, p. 18). If religious faith is the bedrock of a distinctively Ignatian pedagogy, we must ask how this pedagogy might be adapted to religiously diverse contemporary classrooms. To what degree can instructors and students of various faith traditions (including agnostic and atheist) seek to transform the historically established signature pedagogy of Jesuit education for 21st-century U.S. classrooms? And to what degree might a distinctively Ignatian pedagogy seek to transform students and instructors? Furthermore, to what degree is the signature pedagogy of a very specific institutional type relevant to other institutions and to the disciplines that cut across all institutions?

In the first part of this chapter, we contextualize Ignatian pedagogy within the scholarship of teaching and learning. We then turn to the history of Jesuit education, looking primarily at the *Spiritual Exercises.* We conclude by exploring the ways in which this traditional, faith-driven Ignatian pedagogy can be translated into contemporary classrooms.

The Puzzle of a Cross-Disciplinary Signature Pedagogy

The signature pedagogy of Jesuit education is not limited to any one academic discipline, but provides a "way of proceeding"[1] that can be infused throughout the curriculum. However, the concept of signature pedagogies is premised on the idea that different disciplines and professions entail distinct ways of knowing and doing. There are, in Shulman's words, "characteristic forms of teaching and learning" in which "novices are instructed in critical aspects of the three fundamental dimensions of professional work—to think, to perform, and to act with integrity" (2005, p. 52).

So is it meaningful to propose a cross-disciplinary Ignatian signature pedagogy? We think so, because the overriding goal of any signature pedagogy is to prepare students to act in the world in the ways required by the profession or discipline. In the case of Ignatian pedagogy, the "professional" goal, across every discipline and department, is to link the cultivation of intellectual accomplishment and scholarly expertise to the moral and spiritual dimension. We are, in the oft-quoted words of Father Pedro Arrupe, forming "men [and women] for [and with] others" (Arrupe, 1973)—a goal that does not stray far from Shulman's initial formulation. Signature pedagogies tend to be found in the professions, Shulman argues, because "education is not education for understanding alone; it is preparation for accomplished and responsible practice in the service of others. It is preparation for 'good work'" (p. 53). If traditional signature pedagogies are intended to prepare students for good work in the professions, the Ignatian signature pedagogy we describe is meant to prepare students for good work in all professions.

Catholic Mission in Higher Education and the Scholarship of Teaching and Learning

Unfortunately, a disconnect exists between scholarly discussions of Jesuit education on the one hand and efforts to build institutional support for the scholarship of teaching and learning on the other. Scholarly discussions of the aims and methods of Jesuit education are easy to find. The focus of *A Jesuit Education Reader* (Traub, 2008) is, as its subtitle suggests, "contemporary writings on the Jesuit mission in education, principles, the issue of Catholic identity, practical applications of the Ignatian way, and more." These essays offer histories of and visions for the future of Jesuit education; they grapple with issues such as postmodern spirituality, academic freedom, and education for social justice. The section on "Practical Applications" includes thoughtful essays from faculty, describing their approaches to situating their disciplinary objectives within the mission of a Jesuit school. They do not, however, look directly at evidence of student learning. These are teacher narratives rather than inquiries into student learning (see Chick, 2009, for an elaboration on this distinction).

The same trend is visible in three important journals. *Conversations on Jesuit Higher Education* offers thematic issues (on topics such as women in

Catholic education or the core curriculum) filled with vision statements, accounts of particular institutional programs, and personal histories from students and teachers. But there are no inquiries into student learning. Similarly, the peer-reviewed journals *Catholic Education* and the *Journal of Catholic Higher Education* are dominated by descriptions of programmatic approaches, analyses of national problems, and surveys of faculty attitudes toward issues related to Catholic education. Although these journals do include some inquiries into student learning, the studies are rarely conducted by the teachers themselves. To the extent that there is a scholarship of Jesuit teaching and learning, the studies seem to be (to use Pat Hutchings's [2000] taxonomy) "visions of the possible" and efforts toward theory building. Scholarly publications from instructors conducting "what is" or "what works" inquiries related to Jesuit goals or methods in their own classrooms are rare.

Ironically, however, a number of Jesuit colleges and universities are national leaders in the scholarship of teaching and learning (SoTL) movement. Creighton University and Rockhurst College (together with several other colleges) recently sponsored the 8th Annual National CASTL Summer Institute for the Development of Scholars of Teaching and Learning. Centers for Teaching and Learning at Canisius College, Loyola Marymount University, St. Louis University, and Seattle University have well-established programs to support faculty undertaking SoTL inquiries. The Center for New Designs in Learning (CNDL) at Georgetown University—including their "Teaching to the Whole Person" initiative—is a model program for universities looking to see how the scholarship of teaching and learning can invigorate a campus.

But CNDL's "Teaching to the Whole Person" initiative seems to be the exception; as a rule, the scholarship of teaching and learning that has taken root at Jesuit universities has not focused on the Jesuit mission or sought to define a distinctly Ignatian pedagogy. We make this observation not to criticize but to identify an opportunity. In the pages that follow we draw on historical and contemporary writings on Jesuit education to articulate a signature pedagogy that might be further explored in future SoTL inquiries.

Reflection and Action in the Jesuit Tradition

The roots of contemporary Ignatian pedagogy go back centuries. More than 450 years ago, a Basque nobleman named Ignatius Loyola went through a transformational discernment experience that led him from being a soldier to serving God. As a student at the University of Paris he banded with a group of companions; in 1537 they founded a community of priests called "The Society of Jesus"—or "the Jesuits." The Jesuits' numbers grew exponentially, and by 1565 the Society included 3,500 men (O'Malley, 1993, p. 2). Although Ignatius did not plan to start a system of schools, by 1543 a few Jesuits led by Jesuit missionary Francis Xavier had been teaching reading, writing, grammar, and catechism in Goa, India, to about 600 elementary-aged male students (O'Malley, 1993, p. 203). In 1548, the Jesuits opened a school for lay students in Messina, Italy, and Jesuit education soon spread throughout Europe and eventually into Asia and the Americas (O'Malley, 1993, p. 204).

In response to this rapid growth, in 1599 Jesuit collaborators developed the *Ratio Studiorum*; its purpose was to spell out the goals, structure, and modes of the Jesuit educational experience. The *Ratio* prescribed pedagogical choices relating to administration, roles of teachers and students, and classroom practices like disputations, debates, repetitions, exercises, contests, awards, plays, and pageants (Farrell, 1999, p. ix). It also set forth the curriculum: a blend of humanities, the arts, the classics, and physical sciences as well as theology and philosophy. However, the *Ratio* does not elaborate on a pedagogical method that would join spiritual and moral formation to intellectual development. For that we must turn to the *Spiritual Exercises*.

In the *Spiritual Exercises*, Ignatius described and codified his own process of formation as a means of guiding the spiritual formation of others. Ignatius believed that deep reflection on one's experience was a key to discernment, knowledge, and growth. The ideal format for "doing" *The Spiritual Exercises* is a 30-day silent retreat in which retreatants meet daily with a spiritual director who guides them through a sequence of meditations[2] on key moments in the Gospels, using their imaginations; they use their senses to relive the stories and make connections to their own story and need for mercy, healing, forgiveness, love, a sense of call and mission, and so forth.

Particularly important for our purposes is the daily reflection portion of the exercises called the "*Examen of Consciousness*" or *Examen* for short. This practice in conjunction with the meditations is meant to lead persons to better awareness of their own life directions and choices, both simple as well as significant decisions. The *Examen* trains users to reflect in a very direct way using senses, as well as powers of attention and affect. The *Examen* consists of a few simple prompts:

- Become aware of God's presence. Quietly center yourself.
- Review the day with gratitude.
- Pay attention to your emotions, especially the desolations and consolations of the day. Where was I buffeted by sadness or anxiety? What did I find consoling (where have I become aware of the presence of God in joy)?
- Choose one feature of the day: Focus on it, pray from it. Where could I have responded differently?
- Look toward tomorrow. How will I be responsive to those around me? (Hamm, 1994, p. 23)

The practice of the *Examen* is not navel gazing. Instead, these questions suggest four distinct but interrelated processes: Participants must attend to and recollect the *experience* of the day fully, then they must *reflect* on that experience, in order to formulate a course of *action*, which they can later *evaluate.*

To the extent that a signature pedagogy of Jesuit education has been identified, it has been located in this process of experience, reflection, action, and evaluation. In 1986 the International Commission on the Apostolate of Jesuit Education (ICAJE) published *The Characteristics of Jesuit Education.* This document took a broad scope, identifying 10 characteristics, including "care and concern for each individual person" and "lay-Jesuit collaboration"; it also drew an extended parallel (paragraphs 154–160) between the *Spiritual Exercises* and Ignatian pedagogy. In an effort to make those characteristics more accessible and practicable for teachers in the classroom, the ICAJE later published *Ignatian Pedagogy: A Practical Approach.* This document introduces and discusses the "Ignatian pedagogical paradigm"—a paradigm quite explicitly linked to the *Spiritual Exercises.*

> A distinctive feature of the Ignatian pedagogical paradigm is that, understood in the light of the *Spiritual Exercises of St. Ignatius*, it becomes not only a fitting description of the continual interplay of experience, reflection and action in the teaching learning process, but also an ideal portrayal of the dynamic interrelationship of teacher and learner in the latter's journey of growth in knowledge and freedom. (ICAJE, paragraph 23)

The *Examen* is at the heart of Ignatian pedagogy. Its activities constitute a signature pedagogy that can be employed by any educator in search of a means to help students link moral discernment and intellectual excellence. Its focus on learning to pay attention, developing the ability to reflect on one's experience, and then acting and evaluating or questioning one's presuppositions are key learning events appropriate for any educational endeavor—religious or secular—committed to a student's intellectual and moral development.

Key Principles of a Signature Ignatian Pedagogy

We began the chapter by questioning the degree to which a signature pedagogy grounded in a program of religious formation can be adapted for use in contemporary, secular classrooms. To grapple with that question, we unpack the five key terms in the Ignatian pedagogical paradigm—*context, experience, reflection, action,* and *evaluation*—and describe how they can engage students in deep learning across the curriculum.

Context

At the center of the Ignatian paradigm is "context." Historically, this is a legacy of the Jesuit awareness that adaptation to different cultures is crucial. We understand "context" in two dimensions. There is the context of the student's own life situation, who he or she *is* coming into the classroom. This can include a sense of self-identity as well as the student's personal context: economic pressures, relationships with loved ones, and so on. In addition, a larger context surrounds the student in concentric circles: classroom, institution, local, national, and global issues.

An increased awareness of context is relevant not only for teachers (who seek to meet their students where they are) but also for students for whom "the unexamined life" severely limits their choices. As we discuss in the section on reflection, students engaged in this signature Ignatian pedagogy enter into a process of learning to be more attentive to their own experiences. Ultimately, however, the aim of this pedagogy is to help students move beyond a preoccupation with individual context and become responsive to larger social contexts and to the needs of others.

Experience

What does it mean to emphasize the role of student experience in the learning process? In many traditional courses, students sit with their notebooks, writing down what someone else tells them. The Ignatian emphasis on student experience—like so many other critical pedagogies—shifts the focus of the course: The content of the class resides not in the teacher's wisdom but in the breadth of students' learning experiences. For some instructors, experience might mean an out-of-the-classroom experience: service-learning, field trips, clinicals, internships. Other instructors might invite students to participate in research—in the lab, in the field, in the library. Yet other students might be invited to experience a text, to see that text not as a series of pages to be skimmed quickly, but as an opportunity to encounter the ideas and values of another person, removed in time and space.

This broad definition of experience is necessary for a pedagogy that stretches across disciplines. The clinical experiences of a nursing student will be vastly different from the experiences of a chemistry student conducting an experiment or a communications major completing an internship or a philosophy student's encounter with Heidegger. In all these cases, however, experience resides in the student's encounter with people, places, events, and texts that stretch them beyond prior knowledge and experiences.

Reflection

In the original Latin, the term *reflection* (*reflecto*) means literally "to bend back"; it is linked, in sound and in concept, to *respectus*, which means "to look back." The process of reflection demands that our students look back on their experiences with the goal of shedding light on them to understand them better. As instructors, we must help students parse their experiences, asking questions that lead students to attend carefully to their own experience.[3]

Instructors can coach students through the process of reflection in several ways. Instructors can create time and space in what are often overcrowded courses, embracing what Mark Cladis (2006) has termed *slow teaching*. In addition to creating curricular space, instructors can provide writing prompts that encourage students to be attentive. Instructors committed to an Ignatian pedagogy can also return to Ignatius' method in the *Examen* by using sense questions: What did you see, sense, taste, smell, hear?

Some instructors might dismiss such questions as too "touchy-feely"—but an Ignatian pedagogy invites a decidedly corporal revisiting of experience. In the Ignatian classroom, as in the *Examen*, an individual is encouraged to look back on experience—in the clinical, in the lab, in the office, in the text—not simply as a brain disconnected from the world, but as a person living in the physical world with other individuals, many of whom have needs that call out for attention.

Action

Action, as conceived in the Ignatian pedagogical paradigm, is not simply a "to-do" list. When students learn something by reflecting on their experiences (whether reading a text, tutoring in the community, conducting a physics experiment, or learning to balance an account on a spreadsheet) that new-found knowledge leads to some action. Actions might manifest as a concrete activity, but they might also take the form of an understanding, a disposition, a decision, a belief, a commitment, or simply the impetus to try something else (like another experiment) that would build on the previous knowledge. The mental and spiritual movement toward a richer understanding of others is, in the Ignatian paradigm, a valuable action. Action, in short, is the appropriation of the learning that transforms the learner.

As we imagine the implications of this signature pedagogy for secular classrooms and instructors, we recognize that some actions lack any clear moral charge. For instance, if a physics student fully attends to the experience of the lab and reflects carefully on what she observed, her action might simply be an enhanced understanding of Hooke's Law. But, in truth, there's nothing "simple" about such an enhanced understanding. The type of knowledge-in-action encouraged by the Ignatian pedagogical paradigm is the type of deep understanding that enables students to do more than memorize formulas; such action is the mastering of a topic that helps students move from being mere consumers to becoming producers of knowledge. Furthermore, this focus on knowledge-in-action—a value shared by many feminist pedagogues (see, for instance, Bricker-Jenkins & Hooyman 1987)—also helps to highlight an important resonance between the values of Ignatian pedagogy and the commitments of other broad categories of instructors who are neither Catholic nor employed by a Jesuit university.

Evaluation

So far we have described a series of stages in which students have an experience, reflect on that experience, then act (whether through action or by making a mental shift) inspired by their reflection on the experience. One additional, crucial element of this paradigm is a process of evaluation.

> Ignatian pedagogy . . . aims at formation which includes but goes beyond academic mastery. Here we are concerned about students' well-rounded growth as persons for others. Thus periodic evaluation of the student's growth in attitudes, priorities, and actions consistent with being a person for others is essential. (ICAJE, 1993, paragraph 64)

When students themselves engage in this evaluation, they are, in essence, reflecting on their process of reflection (which in turn mediates experience and action)—making the stage of evaluation a type of meta-reflection.

Although the importance of evaluation/meta-reflection is widely recognized (Bransford, Brown, & Cocking, 2000; Yancey, 1998), it is something most instructors are reluctant to grade—perhaps because it is such a deeply personalized process. Instructors do the principle of meta-reflection a disservice by relegating it to an occasional ungraded and largely ignored journal entry. For evaluation to serve its proper role as a key principle of Ignatian pedagogy, instructors must embrace meta-reflection as something that students can do with more or less success and therefore as something that instructors are responsible for coaching and (on some occasions perhaps) even grading. Coaching students on the process of meta-reflection—probing their ideas with them, encouraging them to go beyond a glib "I learned a lot"—is new and, quite frankly, scary for many instructors. We have no easy answers, and no one size fits all portable rubrics.

We do, however, believe that efforts to coach students' meta-reflective processes will benefit from a community of teachers working together. Knowing that a team of like-minded instructors are also assigning and coaching meta-reflective work can help teachers keep the courage of their convictions.[4] What's more, when a cohort of instructors begins to take this approach to evaluation, they might transform their students—and perhaps themselves. Collectively a group of teachers can work to give students practice over time and different contexts and to provide a coherent message that although meta-reflection can be hard work, it can be done well. Although we have located no published scholarly inquiries into the effectiveness of this pedagogy over time at Jesuit institutions (an absence that suggests the need for future research), the broader scholarship on the positive effects of metacognitive reflection (see Chick, Karis, & Kernahan, 2009, for a summary) suggest the promise of this approach.

Conclusion

On our own Jesuit campus we have pockets of faculty in many disciplines committed to enhancing their courses with Ignatian pedagogical practices. We find evidence—in published scholarship (Chubbuck, 2007; Van Hise & Massey, 2010) and through less formally shared inquiries and reflections (e.g., Coppard, Dickel, & Jensen, 2009)—that the Ignatian pedagogical paradigm shapes instructor practice at other institutions as well. However, as Defeo (2009) notes, although knowledge of Ignatian pedagogy is common in certain pockets of Jesuit campuses (such as centers for teaching and learning), it is not ubiquitous. Why would that be, and why would anyone not at a Jesuit institution consider adopting this signature pedagogy?

The relatively low profile of the signature pedagogy that we have described in this chapter can be attributed in part to a lack of education: Some faculty who might adopt it are simply not aware of it. But we also recognize that some faculty are reluctant to adopt it because of its religious origin. Nevertheless, we hope to have demonstrated that this pedagogical approach has relevance not only for teachers who fully accept Ignatius' First Principle: to "want and . . . choose what better leads to the deepening of God's life in me"; it can also be a meaningful pedagogy for instructors who—whatever their own religious (non)beliefs—are committed to their students' moral and spiritual development. One of the goals of the AAC&U's LEAP initiative, for instance, is to promote the development of "ethical reasoning and action" (AAC&U, 2011). Similarly, Parker Palmer's (2007) focus on the ethical and spiritual dimensions of teaching and learning has been well received across the academy. An Ignatian pedagogy grounded in the methods of the *Spiritual Exercises* can help students and teachers work toward such goals; it is, to answer the question we posed in our introduction, an eminently adaptable pedagogy.

But if this is a pedagogy that is easily transformed, it is also a pedagogy that is radically transformative for teachers and students alike. In its fully religious dimensions, it invites instructors to reflect on the consolations and desolations of teaching and to see God in all people, all places—including the most inscrutable or frustrating students. But even in its more secular manifestations, this pedagogy directs instructors' attention to the process of student learning: planning a series of experiences, scaffolding a process of reflection, encouraging action, coaching students in a process of meta-reflection. The gift of this pedagogy transcends the boundaries of the 28 Jesuit colleges and universities and provides guidance for teachers in any profession or discipline committed to the intellectual, moral, and spiritual growth of their students.

Notes

1. See O'Malley (2006) for a delineation of this concept. Reflection on their "way of proceeding" has been key to the Jesuit and Ignatian identity sustained over time.

2. Anticipating that few lay people would have 30 days for such a venture, Ignatius provided for the free use of "adaptations." Some individuals complete the exercises over months or even a year; others participate in abbreviated 5-day, 8-day or weekend retreats.

3. The Ignatian concept of reflection is closely linked with, but not identical to, the type of metacognitive reflection that is often referred to in SoTL literature (see, for instance, Chick et al., 2009; Tsang, 2011). The Ignatian focus on "evaluation" more closely approximates the type of thinking about thinking that characterizes much talk about reflection common in SoTL scholarship. In contrast, the type of reflection we focus on here describes the simple but powerful experience of revisiting one's experiences deliberately and in detail.

4. At Marquette, a faculty learning community focused on Ignatian pedagogy (called Companions in Inspiring Futures) has been wrestling with these very issues. As faculty from disciplines as diverse as nursing, physics, communications, history, philosophy, theology, and engineering come together to imagine visions of the possible, some of our most animated discussions have focused on this process of coaching students in the metareflective, evaluative process.

References

Arrupe, P., S.J. (1973). *Men for others.* Retrieved August 29, 2011, from http://online ministries.creighton.edu/CollaborativeMinistry/men-for-others.html

Association of American Colleges and Universities. (2011). *Liberal education and America's promise.* Retrieved August 29, 2011, from http://www.aacu.org/leap/vision.cfm

Bransford, J. D., Brown, A. L., & Cocking, R. R. (Eds.). (2000). *How people learn: Brain, mind, experience, and school* (Expanded ed.). Washington, DC: National Academy Press.

Bricker-Jenkins, M., & Hooyman, N. (1987). Feminist pedagogy in education for social change. *Feminist Teacher 2*(2), 36–42.

Chick, N. L. (2009). Unpacking a signature pedagogy in literary studies. In R. A. R. Gurung, N. L. Chick, & A. Haynie (Eds.), *Exploring signature pedagogies: Approaches to teaching disciplinary habits of mind* (pp. 36–55). Sterling, VA: Stylus.

Chick, N., Karis, T., & Kernahan, C. (2009). Learning from their own learning: How metacognitive and meta-affective reflections enhance learning in race-related courses. *International Journal for the Scholarship of Teaching and Learning, 3*(1), 1–28.

Chubbuck, S. M. (2007). Socially just teaching and the complementarity of Ignatian pedagogy and critical pedagogy. *Christian Higher Education, 6*(3), 239–265.

Cladis, M. (2006). *Slow teaching.* Retrieved August 29, 2011, from http://www.cfkeep.org/html/snapshot.php?id=12770746101412

Coppard, B., Dickel, T., & Jensen, L. (2009). *Using reflection to foster students' personal and professional formation.* Unpublished presentation. Creighton University.

Defeo, J. A. (2009). *Old wine in new skin: Ignatian pedagogy, compatible with and contributing to Jesuit higher education* (Unpublished/doctoral dissertation).

Farrell, A. P., S.J. (1999). *The Jesuit Ratio Studiorum of 1599.* Retrieved August 29, 2011, from http://www.bc.edu/libraries/collections/collinfo/digitalcollections/ratio/ratiohome.html

Hamm, D., S. J. (1994, May 14). Rummaging for God: Praying backward through your day. *America, 170*(17), 22–23.

Hutchings, P. (Ed.). (2000). *Opening lines: An introduction to the scholarship of teaching and learning.* Menlo Park, CA: Carnegie Foundation for the Advancement of Teaching.

International Commission on the Apostolate of Jesuit Education. (1986). *The characteristics of Jesuit education.* Retrieved August 29, 2011, from http://www.seattleu.edu/uploadedFiles/Core/Jesuit_Education/CharacteristicsJesuitEducation.pdf

International Commission on the Apostolate of Jesuit Education. (1993). *Ignatian pedagogy: A practical approach.* Retrieved August 31, 2011, from www.seattleu.edu/uploadedfiles/core/jesuit_education/ignatian%20pedagogy.pdf

Jesuit Conference of the United States. (2007). *Jesuit Colleges and Universities.* Retrieved August 29, 2011, from http://www.jesuit.org/index.php/main/jesuits-worldwide/education/jesuit-colleges-and-universities/

Mullan, E. (Ed.). (1914). *The Spiritual Exercises of St. Ignatius of Loyola translated from the autograph.* New York, NY: P. J. Kenedy and Sons.

O'Malley, J. W., S. J. (1993). *The first Jesuits.* Cambridge, MA: Harvard University Press.

O'Malley, J. W., S. J. (2006, July 13–Aug 7). Ignatius' special way of proceeding. *America, 195*(3), 10–12.

Palmer, P. (2007). *The courage to teach: Exploring the inner landscape of a teacher's life (10th anniv. ed.). San Francisco, CA: Jossey-Bass.*

Shulman, L. (2005, Summer). *Signature pedagogies in the professions. Daedalus,* 52–59.

Traub, G. W., S.J. (2008). *A Jesuit education reader: Contemporary writings on the Jesuit mission in education, principles, the issue of Catholic identity, practical applications of the Ignatian way, and more.* Chicago, IL: Loyola Press.

Tsang, A. K. L. (2011). In-class reflective group discussion as a strategy for the development of students as evolving professionals. *International Journal for the Scholarship of Teaching and Learning* 5(1), 1–20.

Van Hise, J., & Massey, D. W. (2010). Applying the Ignatian pedagogical paradigm to the creation of an accounting ethics course. *Journal of Business Ethics* 96, 453–465.

Yancey, K. B. (1998). *Reflection in the writing classroom.* Logan: Utah State University Press.

11

A SIGNATURE FEMINIST PEDAGOGY

Connection and Transformation in Women's Studies

Holly Hassel and Nerissa Nelson

Women's studies as an interdisciplinary field of study emerged out of the social and political feminist movements of the 1960s' "second wave." Often considered the academic arm of feminist activism, women's studies emerged in the academy as early as 1970, when women faculty at San Diego State University (SDSU) began teaching women's studies courses on a voluntary basis, establishing the first Women's Studies Department at SDSU that same year. As Robyn Wiegman explains, women's studies was less a formal part of the institution than it was "an ensemble of courses listed on bulletin boards and often taught for free by faculty and community leaders" (Wiegman, 2002, p. 18). The National Women's Studies Association was founded in 1977 and held its first convention in 1979 (Shaw & Lee, 2008, p. 3). At the time, women's studies as a field emerged out of resistance to the male-dominated and male-centered curricula typical of much of higher education as well as what the earliest practitioners viewed as patriarchal methods of teaching and learning. Women's studies courses aimed to create a curriculum acknowledging women's experiences and contributions to academic disciplines and sought to use the feminist consciousness-raising model in an academic setting, honoring the voices and personal experiences of students as part of the educational enterprise.

The activist mantra "the personal is political" extended to the academic study of women's issues, as individual experience was used as a way of understanding social structures that supported or promoted patriarchy within and outside of the university walls. The aim of such courses was partly to make women's lives and contributions visible and partly to make a space for women within what had been a traditionally masculine domain—higher education. Feminist writer Adrienne Rich declared in her 1979 essay "Toward a Woman-Centered University" that "Women in the university heretofore need to address themselves . . . to changing the center of gravity of the institution as far as possible; to work toward a woman-centered university because only if that center of gravity can be shifted will women really be free to learn, to teach, to share strength, to explore, to criticize, and to convert knowledge to power" (Rich, 1979, p. 128). In the same essay, she outlined the contours of a "woman-centered university" both in the content of the curriculum and the style of the feminist classroom, which she calls explicitly "antihierarchical" (p. 145). These early characterizations still hold true today, but in the past decade, increasing numbers of academic programs have moved toward broader definitions of the field, renaming departments "Women's and Gender Studies" or "Gender Studies," encompassing what they believe is a more expansive academic field than the feminist-focused efforts of early women's studies programs. Many of these programs place the study of identity (through multi- and interdisciplinary lenses) as the center of inquiry, focusing on both men and women as gendered beings; however, women's studies as a field continues to take a feminist approach to the study of gender, places women's lives at the center of inquiry, and looks at power and identity as two central concepts in understanding social structure—particularly gender *as a system.*

As an "inter-discipline," or an interdisciplinary field of study, women's studies by definition has reacted against traditional, disciplinary ways of teaching and ways of knowing and has drawn from multiple disciplines within the humanities, social sciences, and natural sciences to answer key questions about women's experiences, cultural status, and perspectives. The signature pedagogy in women's studies is feminist in nature, focused on helping students bridge the gap between the personal and political within an academic context.[1] The editors of the 2009 volume *Exploring Signature Pedagogies* cite Lee Shulman's definition of signature pedagogies in establishing the scope of their book's inquiry: " 'elements of instruction and of socialization' that teach disciplinary novices 'to think, to perform, and to act with integrity' within the [inter]discipline" (Gurung, Chick, & Haynie, 2009, p. 3). They further invoke Lendol Calder's advice that "instructors invested in signature pedagogies will encourage students 'to do, think, and value what practitioners in the field are doing, thinking, and valuing'" and that they "disclose important information about the personality of a disciplinary field—its values, knowledge, and manner of thinking—almost, perhaps its total world view" (pp. 3–4). A feminist signature pedagogy invites students to develop a gender consciousness (in Shulman's model, the "deep structure" of the field) and ultimately a feminist consciousness (the "implicit structure") through the use of pedagogical methods (the "surface structure") that create connections between theory and practice—praxis—a central principle of the women's studies classroom (another part of the "deep structure"). Shulman's concept of the "implicit structure" is echoed in women's studies' value system: By helping students develop a critical apparatus for understanding gender as a system—complicated by dynamics of power, privilege, and categories of identity—teaching and learning in women's studies emphasizes critical reflection at the intersection of the personal and the political. Over the last three decades, the deployment of these signature pedagogies by feminist educators has not been without intra-field tensions, which are reflected in the scholarship on pedagogical approaches within women's studies courses.

Feminist Pedagogy Literature: "What We Do" and "What We Should Do" Best Practices

Feminist practitioners have established a strong body of research defining feminist pedagogy within and beyond women's studies courses (see Akyea & Sandoval, 2004; Chick & Hassel, 2009; Clegg, 2006; Colwill & Boyd, 2008; Crawley, Lewis & Mayberry, 2008; Crowley, 2009, for contemporary contributions to the discussion; and Shrewsbury, 1993; Bricker-Jenkins & Hooyman, 1987; and hooks, 1989, for more foundational texts in the field). Much of the current literature on feminist pedagogies in women's studies courses centers on the evolution of best practices over the last 40 years. For example, Crawley, Lewis, and colleagues (2008) propose that a fundamental and institutional change can occur through conversations across disciplines with the ultimate goal of "offering our students an academy in which feminist pedagogies are omnipresent, multi-faceted and synergistic" (p. 11). As a result, the very nature of feminist pedagogy is a departure from the traditional "banking concept of education" (Freire, 1970), embracing what feminist scholars outline as key elements of feminist pedagogies: participatory learning, validation of personal experience, development of political/social understanding and activism, critical thinking/open mindedness, reflexivity (consciousness-raising), action orientation (social change), social construction of knowledge, attention to affect (refusal to separate the rational from the emotional), use of situation at hand (local and global connections), empowerment, inclusion, collaboration, community and leadership (Crawley, Curry, Dumois-Sands, Tanner, & Wyker, 2008; Maher, 1987a; Markowitz, 2005; Shrewsbury, 1993; Stake & Hoffman, 2000). Even more recent approaches include ecofeminism, service-learning, and discourse studies (Jacobs, 2008). In essence, student connections with each other, with the instructor, with the material, and with the world outside the classroom walls are stressed as strongly as the course content and more traditional academic material.

A closer examination of the feminist pedagogy literature reveals distinctive themes that define or describe common pedagogical approaches in the field of women's studies: the caring model, community and leadership, collaborative connections, liberatory/gender models, feminist assessment, theory to practice, and pedagogical innovations. The caring model (exemplified by Akyea & Sandoval, 2004; and Ropers-Huilman, 1999) emphasizes personal relationships within a classroom community; community and leadership (such as in Shrewsbury, 1993, or Duncan & Stasio, 2001) focuses on helping students become empowered as both members of a community and as leaders within that community involved in shared decision making; collaborative connections (see Colwill & Boyd, 2008; Chick & Hassel, 2009; Jacobs, 2008) stress different forms of collaboration among and between instructors and students. Other examples of prevailing themes include the liberatory/gender models (see Maher, 1987b), which draw from Freirean liberation pedagogy to challenge oppression and foster empowerment; writers interested in feminist assessment (Akyea, for example) work to categorize learning outcomes, knowledge, and skills that are transformative and constructive with the end goal of students making better choices in their lives; Blake and Ooten (2008) is one example of writers interested in "theory to practice," the ways that feminist educators can and should blend theoretical and historical contexts with practice, although this concept pervades the literature. A number of publications introduce pedagogical innovations (for example, use of student-centered techniques) and identify teachable moments (Crawley, Curry, et al., 2008; Feigenbaum, 2007) in which the writers describe specific pedagogical practices that will actualize inside and outside the classroom the core values of "what . . . we [are] teaching and what . . . our students [are] learning" in the women's studies classroom (Gurung et al., 2009, p. 1). These approaches are discussed in more detail in the next section.

The articulation of a feminist pedagogy has not been without intra-field conflict. The expressive model of feminist pedagogy that emerged in the 1970s attracted criticism from both within and outside of women's studies. These critics charged that the sharing of personal experience and self-disclosure lacked rigorous critical thinking and viewed it as a "therapeutic pedagogy" (Lehrman, 1993). This "expressive" pedagogical approach modeled the social movement of consciousness-raising in an academic setting, encouraging students to connect those individual experiences to patterns of oppression that exist in larger society. A newer approach to teaching and learning in women's studies blends the expressive with the more traditionally academic. Although both models agree that students are partners in the process of knowledge construction, the latter emphasizes that feminist assessment needs to be "illuminating and transforming so as to provide knowledge and skills students need to make informed choices in their lives" (Akyea & Sandoval, 2004).

Further, the scholarship of teaching and learning (SoTL) literature in women's studies—work that qualitatively or quantitatively measures the impact of teaching and the assessment of student learning—is still developing. The majority of feminist pedagogy literature[2] continues to focus on best practices of "what we do" and discussion of "what we should do." Of work that fits traditional definitions of SoTL, it is important to note that there are two approaches to feminist pedagogy: Qualitative SoTL might use humanities methods that rely on student voices, student-centered assignments, texts, or evaluations that are systematic but not necessarily empirical or clinical methods. This body of literature poses a "hypothesis" or a question that is investigated, but it does not necessarily use a social science–driven methodology to answer that question or hypothesis. Quantitative SoTL relies on a systematic, objective, and measurable form of evaluation that reveals the effects of teaching methods. Researchers employing this model rely on more traditional quantitative measurements and study designs—pretests and posttests, course grades, and surveys and/or questionnaires.

The relative dearth of SoTL scholarship in women's studies should not come as a surprise, given that SoTL traditionally calls for "objective and measurable forms of evaluation" (Gurung et al., 2009, p. 2)—a methodology that is rejected by many feminist researchers. Maher (1987a), after discussing models of feminist pedagogies, explains the reason for this rejection: "[F]eminist methodology . . . challenges the ideals of universality and objectivity, not only because they are impossible to achieve, but because they are not useful in capturing the complexity and variety of human experience" (p. 191). Maher's position is far from being the exception. In their review of studies analyzing feminist methodology in the field of sociology, Cook and Fonow (1986) argue that one core principle of feminist epistemology is the "need to challenge the norm of 'objectivity' that assumes a dichotomy between the subject and object of research" (p. 2). As a result, traditional, statistics-driven social science models are not extensively represented in the literature on SoTL in women's studies; however, neither have humanities-focused researchers taken up the work of SoTL in women's studies with much vigor, suggesting that the field has ample opportunity to more fully investigate the effectiveness, impact, and value of teaching and learning in women's studies.

Guiding Themes and Traditional Pedagogies in Women's Studies

Teaching and learning in the feminist classroom depend on the dominant and long-standing model of caring, student-centeredness, shared experiences, inclusivity, and collaboration. Students entering their first women's studies course might never have experienced such a learning environment, where the structure of the class is driven by mutual caring (about other students' intellectual development and emotional lives, caring between the instructor and students), collaboration, and shared experiences, values that differ significantly from the traditional pedagogies that still predominate in many disciplines and where authority rests entirely with the teacher.

For feminist educators, this inclusive learning environment, where voice, shared experiences, collaboration, and caring are considered, changes classroom dynamics in comparison to a more traditionally structured classroom. Ropers-Huilman (1999) discusses power and caring in the feminist classroom and how "feminist teachers and students can model to each other the complexities of using our power to care about each other and the educational environments that we create" (p. 133). A caring teacher, however, is not to be confused with one who is permissive or accommodating to students, as Akyea and Sandoval (2004) explain. A misinterpretation of caring, where the teacher might have pity on a student or a student's circumstances, or is overly sympathetic, might even create a situation of inequity. Caring, as they describe, "means providing clear and honest feedback (without sarcasm, sympathy or pity) on students' products or performance" (p. 10). In this way, "caring" as a feminist pedagogical value means identifying and responding to the individual learning, and sometimes affective, needs of the student as it relates to both the personal and the academic.

Leadership, community, and critical thinking are also significant traditional elements in feminist pedagogy, encouraging students to focus on finding connections with the instructor, with other students, and between the course material and their own lived experiences, and to take on leadership roles within and outside of the classroom. In practice, this is demonstrated where students take an active role in formulating and developing the goals and objectives of a course, learn about the process of negotiation, build community through group work, and be otherwise involved in the decision-making process about the structure or content of the course (Duncan & Stasio, 2001; Shrewsbury, 1993). For example, Crawley, Curry et al. (2008) describe two student-centered techniques to foster personal and community engagement, as well as critical thinking. Specifically, they devised two assignments: "Lecturing with questions" starts with the major debates in the discipline, moves to an interactive method of questioning, and ends with questions that put students in the roles of the authors from the readings. In "autoethnography" and "feminifesto" assignments, students are asked to write about gender experiences and issues. The autoethnography focuses on a sociological exercise asking students to write a personal "collection" of scenes and responses based on persistent memories a student has experienced. The "feminifesto" requires students to pick an issue about gender inequality they feel passionate about. Drawing from class readings, students weave theory to make their own claims rather than pure description of a particular theorist, allowing for some creativity and self-reflection in the process. Taking the place of more traditional research papers, these assignments were designed to get students "to do" disciplinary work and to think differently from what might be called prescriptive type of assignments or "static curriculum" (p. 29). Most feminist educators strive for what Crawley, Curry et al. (2008) calls "full contact pedagogy," or "to engage them [students] so fully in the given discipline we are teaching that they can claim it as a scholar would" (p. 13)—reflecting the goals of a signature pedagogy.

Clegg (2006) asks, what sorts of pedagogy should we be developing to delve deeper into ways of knowing and doing? For women's studies, there does not appear to be a conclusive answer to Clegg's question. Although there are established pedagogical practices in women's studies, as mentioned before, there is still little evidence measuring how effectively we are helping students understand gender as a system or moving into the implicit structure of feminist consciousness as a habit of mind. The most common ways of teaching in women's studies include reading, writing, speaking, dialogue, development of critical thinking, group work, and shared authority, but the assessment of the overall effectiveness of such pedagogical approaches seems thus far to be more anecdotal than measurable and generalizable. Commonly employed women's studies pedagogy points in the direction of established ways of knowing and doing within the field, but right now, the field lacks longitudinal research examining the development in students of a feminist consciousness that is carried beyond the classroom.

Key Elements of a Feminist Signature Pedagogy in Women's Studies

Although feminist pedagogy in women's studies is not a singular signature pedagogy, there are a number of key practices rooted in the values of the interdisciplinary field: For example, values like collaboration reflect the interconnectedness of the multiple disciplines that make up women's studies and reveal the way the field itself has evolved in the last three decades. Women's studies' signature pedagogy continues to evolve, but using Shulman's three-pronged definition, it's clear that there are definitive surface structures, deep structures, and implicit structures that inform teaching and learning in this interdisciplinary field. Surface structures in women's studies are dialogic and student-centered and involve distributed authority, mirroring the field's focus on connection and collaboration.

The deep structures of women's studies assume that one of the primary goals of a course in the field is to help students develop a gender consciousness—to see themselves as gendered beings in the world and the cultivation of the critical apparatus to position that gendered experience within a larger context—and ultimately a feminist consciousness. This objective matches the interdisciplines' historical emphasis on challenging forms of oppression and patriarchal hegemony.

A feminist consciousness is also part of the implicit structure of women's studies, what Crawley, Lewis, et al. (2008) usefully define as "an epistemological stance," one that is "attentive to power differences that create inequalities" but that is also a shift "away from a history of androcentric bias in the sciences, social sciences, and humanities" (p. 2). Crawley, Lewis et al. (2008) go on to explain feminist teaching and learning as "a way of orienting to academic work that is attuned to power relations, both within the academy and within knowledge construction itself" (p. 2), following in the tradition of the feminist social movement, which similarly challenged unequal power distribution and oppressive social structures. Ultimately, feminist educators hope to cultivate in students this feminist epistemological stance so that students leave the course equipped to approach their future learning inside and outside the classroom through a feminist lens.

A number of signature methods enact these values and principles. The deep structures in women's studies are rooted in core values that are manifested in pedagogical approaches that help students think and see in ways that reflect a feminist consciousness. At the core of women's studies is an emphasis on inclusion, collaboration, and shared experience. Feminist practitioners enact this focus in the classroom through a heavy use of large group and small group discussion, a minimal use of instructor lecture, and innovative discussion techniques like the fishbowl (see Young, 2007 or Piles, 1993 for a brief introduction to this technique), round-robin, or discussion chain (in the case of online courses—see Chick & Hassel, 2009). In a fishbowl discussion, a small group of students sits in a small circle in the middle of the rest of the students, in a large circle. An empty chair in the inner circle provides an entrée for students (or the professor) in the larger group to introduce new ideas, but the inner circle remains responsible for exploring an idea, topic, or reading that is the focus for that day. Round-robin discussions ask each student to contribute to a discussion by taking turns individually responding to the day's reading, question, or topic before the class moves to an open discussion, and a discussion chain requires the students to build on each other's contributions, again, before moving to a whole-class conversation about the topic. Each of these techniques places student voices (another women's studies core value) at the center of the conversation and highlights the dialogic and conversational nature of the feminist classroom, where the instructor is typically a facilitator and participant rather than a pedagogue.

Equally as important to women's studies is the notion of "agency," or a process of empowerment involving the rejection of social expectations about gender roles, where students are able to make autonomous decisions about gender outside of social constrictions. Empowerment, consciousness-raising, agency, and becoming change agents through sometimes uncomfortable and challenging discussions are all at the core of the feminist, women's studies classroom and part of the "deep structure" of a feminist signature pedagogy. Feminist educators enact this deep structure through a variety of student-directed activities that cultivate leadership skills and encourage students to develop their independent interests within women's studies. Field research or service-learning activities that connect students' learning inside the classroom to the world outside are common, reflecting what Crawley, Lewis et al. (2008) have described as the "action orientation" of feminist pedagogy. In women's studies courses, these can include mentoring programs, volunteer work, internships with feminist agencies in the community, ranging from women's shelters to family planning clinics, or consciousness-raising projects that invite students to identify a key theme or topic within the course and raise awareness within their communities. They typically involve not just collaboration with an outside group but also an academic assignment that asks students to apply key concepts from feminist theory or reading assignments from the class to their experience with action research.

For women's studies courses specifically (in contrast with discipline-specific courses that are cross-listed or that employ feminist pedagogy within their home disciplines, for example, a course on women in literature or women in the arts), other pedagogical features are deeply embedded in the understanding of the course content and reflective of the implicit structure of a feminist signature pedagogy characterized by a feminist epistemological stance. In practice, practitioners of feminist pedagogy in women's studies ground the content of women's studies courses in the pedagogical values described previously and help students develop an understanding of key concepts like the structure and gendered nature of institutions; gender and patriarchy as a system in which both men and women participate; feminist consciousness; social privilege and oppression based on categories of identity like race, gender, ability, sexual orientation, religion, ability, age; and so on.

In order to do this, instructors routinely employ pedagogical techniques that invite students to think like feminist scholars do, as Crawley, Lewis et al. (2008) have observed, using and discussing the role of reflexivity, or "constant awareness of one's own place in the power relations that comprise all academic pursuits" (p. 3)—and beyond. In the classroom, then, this might take the form of gender moments journals that ask students to document and reflect on the way gender is enacted in their everyday lives, or reflective narratives that ask students to discuss their own experiences as gendered beings and connect those experiences with course content.

Conclusion

Feminist educators in women's studies have developed a rich body of scholarly literature attentive to teaching and learning both within the interdisciplinary field of study and extending beyond to feminist research and teaching across and within the traditional disciplines. Feminist scholars have typically used reflective, theoretical, or descriptive approaches more along the lines of "scholarly teaching," or a reflective and analytical approach to teaching self-improvement than the scholarship of teaching and learning (Richlin, 2001), where teacher-scholars employ the rigorous research models they use in their own disciplinary scholarship to assess, evaluate, modify, propose, or reflect on teaching and learning in their classrooms. In this way, the field still has additional work to do in documenting the effectiveness of particular pedagogical approaches in cultivating the field's ways of thinking and knowing. At the same time, there is clearly a shared value system about what feminist educators in women's studies should be asking students to do and know after leaving a women's studies course.

Notes

1. Though feminist pedagogy is the style most frequently used in women's studies courses, feminist pedagogical approaches can be found across the disciplines.
2. For example, see journals such as *Feminist Teacher*.

References

Akyea, S. G., & Sandoval, P. (2004). A feminist perspective on student assessment: An epistemology of caring and concern. *Radical Pedagogy*. Retrieved from http://radicalpedagogy.icaap.org/content/issue6_2/akyea-sandoval.html

Blake, H., & Ooten, M. (2008). Bridging the divide: Connecting feminist histories and activism in the classroom. *Radical History Review, 102*, 63–72.

Bricker-Jenkins, M., & Hooyman, N. (1987). Feminist pedagogy in education for social change. *Feminist Teacher, 2*(2), 36–42.

Chick, N., & Hassel, H. (2009). "Don't hate me because I'm virtual": Feminist pedagogy in the online classroom. *Feminist Teacher, 19*(3), 195–215.

Clegg, S. (2006). "Cross-disciplinary pedagogies and the project of the personal in global higher education." Panel discussion at the *International Society for the Scholarship of Teaching and Learning (ISSoTL) Conference.*

Colwill, E., & Boyd, R. (2008). Teaching without a mask? Collaborative teaching as feminist practice. *Feminist Formations, 20*(2), 216–246.

Cook, J., & Fonow, M. M. (1986). Knowledge and women's interest: Issues of epistemology and methodology in feminist sociological research. *Sociological Inquiry, 56*, 2–29.

Crawley, S. L., Curry, H., Dumois-Sands, J., Tanner, C., & Wyker, C. (2008a). Full-contact pedagogy: Lecturing with questions and student-centered assignments as methods for inciting self-reflexivity for faculty and students. *Feminist Teacher, 19*(1), 13–30.

Crawley, S. L., Lewis, J. E., & Mayberry, M. (2008b). Introduction—Feminist pedagogies in action: Teaching beyond disciplines. *Feminist Teacher, 19*(1), 1–12.

Crowley, Karlyn. (2009). Pedagogical intersections of gender, race, and identity. In R. A. R. Gurung & L. R. Prieto (Eds.), *Getting culture* (pp. 137–148). Sterling, VA: Stylus Publishing, LLC.

Duncan, K., & Stasio, M. (2001). Surveying feminist pedagogy: A measurement, an evaluation, and an affirmation. *Feminist Teacher, 13*(3), 225–239.

Feigenbaum, A. (2007). The teachable moment: Feminist pedagogy and the neoliberal classroom. *The Review of Education, Pedagogy, and Cultural Studies, 29*, 337–349.

Freire, P. (1970). *Pedagogy of the oppressed.* New York, NY: Herder and Herder.

Gurung, R. A., Chick, N. L., & Haynie, A. (Eds.). (2009). *Exploring signature pedagogies: Approaches to teaching disciplinary habits of mind.* Sterling, VA: Stylus Publishing, LLC.

hooks, b. (1989). *Talking back: Thinking feminist, thinking black.* Cambridge, MA: South End Press.

Jacobs, L. (2008). Re-claiming what we know: Pedagogy and the f-word. *Thirdspace: A Journal of Feminist Theory and Culture, 8*(1), 1–6.

Lehrman, K. (1993). Off course. *Mother Jones*, 45–68.

Maher, F. A. (1987a). Inquiry teaching and feminist pedagogy. *Social Education, 51*(3), 186–192.

Maher, F. A. (1987b). Toward a richer theory of feminist pedagogy: A comparison of "liberation" and "gender" models for teaching and learning. *Journal of Education, 169*(3), 91–100.

Markowitz, L. (2005). Unmasking moral dichotomies: Can feminist pedagogy overcome student resistance? *Gender and Education, 17*(1), 39–55.

Piles, M. (1993). The fishbowl discussion: A strategy for large honors classes. *English Journal, 82*(6), 49–50.

Rich, A. (1979). *On lies, secrets, and silence: Selected prose 1966–1978.* New York, NY: W.W. Norton and Co.

Richlin, L. (2001). Scholarly teaching and the scholarship of teaching. In C. Kreber (Ed.), *New directions for teaching and learning: No. 86. Scholarship revisited: Perspectives on the scholarship of teaching and learning* (pp. 57–68). San Francisco, CA: Jossey-Bass.

Ropers-Huilman, B. (1999). Scholarship on the other side. *NWSA Journal, 11*(1), 118–135.

Shaw, S., & Lee, J. (2008). *Women's voices, feminist visions: Classic and contemporary readings* (4th ed.). New York, NY: McGraw Hill.

Shrewsbury, C. M. (1993). What is feminist pedagogy? *Women's Studies Quarterly, 3,* 8–16.

Stake, J. E., & Hoffman, F. L. (2000). Putting feminist pedagogy to the test. *Psychology of Women Quarterly, 24,* 30–38.

Wiegman, R. (2002). Academic feminism against itself. *NWSA Journal, 14*(2), 18–37.

Young, J. (2007). Small group scored discussion: Beyond the fishbowl or, everybody reads, everybody talks, everybody learns. *History Teacher, 40*(2), 177–181.

12

MAPPING AN EMERGING SIGNATURE PEDAGOGY FOR DISABILITY STUDIES

Sheila O'Driscoll

Disability studies is a relatively new field of scholarship that critically examines issues related to the dynamic interplay between disability and various aspects of culture and society. The emergence of disability studies as an academic discipline has been both rapid and extensive, but its roots are in the activism and experiences of disabled people (Albrecht, Seelman, & Bury, 2001). The most significant issues academically and politically have arisen from the development of a social interpretation (Finkelstein, 2001a) or "social model" of disability (Oliver, 1990b), which began officially in the United Kingdom (UK) with a proclamation by the Union of Physically Impaired Against Segregation (UPIAS) in 1976 and the founding of the Society for Disability Studies (SDS) in the United States, in 1982 (Danforth & Gabel, 2008). This social interpretation of disability tends to relocate the "problem" from the individual to society. It seeks to challenge the more traditional medical, scientific, and psychological models of disability by questioning the social process of disability within our collective societies (Campbell & Oliver, 1996), thereby developing an understanding of the impact that these models have, not only on the lives of a person living with a disability, but the implications for policy, employment, education, legislation, and research (Oliver, 1990b). The social model of disability centers on a seemingly simple question and one that informs the discussion in this chapter: What is a disability? (Gallagher, 2004).

Disability studies is less well-defined than other social sciences because of its interdisciplinary nature. Its pedagogical literature is in the early stages of development and draws on scholarship from the critical sociology tradition of the United Kingdom (e.g., Barnes & Mercer, 2003; Finkelstein, 1980; Oliver, 1990b; Oliver & Barnes, 1998); feminist literature on disability (e.g., Fawcett, 2000; Ferri, 2008; Linton, 1998; Lonsdale, 1990; Morris, 1996; Thomas, 1999; Wendell, 1996); humanities scholarship (e.g., Davis, 1997; Siebers, 2006; Ware, 2008); cultural studies (e.g., Riddell & Watson, 2003); the social sciences (e.g., Giddens, 2006; Priestley, 2003; Zola, 1982); and disability studies in education (e.g., Danforth & Gabel, 2008; Gabel, 2002; Gabel & Peters, 2004; Gallagher, 2004; Taylor, 2008).

Some of these scholars emphasize the social oppression of disabled people; others view disability in terms of culture and identity (Barton & Oliver, 1997; Shakespeare & Watson, 2002). Taylor (2008) contends that although there are important differences in these social interpretations of disability, they share a common understanding of disability as a social phenomenon. The fundamental paradigm of disability studies is distinct from rehabilitation, medical sociology, psychology of deviance, special education, and the allied health sciences, which are informed by the medical model of disability (Pfeiffer & Yoshida, 1995).

Articulating a signature pedagogy for disability studies is a challenging task involving complex questions of teaching methods, personal attitudes, and interpersonal morality (Danforth & Gabel, 2008). A discipline's signature pedagogy provides important information about the personality of a professional field (Calder, 2006). In the context of disability studies, this is not just a discussion about the way "disability" is understood, "but an argument about the nature of all human beings—the essentials of being human" (Finkelstein 1972, p. 2). Whereas professions like medicine and law are explicit about teaching their students to think like disciplinary experts, the learning process for students in an introductory program in disability studies is more complex. It relates to learning as a shared responsibility not only between students but also between teachers and students, which Savin-Baden and Howell Major (2004) contend enables all those engaged in such a program to develop a sound understanding of the content and process of learning.

This chapter elucidates and maps a suitable signature pedagogy for the discipline of disability studies, with a focus on introductory programs. This requires a pedagogical approach that introduces complexity into the classroom from the outset and provokes a conversation about how "we look at disability" with a series of broad, provocative questions about disability and the life experiences of disabled people (Albrecht et al., 2001; Ben-Moshe, Cory, Feldbaum, & Sagendorf, 2009; Ware, 2008).

The Social Model of Disability

The earliest formal expression of the social model originated in the disabled people's movement of the UK in 1975. In their manifesto, which drew upon their individual and collective experience, entitled *The Fundamental Principles of Disability,* they claimed that disability was something imposed on the lives of people with "impairments" by a society intolerant of any form of biological flaw whether real or imagined (UPIAS, 1976). This manifesto contains several key elements succinctly outlined by Shakespeare and Watson (2002). First, it claims that disabled people are an oppressed social group; second, it distinguishes between the impairments that people have and the oppression they experience. Finally, it defines *disability* as the social oppression, not the form of impairment. Oliver (1990a), the originator of the social model of disability, emphasizes the importance of these distinctions, noting that "if disability is defined as social oppression, then disabled people will be viewed as the collective victims of an uncaring society rather than as individual victims of circumstance" (Oliver, 1990a, p. 2).

Britain's first disability studies course was developed by an interdisciplinary team at the Open University (OU) in 1975 (Oliver, 1996). The OU was an appropriate location for the new course and its emergence signaled a new and innovative approach to university education (Swain, French, Barnes, & Thomas, 2004). As a correspondence university, OU publicity and course materials are accessed by a very large audience; thus, ideas disseminated by the first and subsequent courses penetrated the consciousness of a large body of disabled people as well as practitioners working with disabled people. A consequence was that the language of disability studies increasingly became common currency. The OU developed a wealth of material, much of it generated by disabled people, which provided the basis for the development of disability studies courses and professional training schemes across the UK (Barnes, Oliver, & Barton, 2002).

Barnes and Mercer (2003) argue that the introduction of the social model and the development of disability studies posed a direct challenge to the kind of orthodox thinking generated by scholars working in the established disciplines of medicine, sociology, and psychology. In essence, their argument, which informs this chapter, is that the concept of disability is socially constructed. From this standpoint, disability is not a characteristic that exists in a person or a pathological condition that can be objectively diagnosed by trained professionals using standardized instruments (Taylor, 2008). Rather than transmitting information, or giving instructions, constructivist educators begin by posing problems and asking questions (Gallagher, 2004).

The Minority Group Model: Disability Studies in the United States

North American academics and activists have also developed a social approach to the study of disability by focusing on the concept that disability as a social construct uses a minority group model (Linton, 1998). This model signifies neither a denial of the presence of impairments nor a rejection of the utility of intervention and treatment. Instead it separates impairments from the negative attributions to which disability has been socially and politically attributed (Mutua & Smith, 2008).

Introduced to the mainstream academic agenda in the United States and Canada in the 1970s (Albrecht, et al., 2001), the link between disability activism and the disability studies academy was instrumental in this process because they shared the same problems and a common methodology (Pfeiffer & Yoshida, 1995). Gabel and Peters (2004) observe that members of this minority group model were influenced by the U.S. civil rights movement when they claimed that the disabled experienced marginalization, disenfranchisement, and stigmatization.

An understanding of disability in the United States requires that U.S. values and ideologies are taken into account, because they influence the ways in which disability is socially constructed. The emphasis on individualism, capitalism, and the U.S. brand of democracy affect how disability is defined, and Albrecht et al. (2001) claim that the title "disability studies" designates a much broader field of study in the United States, one that encompasses a range of social scientific and rehabilitative disciplines as well as the perspectives of disabled activists. One of the founding fathers, Irving K. Zola, founded the *Disability Studies Quarterly* and cofounded the Society for Disability Studies (SDS) (Albrecht et al., 2001). Professor Zola, a social scientist who had an acquired disability, focused on the lived experiences and perceptions of people with impairments as a means of discovering the social dynamics of disability (Zola, 1982).

Although both early social interpretations of disability (the traditional British version of the social model and the minority group model in the United States) were concerned with the collective experience of disabled people, subtle distinctions in discourse emerged, stemming from political and cultural differences (Barnes, Mercer, & Shakespeare, 1999; Gabel, 2005; Linton, 1998; Meekosha, 2004; Snyder, Brueggemann, & Thomson, 2002). Shakespeare and Watson (2002) argue that the North Americans' social approach has not gone as far as the British social model. They cite the work of U.S. scholars, such as Hahn (1985) and Wendell (1996), as making important social, cultural, and political contributions to disability, but argue that the literature did not recognize the firm distinction between the medical (impairment) and social (disability), which is the key to the British social model.

Armstrong and Barton (1999), in their publication *Disability, Human Rights and Education,* make an important contribution to the global approach to disability studies. Applying the concept of human rights to issues of disability and education in countries such as Zimbabwe, Australia, China, and Trinidad and Tobago, they highlight "the contested notion of human rights, the social construction of difference, the importance of the constant re-patterning of social experience in the light of historical and contemporary change, the nature of policy and the interface of all these with education" (p. 5). In Australia the field of disability studies has been influenced by both the British and U.S. traditions, but Meekosha (1998) argues that neither of these is of major help in examining issues such as the almost totally unexplored space of indigenous disability. Cross-cultural approaches are important, providing very interesting insights and ideas on disability, human rights, and education, and it begs the question, what can Western nations learn from educators in the East or South who apply disability studies to their everyday practice (Danforth & Gabel, 2008)?

Disability Studies and the Scholarship of Teaching and Learning (SoTL)

Despite the growing influence of disability studies over the last three decades, it is a discipline that was largely ignored by educational researchers until the nineties, when disability research began to evolve in parts of Europe, Australia, and New Zealand. In 1999, the American Educational Research Association (AERA) founded Disability Studies in Education (DSE) (Gabel, 2005). This marked the formal beginning of what has become a growing movement in educational research, theory, and practice (Gabel & Peters, 2004). These scholars sought to examine the ethical, social, and political problems resulting from the domination of positivist writings in journals. They explored alternative ways of envisioning and writing about the lives and possibilities of persons with disabilities (DSE, p. 1). They described Disability Studies in Education as an intellectual and practical tradition that has emerged at the intersection of disability studies and educational research, creating a general orientation to disability as a social and political phenomenon within the context of teaching and learning (Danforth & Gabel, 2008). New ways of thinking, talking about, and enacting practice have emerged in the form of problematic questions concerning disability and education. Such questions consider: "In what ways does disability studies inform pedagogy and practice" (Danforth & Gabel, 2008, p. 5)? As Ferri (2008) observes, in moving away from the traditional models of disability (the preferred choice of special education research and scholarship), "we ask students (and ourselves) to give up certainties but in the process we gain complexity, we give up having easy answers but get better at asking hard questions" (p. 304).

The overarching goals for an introductory module on a program in disability studies are best described by Swain et al. (2005): to enable critical thought, reflection, and personal growth; to explore the experiences and lives of disabled people by examining the barriers that disabled people face in the social world; and to take the social model as the foundation for an enquiry-based approach to the study of disability in a social world. These goals reflect the deep structure of the discipline, which is a core requirement for a signature pedagogy. Such goals require specific pedagogical techniques that are unique to the discipline if they are to be considered a signature pedagogy.

Problem-Based Learning

The idea of learning through solving problems is not new. Savin-Baden and Howell Major (2004) suggest that the development of knowledge as a process through which students reflect on complex questions, conduct original investigations, and consider how they might be investigated, is drawn from early philosophical ideas dating back to the 7th century BC.

One of the main principles of problem-based learning is the focus on learning as a shared responsibility. The acknowledgment that nobody, including the instructor, is responsible for knowing everything enables those engaged in such a community to gain a sound understanding of both the content and process of learning. These learning communities are considered as communities of practice, where students are constructing understanding of what it means to be a professional (Savin-Baden & Howell Major, 2004). Problem-based learning is part of the move from the teaching paradigm to the learning paradigm (Barr & Tagg, 1995). It symbolizes an integrative approach to learning and draws on a number of learning theories, while at the same time acknowledging the importance of learning through experience. In proposing problem-based learning as a suitable signature pedagogy for disability studies, there seems to be no particular approach to this teaching method. Savin-Baden and Howell Major (2004) maintain that problem-based learning does not have defined characteristics and is an approach to learning that affects the pedagogical environment into which it is placed, in terms of the discipline and tutors.

Students in disability studies courses are encouraged to reflect and engage with problems in a way that transcends taken-for-granted preconceptions and prejudices, a process that Shulman (2005) suggests as a universal feature of signature pedagogies. For example, they might be asked to reflect on the power of the medical profession, which gives them control over fundamental aspects of disabled people's lives: where they should live, whether they should work or not, what kind of school they should go to, the kinds of benefits and services they should receive, and, "in the case of unborn children whether they should live or die" (Oliver, 1996, p. 36).

Research has shown that problem-based learning facilitates thinking about material rather than simply memorizing it, thereby prompting a deep approach to learning (Bernstein, Tipping, Bercovitz, & Skinner, 1995). It engages the learner's feelings, thoughts, experiences, relationships, and cultural, educational, and employment backgrounds, values, and beliefs; in other words, everything that makes a person unique (Brockbank & McGill, 2007). For students of disability studies, problem-based learning reflects a commitment to the social model of disability, enabling lecturers to bring to the classroom diverse and interdisciplinary perspectives from the world of disability, while simultaneously encouraging students to explore and critically engage with the lived experiences of disabled people.

In problem-based curricula, the starting point should be a set of problem situations that will equip students to become independent inquirers, who see that there are other ways of knowing besides their own perspective (Savin-Baden & Howell Major, 2004). To date, there are no "recipes" for teaching a disability studies program, and there are a limited number of textbooks and readings in teacher education that begin with a disability studies perspective (Ferri, 2008, p. 289). However, despite limited resources and a lack of available models, educators have begun the task of infusing their curriculum with a disability studies perspective. Some of their reflections and that of their students inform the last section of this chapter, and they also mirror the experiences of this author, who teaches introductory programs in disability studies throughout the south of Ireland.

Teaching Disability Studies: Mapping the Terrain

Solis and Connor (2008) argue that scholarship in disability studies has developed into an academic discourse and has been criticized for a lack of relevance to the lives of disabled people, sometimes by disabled people themselves. Critique has been a basic characteristic of disability studies, and Ferri (2008) observes that disability studies scholars are better at critiquing dominant models than offering clear-cut alternatives. While acknowledging that the pedagogical literature is relatively limited and is in the early stages of development, the final part of this chapter seeks to engage with these issues with first-person accounts of the teachers and students who have written of their experiences in disability studies programs.

Gabel (2005) offers a working definition of disability studies as "the use and application of disability studies assumptions and methods to educational issues and problems" (p. 10), and Broderick, Reid, and Weatherly Valle (2008) note from their research that disability scholars indicate that the perspective of disability studies informs their current practice in a number of ways, as exemplified by a professor with a significant disability who reports:

> My commitment to disability studies has caused me to repudiate much of the framework underlying Special Education as a discipline even though it is the intellectual arena and medium in which I operate. The result is that students are so challenged by the information they are presented they are not quite sure how to proceed. The one thing that is certain is that students are questioning everything they are presented and they are being given license to assume a role not only as educational advocates for the youths they serve but as advocates for the preservation of their own intellectual integrity . . . they have begun to understand how they have been enculturated in a belief system that at least one professor challenges them to question. (p. 141)

Another teacher with two years of teaching experience responded:

> My definition of learning disability is the result of my personal experience growing up with a visual perceptual learning disability. Through the medical model lens, I learned to associate disability within myself and I worked hard to rid myself of the ugliness I associated with Disability. (p. 145)

Another disability studies scholar (Ferri, 2008) outlines how she frames her courses with the specific aim of critiquing the medical model of disability. She begins by troubling rather than reifying identity categories, exposing the interconnectedness of issues of disability, race, class, gender, and sexuality. This is followed by the use of autobiography and narrative to broaden and complicate students' ideas about sources of expertise on disability, and, finally, she seeks to trouble students' assumptions about disability by highlighting how the categories of ability and disability are constructed. Her overall goal is to create a disruption in the students' knowledge of disability and she draws on a problem-based learning perspective to show that in class "we struggle together," and "we think together about how to work towards making general education more accessible" (p. 300), thus engaging in one of the overarching goals for problem-based learning, a community of practice (Savin-Baden & Howell Major, 2004).

Ferri (2008) observes that "students often take a disability course to learn about disability as a discrete form of knowledge" (p. 296). This quote succinctly outlines the experience of two students from Ryerson University (Paterson, Hogan & Willis, 2008) and is typical of many students who register in a program of disability studies, who are working in the "industry" of disability. The first student who came to the school of disability studies, hoping to become a better support worker and advocate, stated that she defined disability as something that did not personally affect her; it was just the people she supported who needed help. However, as she progressed through the disability studies program, she documents that, "my definition of disability became more complex," which returns to one of the questions posed earlier in the chapter in relation to the importance of definitions of disability outlined by Oliver (1990a).

The second student from the same university documents that questioning her own personal history was a very unsettling experience: "Disability studies was supposed to help me learn and understand the dynamics of other people's disabilities. I didn't expect it to make me question my own personal history and current way of living" (Paterson, Hogan, & Willis, 2008, p. 2). She added that as a support worker, "It can be very unsettling to confront how one's role within the system may be part of the problem" (p. 3).

Conclusion

Given the values, practices, attitudes, assumptions, and beliefs that disability scholars bring to their discipline, using a social constructionist perspective and informed by the social model of disability, it is not surprising that these are also the key characteristics of the emerging signature pedagogy as described in this chapter. Although disability studies approaches differ, scholars share an important commonality: a rejection of the medical model of disability in favor of more social and political understandings of disability. Engaging in disability studies scholarship encompasses more than the dilemmas it poses in an educational context. It is a redefining experience, adding value to individual lives and clarifying what it means to be human. In other words, "the issue of disability is not about disability it is about all of us in a just society" (Danforth & Gabel, 2008, p. 72).

References

Albrecht, G. A., Seelman, K. D., & Bury, M. (Eds.). (2001). *The handbook of disability studies.* London, UK: Sage.

Armstrong, F., & Barton, L. (1999). *Disability, human rights and education: Cross-cultural perspectives.* Buckingham, PA: Open University Press.

Barnes, C., & Mercer, G. (2003). *Disability.* London, UK: Polity Press.

Barnes, C., Mercer, G., & Shakespeare, T. (1999). *Exploring disability: A sociological introduction.* Cambridge, MA: Polity Press.

Barnes, C., Oliver, M., & Barton, L. (Eds.). (2002). *Disability studies today.* London, UK: Polity Press.

Barr, R. B., & Tagg, J. (1995). From teaching to learning—a new paradigm for undergraduate education. *Change Magazine,* 27(6), 12–25.

Barton, L., & Oliver, M. (1997). *Disability studies, past, present and future.* Leeds, UK: Disability Press.

Ben-Moshe, L., Cory, R. C., Feldbaum, M., & Sagendorf, K. (2009). *Building pedagogical curb cuts: Incorporating disability into the university classroom and curriculum.* Syracuse, NY: The Graduate School, Syracuse University.

Bernstein, P., Tipping, J., Bercovitz, K., & Skinner, H. A. (1995). Shifting students and faculty to a PBL. Curriculum: Attitudes changed and lessons learned. *Academic Medicine, 70,* 245–247.

Brockbank, A., & McGill, I. (2007). *Facilitating reflective learning in higher education* (2nd ed.) Buckingham, PA: Open University Press.

Broderick, A. A., Reid, D. K., & Weatherly Valle, J. (2008). Disability studies in education and the practical concerns of teachers. In S. Danforth & S. Gabel (Eds.), *Vital questions facing disability studies in education* (pp. 133–160). New York, NY: Peter Lang.

Calder, L. (2006). Uncoverage: Toward a signature pedagogy for the history survey. *Journal of American history* 1067–1078. Bloomington, IN: The Organization of American Historians.

Campbell, J., & Oliver, M. (1996). *Disability politics: Understanding our past, changing our future.* London, UK: Routledge.

Danforth, S., & Gabel, S. (2008). *Vital questions facing disability studies in education.* New York, NY: Peter Lang.

Davis, L. (Ed.). (1997). *The disability studies reader.* London, UK: Routledge

Fawcett, B. (2000). *Feminist perspectives on disability.* Essex, UK: Pearson Education Limited.

Ferri, B. A. (2008). Why teach disability studies in education? Teaching to trouble. In S. Danforth, & S. Gabel (Eds.), *Vital questions facing disability studies in education* (pp. 289–306). New York, NY: Peter Lang.

Finkelstein, V. (1972). *The psychology of disability.* The Disability Studies Archive UK, Centre for Disability Studies, University of Leeds. Retrieved from www.leeds.ac.uk/disability-studies/archiveuk/archframe.htm

Finkelstein, V. (1980). *Attitudes and disabled people; issues for discussion.* New York, NY: World Rehabilitation Fund.

Finkelstein, V. (2001a). *The social model of disability repossessed.* The Disability Studies Archive UK, Centre for Disability Studies, University of Leeds. Retrieved from www.leeds.ac.uk/disability-studies/archiveuk/archframe.htm

Finkelstein, V. (2001b). *A personal journey into disability politics.* The Disability Studies Archive UK, Centre for Disability Studies, University of Leeds. Retrieved from www.leeds.ac.uk/disability-studies/archiveuk/archframe.htm (accessed August 2003).

Gabel, S. (2002). Some conceptual problems with critical pedagogy. *Curriculum Inquiry, 32*(2), 177–201.

Gabel, S. L. (Ed.). (2005). *Disability studies in education: Readings in theory and method.* New York, NY: Peter Lang.

Gabel, S. L., & Peters, S. (2004). Presage of a new paradigm; beyond the social model of disability toward resistance theories of disability. *Disability and Society, 19,* 571–596.

Gallagher, D. J. (2004, Spring). The importance of constructivism and constructivist pedagogy for disability studies in education. *Disability Studies Quarterly, 24*(2), 1–14.

Giddens, A. (2006). *Sociology* (5th ed.). London, UK: Polity Press.

Hahn, H. (1985). Toward a politics of disability: definitions, disciplines, and policies. *The Social Science Journal, 22*(4), 87.

Linton, S. (1998). Disability studies/not disability studies. *Disability and Society, 13*(4), 525–540.

Lonsdale, S. (1990). *Women and disability.* London, UK: Campbell.

Meekosha, H. (2004). Body battles: Bodies, gender and disability. In T. Shakespeare (Ed.), *The disability reader: Social science perspectives* (pp. 163–180). London, UK: Cassell.

Morris, J. (1996). *Pride against prejudice: A personal politics of disability* (3rd ed.). London, UK: McNamara.

Mutua, K., & Smith, R. M. (2008). Disrupting normalcy and the practical concerns of classroom teachers. In S. Danforth & S. Gabel, *Vital questions facing disability studies in education* (pp. 121–160). New York, NY: Peter Lang.

Oliver, M. (1990a). *The politics of disablement.* London, UK: Macmillan Press.

Oliver, M. (1990b). *The Individual and Social Models of Disability.* Paper presented at Joint Workshop of the Living Options Group and the Research Unit of the Royal College of Physicians [online], Leeds University. Retrieved from http://www.leeds.ac.uk/disability-studies/archive/Oliver/insocialdisability.pdf

Oliver, M. (1996). *Understanding disability: From theory to practice.* New York, NY: Palgrave.

Oliver, M., & Barnes, C. (1998). *Disabled people and social policy: From exclusion to Inclusion.* New York, NY: Longman.

Paterson, J., Hogan, J., & Willis, H. (2008, Fall). Vision, passion, action: Reflections on learning to do disability studies in the classroom and beyond. *Disability Studies Quarterly, 28*(24), 1–11.

Pfeiffer, D., & Yoshida, K. (1995). Teaching disability studies in Canada. *Disability and Society, 10*(4), 475–500.

Priestley, M. (2003). *Disability: A life course approach.* Cambridge, UK: Polity Press.

Riddell, S., & Watson, N. (2003). *Disability, culture and identity.* London, UK: Prentice Hall.

Savin-Baden, M., & Howell Major, C. (2004). *Foundations of problem-based learning.* Maidenhead, UK: Open University Press.

Shakespeare, T., & Watson, N. (2002). The social model of disability: An outdated ideology? *Research in Social Science and Disability*, 2, 9–28.

Shulman, L. S. (2005, February). *The signature pedagogies of law, medicine, engineering, and the clergy: Potential lessons for the education of teachers.* Math science partnership workshop, Irvine, California. Retrieved from http://hub.mspnet.org/index.cfm/11172

Siebers, T. (2006, Spring/Summer). Disability Aesthetics. *Journal for Cultural and Religious Theory* 7(2), 63–73.

Solis, S., & Connor, D. J. (2008). Theory meets practice: Disability studies and personal narratives in school. In S. Danforth & S. Gabel (Eds.). *Vital questions facing disability studies in education* (pp. 103–119). New York, NY: Peter Lang.

Snyder, S. L., Brueggemann, B. J., & Thomson, R. G. (2002). *Disability studies: Enabling the humanities.* New York, NY: Modern Language Association of America.

Swain, J., French, S., Barnes, C., & Thomas, C. (2004). *Disabling barriers—Enabling environments* (2nd ed.). London, UK: Sage.

Swain, J., French, S., & Cameron, C. (2005). *Controversial issues in a disabling society* (2nd ed.). Maidenhead, UK: Open University Press.

Taylor, S. J. (2008). Before it had a name: Exploring the historical roots of disability studies in education. In S. Danforth & S. Gabel (Eds.), *Vital questions facing disability studies in education* (pp. xiiii–xxiii). New York, NY: Peter Lang.

Thomas, C. (1999). *Female forms, experiencing and understanding disability.* Buckingham, PA: Open University Press.

UPIAS. (1976). *Fundamental principles of disability.* London, UK: Union of Physically Impaired Against Segregation.

Ware, L. (2008). Why teach disability studies in education? In S. Danforth & S. Gabel (Eds.), *Vital questions facing disability studies in education* (pp. 271–287). New York, NY: Peter Lang.

Wendell, S. (1996). *The rejected body, feminist and philosophical reflections on disability.* London, UK: Routledge.

Zola, I. K. (1982). *Missing pieces: A chronicle of living with a disability.* Philadelphia, PA: Temple University Press.

PART FOUR

PROFESSIONS

13

COMPETENCE AND CARE

Signature Pedagogies in Nursing Education

Thomas Lawrence Long, Karen R. Breitkreuz, Desiree A. Diaz, John J. McNulty, Arthur J. Engler, Carol Polifroni, and Jennifer Casavant Telford

A registered nurse should exercise sound, compassionate clinical judgment; demonstrate deep and broad knowledge of health and illness; and be a technically skilled health care provider, who works effectively with patients and families in a complex medical, ethical, legal, and professional landscape. The nursing profession has periodically reflected deeply on the nature of nursing education and has proposed new directions in the teaching of nursing. The *Goldmark Report* (1923), funded by the Rockefeller Foundation, paved the way for college- and university-based nursing programs; prompted by the success of the World War II cadet nurse program, the *Montag Report* (1951) initiated the movement toward associate degree nursing programs; the National Commission for the Study of Nursing and Nursing Education's *Lysaught Report* (1970) prompted research-based education of nurses and research into nursing education. Now the Carnegie Foundation for the Advancement of Teaching has funded another watershed study: *Educating Nurses: A Call for Radical Transformation* (Benner, Sutphen, Leonard, & Day, 2010) finds that, although U.S. nurse educators are very effective in teaching ethics and professionalism and are often successful when they integrate theory and clinical courses, they are "not generally effective in teaching nursing science, natural sciences, social sciences, technology, and humanities" (p. 12). At each turning point in the history of nursing education, nurse educators have assessed learning outcomes and the methods used to achieve them with the same critical eyes that they apply to evidence-based clinical nursing practice. Today nurse educators are examining the field's signature pedagogies, like clinical rotations and simulation, and are turning to new approaches, like narrative and problem-based pedagogies or study-abroad experiences.

Emerging Themes in Nursing Pedagogy

As a practice-based discipline, simultaneously a pure science and an applied science, nursing needs pedagogical approaches different from those disciplines that teach mainly science content like biology, chemistry, and physics, or mainly applied science like engineering and architecture. The default pedagogy of didactic instruction alone is insufficient to teach the knowledge and skills one needs to be a nurse, much less to cultivate the professional ethos of nursing. Depending on the topic, health information tends to grow exponentially, and students find the most accurate and current information that they will use in their clinical experiences through online databases like the Cumulative Index to Nursing and Allied Health Literature (CINAHL) or articles and research reports from reliable sources like the National Institute of Nursing Research or the Centers for Disease Control and Prevention, rather than in quickly outdated textbooks or lectures. In addition to this scientific knowledge, students need to practice skills and apply knowledge in low-risk settings (like a simulation lab) before they can safely work in clinical settings with patients and families. Signature pedagogies for nursing education, therefore, have to teach health science knowledge, clinical practice skills, and critical thinking, while inculcating an ethos of compassionate and ethical behavior. The two emerging themes discussed here also recognize the dynamic tension in nursing education between default approaches, like didactic lectures, and signature process approaches, like debriefing sessions in clinical or simulation activities (Gwele, 1996), in other words, between covering content and fostering critical clinical thinking and practice (Ironside, 2004).

The sheer quantity of clinical health science knowledge prompts some faculty to revert to a default pedagogy of lectures, textbooks, and PowerPoint slides. This tendency is exacerbated by the fact that nursing degree programs have strict limits on the maximum number of students who can be enrolled in clinical courses. As a result, clinical science theory courses tend to be large lecture classes with as many students as can fit into a lecture hall, and with assessments typically using multiple-choice questions. However, students in such courses might not be actively engaged or induced to think critically.

In recent years, narrative pedagogy and problem-based learning have emerged as pedagogies that engage nursing students actively and critically. Both narrative pedagogy and problem-based learning engage nursing students' imaginations, empathy, and clinical judgment. The power of stories to engage our imagination and our empathy is used to employ "multiple epistemologies (knowledge), exploring ways of knowing and practices of thinking, and interpreting as central to understanding the nature of experiences" (Diekelmann, 2001, p. 54). Narrative pedagogy considers the experience of all involved in the conversation: the student, the faculty member, the patient, the family, and the clinical group as a whole (Bankert & Kozel, 2005; Chan, 2008; Diekelmann, 2001; Kawashima, 2005). Stories include students' own writing (Chirema, 2007), patients' writing, and published fiction and nonfiction narratives that students read and discuss (Cagle, Walker, & Newcomb, 2006; Sakalys, 2002). The participants focus on the narratives in order to analyze, critique, interpret, explain, and understand the information presented and experienced. Through this highly personal and interpretive process, the student learners are able to recognize what they know and to realize when more knowledge is needed through further exploration and investigation. Narrative is becoming significant in nursing education, both as a means of students' reflection on the experience of patients and as a means of communicating with patients and their families (Benner et al., 2010). Narrative pedagogies can lead students into critical reflection about learning that expands their knowledge beyond the traditional content focus and to the critical interpretation essential to nursing practice (Ironside, 2006; Scheckel & Ironside, 2006). They are valuable in the formation of a nursing student's ethical awareness (Diekelmann & Diekelmann, 2000). Narratives also serve as a valid source of data in assessing students' cultural competence (Wong & Blissett, 2007), which is an essential professional quality in nursing. Narrative pedagogies might help inculcate a less isolating and competitive climate in nursing schools and help combat the fraught student-teacher relationships that can result from competency-based pedagogies (Andrews et al., 2001). And as nursing education acknowledges its global and multicultural dimensions, narrative pedagogies also might be generalizable across cultures, having been used effectively outside of Western contexts (Chan, 2008; Kawashima, 2005; Wong, Kember, Chung, & Yan, 1995).

Problem-based learning is "a pedagogical method that provides students with practical, real-life problems to solve. These problems are typically open-ended in nature, generally possessing many possible solutions" (Visconti, 2010, p. 27). Problem-based learning, originally used in medical schools decades ago and adapted more recently by nurse educators (Baker, 2000), begins with a short health care vignette followed by a series of four questions: (1) "What do you know?"; (2) "What else do you need to know to address the problem?"; after which participants gather the needed information and are asked, (3) "Now that you know this, what does it mean?"; and finally, (4) "What are you going to do as a result of this?" As in narrative pedagogy, the learner is actively engaged in problem-based learning, although the faculty member needs to be expert enough to "Go where the students go" and to redirect them when needed. Problem-based learning focuses on supplying information rather than discovering and applying information, and this stimulates continued exploration and provides new knowledge (Niemer, Pfendt, & Gers, 2010).

Not unique to nursing education, narrative pedagogy and problem-based learning show promise in engaging students in the affective and cognitive domains, stimulating empathy and critical thinking. They build on nurse educators' adaptation of what might be called liberal arts pedagogies.

Liberal Arts Pedagogies

Historically nursing has appropriated pedagogies from diverse disciplines that might seem, at first glance, not to be associated with a health science. A relatively new profession and even newer academic discipline, nursing has adapted previous education theories and practices while at the same time defining itself in distinction from other professions and disciplines. Expanding Carper's (1978) groundbreaking study of ways of knowing, Chinn and Kramer (2008) have defined five ways of knowing unique to nursing: emancipatory knowledge (their addition to Carper's four), ethical knowledge, personal knowledge, aesthetic knowledge, and empiric knowledge. Empiric knowing is that most familiar to the natural and health sciences and is constituted by the scientific method. Emancipatory knowing engages critical thinking about the social and political (and explicitly social justice) dimensions of health, illness, and disease. Ethical knowing engages the nurse's understanding of professional and legal obligations. Personal knowing reflects each nurse's life story and culture. Aesthetic knowing refines practiced skill into an art and privileges intuition and tacit knowledge. Knowledge development in each of the first four domains lends itself particularly well to pedagogies derived from the liberal arts, which are already embedded in many baccalaureate nursing curricula (Anthony & Templin, 1998; Arlton, Ernst, & Sunderwirth, 1990; Hagerty, 1992; Hanson, 1989; Sohn, 1986) because of the liberal arts' emphasis on interpretation, their capacity for ambiguity, and their appreciation of subjectivity.

Aesthetic pedagogies derived from the fine and performing arts and from creative writing have been employed extensively in nursing education in order to engage emancipatory, ethical, and personal knowing, as well as to develop students' facility with nursing practice as an art as well as a craft. Aesthetic pedagogies include both viewing art or performance and participating in its production as a means of enhancing nursing students' professional responses to patients (see Chinn & Watson, 1994). Viewing visual art has provided an occasion for exploring tacit knowledge about patients and patient care with older adults (Blomqvist, Pitkälä, & Routasalo, 2007) and for examining communication with patients (Wikström & Svidén, 2007). Other uses of aesthetic pedagogies include group discussion of visual art and workshop creation of art to engage linguistic and extralinguistic forms of knowledge in empathic engagement with patients' constraints and challenges (Casey, 2009); students drawing images of their critical care patients as a means of expressing the students' experience of human suffering (Eifried, Riley-Giomariso, & Voigt, 2001); using commercial films (Raingruber, 2003), poetry (Kidd & Tusaie, 2004), and drama (Wasylko & Stickley, 2003) to promote empathy and critical reflection in mental health nursing; and patients' using creative media in order for their clinical nursing students to learn about the experiential varieties of chronic illness (Michael & Candela, 2006).

These adaptations of liberal arts pedagogies in a nursing education context prepare clinical practice nurses who think critically and act compassionately and ethically. The place where nursing students begin to put these dispositions into skilled practice is in the supervised clinical setting, a signature pedagogy requiring its own techniques.

Clinical Education Pedagogies

Clinical education is vital in teaching undergraduate nursing students because it provides opportunities for them to practice many essential skills and dispositions, such as forging relationships with patients and families, developing interpersonal skills, learning the art of engagement and involvement, understanding themselves as instruments of care, and deepening their understanding of the experiential aspects of illness and injury (Benner et al., 2010; Tanner, 2010). Traditionally, such education has followed a "total patient care" pedagogy, which was introduced in the 1930s (Goodrich, 1973). In this model, nursing students provided all necessary care to individual patients. The rationale for this approach was that, in addition to learning how to provide high-quality care, students would also learn empathy. Although that approach is still followed in most schools of nursing, today's health care environment confronts nurse educators with many challenges to providing clinical education, especially in the traditional format. These include lack of available clinical placements, a paucity of qualified nursing faculty (American Association of Colleges of Nursing, 2007), and the need to balance student learning with patient safety (Tanner, 2010).

Despite the challenges of clinical pedagogy, many kinds of learning occur in this setting: Students in supervised clinical education learn to connect theoretical knowledge with clinical situations (Benner, 1984; Benner, Tanner, & Chesla, 2009); they develop essential psychomotor nursing skills (Tanner, 2010), like how to take blood pressure readings and other vital signs; students also hone their clinical judgment through experiential learning (Tanner, 2006), in which clinical experiences are followed by conferences to debrief students. Finally, by dealing with patients from diverse social, economic, ethnic, or cultural backgrounds in a variety of health care settings, students formulate a realistic understanding of the cultures of health care and nursing (Tanner, 2010).

One way to improve clinical education is through clinical partnerships. In this model, the formation of dedicated education units (DEUs) can dramatically increase both educational capacity and student and staff satisfaction (Tanner, 2010). Because clinical nurses typically have no background in teaching and learning, these DEUs are staffed by nurses interested in being educators, who are supported by faculty who help them develop as educators to employ appropriate clinical pedagogies (Tanner, 2010). Benner and colleagues (2010) recommend several other ways to enhance the clinical experience of nursing students: (1) introducing nursing students to nursing early in their education, (2) broadening the clinical experience, (3) preserving post-clinical conferences and small patient-care assignments, (4) developing pedagogies that keep students focused on their patient's experience, (5) varying the means of assessing student performance, (6) promoting and supporting learning the skills of inquiry and research, (7) redesigning the ethics curricula, and (8) supporting students in becoming agents of change.

Clearly, the pedagogical approaches to clinical nursing education must incorporate the realities of today's health care environment. Attention to the clinical pedagogies that will form undergraduate nursing students is of long-term importance and deserves the profession's focused attention. A well-established way of preparing students for their clinical settings and refining their clinical skills is the clinical simulation, which is widely used in preprofessional education and professional continuing development.

Simulation Pedagogies

Simulation as a teaching strategy has been used for many decades in different professional and technical fields. Although nurse educators used infant dolls and specially made adult mannequins, high-fidelity nursing simulation technology began with cardiopulmonary resuscitation and simulated clinical scenarios (American Heart Association, 2006; Cooper & Taqueti, 2004). Simulation pedagogies in nursing are now standard practice, employing a continuum of complexity from low-fidelity to high-fidelity, with an increased use of high-fidelity simulations in nursing that focus on improved patient outcomes (Cannon-Diehl, 2009). Simulation pedagogies are based on adult learning principles derived from an *andragogical* framework (a term coined by Knowles [1968]), which establishes that adults (unlike children) learn through experiences before organizing those experiences conceptually (Jeffries, 2005; Knowles, Holton, & Swanson, 1998; Kolb, 1984; Mezirow, 2000). Accordingly, Jeffries (2005) develops a simulation framework that defines its application and research.

Simulation pedagogies extend beyond the immediate simulation to post-simulation metacognitive learning activities, including reflection and debriefing. Several pedagogical theories explain the effectiveness of reflection and debriefing. Lockyer, Gondocz, and Thivierge (2004) propose that reflection allows one to transform learner knowledge into clinical application, which is the goal for nursing simulation. Concomitant critical thinking skills in nursing students cause a ripple effect in positive patient outcomes, and patient outcomes improve as novice nurses think critically in the field (Khosravani, Manoochehri, & Memarian, 2005; Lasater, 2007). Active participation in simulation advances students' learning and provides a frame of reference in clinical practice (Fuzard, 1995; Ost et al., 2001; Wallin, Meurling, Hedman, Hedegard, & Fellander-Tsai, 2007).

However, simulation pedagogies are expensive in time and money. Costs include the simulation technologies, the labor to maintain them, and the faculty to create and manage simulations that are integrated into the curriculum (Nehrig & Lashley, 2004). Although a cost-benefit analysis in a medical education systematic review (Issenberg et al. 2005) reported favorably on simulation pedagogies, further research on actual patient outcomes is warranted. One study, using a multidisciplinary sample, supported the contention that simulation pedagogies improve patient safety (Langdon & Cunningham, 2007). Systematic reviews and state-of-the-science documents will set the course for the direction of simulation (Cannon-Diel, 2009; Gaba, 2004; Issenburg et al., 2005), calling on researchers to increase the rigor of research on the efficacy of simulation pedagogies, particularly concerning the relative merits of varying degrees of fidelity, their frequency, and their integration into clinical and didactic course work. Although global health education systems mandate certain forms of simulation and the international Society for Simulation in Healthcare has taken the lead in formulating a plan for implementing simulation pedagogies, in the United States individual state boards continue to diverge in their views on the significance and importance of simulation (Nehrig & Lashley, 2007).

Although these clinical skills are indispensable in nursing practice, the increasingly complex multicultural health care settings in which nurses are employed and the global nature of the nursing profession have more recently required new nursing pedagogies for cultural competence. Clinical simulations can include cultural dimensions with ethnically diverse standardized patients or even mannequins. However, cultural immersion experiences are more likely to be pedagogically useful. One of the more challenging logistically of these, but one that appears highly effective, is the study-abroad experience in nursing.

Study Abroad Pedagogies

As an emerging signature pedagogy, study abroad offers unique teaching and learning opportunities for nursing educators and students. Students learn about issues in global health and nursing, are able to practice communicating and caring for clients in cross-cultural settings, and gain an understanding of global cultural differences in approaching nursing care. Students increase their academic knowledge and skills and experience personal growth (Frisch, 1990; Thompson, Boore, & Deeny, 2000). Other positive outcomes include increased intercultural sensitivity, improved communication skills, professional growth, changed perceptions of the professional nurse role, and development of culturally focused nursing practice (DeDee & Stewart, 2003; Evanson & Zust, 2004; Lee, 2004; Walsh & De Joseph, 2003; Zorn, 1996). Although the development of culturally competent nurses has been a goal of professional nursing education for many years (De Leon Siantz & Meleis, 2007), the strict curricular and clinical requirements of undergraduate nursing programs often limit opportunities for the nursing students to study abroad.

Leininger (1988) and others have defined *cultural competence* as a nurse's ability to offer supportive care to people from a variety of cultures. Nevertheless, definitions of *cultural competence* vary, and outcomes have been difficult to assess (Currier, Lucas, & Saint Arnault, 2009). Nurse educators commonly teach cultural competence by including cultural content surrounding health beliefs and practices in on-campus nursing course work, and, although these approaches can teach basic concepts about cultural differences, they pale in comparison to the holistic learning that occurs in a study-abroad experience. Currier, Lucas and Saint Arnault (2009) encourage nursing professionals to broaden their perspective from cultural competence to global competence. The concept of *global competence* is important because it informs the ways we educate nursing students to interact with patients from other cultures, including those within the United States (Green & Olson, 2003; Hunter, White, & Godbey, 2006). Even if a U.S. nursing student does not go on to work abroad in clinical practice, the study-abroad experience can provide a cultural resilience that is applicable in the multicultural settings at home.

To date, nursing study-abroad research, for the most part, has employed qualitative assessments of students' perceptions of personal and professional development. Researchers have begun, however, to link concepts of cross-cultural learning with the outcomes in study-abroad programs. For example, Caffrey et al. (2005) compared students who had cultural content integrated into their nursing curricula with those who studied the same curricula with an additional five-week immersion experience and found that those who were immersed in another culture perceived more gains in cultural competence. Thompson et al. (2000) compared experiences for nursing students studying in developed or in developing nations and found that students studying in developing countries report higher impact in how they evaluate world issues and incorporate intercultural dimensions into their nursing practice. These researchers also report significant changes in how students view socioeconomic and personal-relational dimensions of their patients' lives through the students' interaction with other cultures.

NCLEX-RN Preparation Pedagogies

Upon completion of their formal education, graduates from schools of nursing in the United States must pass an examination prior to becoming licensed as registered nurses. The National Council of State Boards of Nursing (NCSBN) develops, administers, and analyzes results of this exam, the National Council Licensure Examination for Registered Nurses (NCLEX-RN), which is designed to test the knowledge, skills, and abilities essential to the safe and effective practice of nursing at the entry level (NCSBN, 2010). Although most nursing graduates pass the NCLEX-RN on the first attempt, as many as 5 to 15% of a school's recent graduates might fail. NCLEX-RN questions frequently include distracters (data that are not particularly germane or important to a critical issue) and often ask students to rank items in order of sequence or significance (requiring students to prioritize using clinical judgment). In examining the range of NCLEX-RN preparation pedagogies, a review of the literature suggests three types, each with its own benefits: knowledge-driven, process-driven, or holistic pedagogies.

Knowledge-driven NCLEX-RN preparation pedagogies acknowledge the explosion of information in the life sciences, health care technologies, health care delivery systems, and nursing science that are now needed in clinical nursing practice (Diekelmann, 2002; Giddens & Brady, 2007). Since the 1990s the proliferation of test preparation and standardized testing in nursing programs (provided by such commercial vendors as HESI, ATI, Kaplan, or NLN) indicates that many faculty are adhering to the traditional pedagogical approach of reviewing content-specific material as preparation for the NCLEX-RN licensing exam. The use of specific standardized tests in content areas like medical-surgical nursing, maternity, pediatrics, community, and mental health nursing, followed by remediation in content-specific material, accompanies this traditional approach. Knowledge-driven test preparation is designed to identify a student's strengths or weaknesses in specific content areas.

Another pedagogy of NCLEX-RN preparation is a *process-driven* approach that employs general test-taking strategies as well as taking the test on computers. Frith, Sewell, and Clark (2008) describe the development of an Integrated Clinical Concepts course provided for an eight-week period prior to graduation that focused on application of content to case studies as well as strategies for reducing test anxiety and negative self-talk. Significant improvements in NCLEX-RN pass rates were noted in comparison to a control group that did not receive the intervention. Ashley and O'Neil (1991) found that focusing on test-taking strategies with students during the second semester of their senior year had a positive effect on students' being able to pass the NCLEX-RN. Since 1994, the administration of the exam has moved from pencil and paper to an online computerized version, which has allowed the NCSBN to ask alternate styles of questions, such as fill-in-the-blank, calculation, multiple response, and drag-and-drop questions, and questions based on audio clips and graphics, requiring a different approach by the student to answer questions successfully. DiBartolo and Seldomridge (2008) suggest that periodic computer-based testing should become part of the curriculum to enhance student comfort with this style of test administration, and anecdotal evidence indicates that practice with online exams has helped to allay student anxiety and promote success on NCLEX-RN (March & Ambrose, 2010). Given that many students are accustomed to taking standardized tests on which there is simply one clearly correct response, the process-driven pedagogy is designed to help students apply their knowledge successfully in a more complex test situation. However, a lack of rigorous empirical research prevents us from confidently concluding that these types of preparation would be effective generalizable strategies for NCLEX-RN success.

The final test-prep pedagogy in the nursing literature takes a *holistic* view of the individual preparing to take the licensing exam. Arathuzik and Aber (1998) investigated factors that are associated with NCLEX-RN success and found that many other variables in a student's life outside the curriculum (including family responsibilities, emotional distress, fatigue, financial and work burdens) can have a negative impact on her ability to pass the test.

Teaching and learning complex and constantly updated health information, inculcating a professional ethos characterized by empathy, ethical behavior, and social justice, and preparing skilled health care practitioners to use sound clinical judgment, are the challenges of nursing education. Its signature pedagogies include teaching clinical science and professionalism by adapted liberal arts pedagogies, supervising clinical practicums, providing appropriate clinical simulations, exploring cultural diversity through study-abroad experiences, and preparing students for certification as registered nurses in the NCLEX-RN exam. In addition to these daunting aims, the changing demographics of nursing students and subsequent nursing workforce (including more men and more underrepresented racial, ethnic, and economic groups) requires new approaches to effective teaching and learning of nursing science. As a field that adapts and synthesizes knowledge and methods from other disciplines as well as defining its own theories and methods, nursing education will continue to refine its signature pedagogies by building an evidence base for their effectiveness and by critiquing the merely habitual pedagogies of the past that might need to be revised or retired.

References

American Association of Colleges of Nursing. (2007). *Enrollment growth slows at U.S. nursing colleges and universities in 2007 despite calls for more registered nurses.* Retrieved August 30, 2010, from http://www.aacn.nche.edu/Media/NewsReleases/Archives/2007/enrl.htm

American Heart Association. (2006). *Advanced cardiovascular life support.* Dallas, TX: American Heart Association National Center.

Andrews, C. A., Ironside, P. M., Nosek, C, Sims, S. L., Swenson, M. M., Yeomans, C, et al. (2001). Enacting narrative pedagogy: The lived experiences of students and teachers. *Nursing and Health Care Perspectives, 22*(5), 252–259.

Anthony, M. L., & Templin, M. A. (1998). Nursing faculty teaching in the general education sequence: The value of liberal arts as a component of professional nursing practice. *Journal of Nursing Education, 37*(7), 321–323.

Arathuzik, D., & Aber, C. (1998). Factors associated with National Council Licensure Examination—registered nurse success. *Journal of Professional Nursing, 14*(2), 119–126.

Arlton, D., Ernst, M., & Sunderwirth, S. (1990). General education in the professional curriculum: Faculty perceptions of contributions. *The Journal of Allied Health, 19*(1), 49–57.

Ashley, J., & O'Neil, J. (1991). The effectiveness of an intervention to promote successful performance on the NCLEX-RN for baccalaureate students at risk for failure. *Journal of Nursing Education, 30*(8), 360–366.

Baker, C. M. (2000). Problem-based learning for nursing: Integrating lessons from other disciplines with nursing experiences. *Journal of Professional Nursing, 16*(5), 258–266.

Bankert, E., & Kozel, L. V. (2005). Transforming pedagogy in nursing education: A caring learning environment for adult students. *Nursing Education Perspectives, 26*(4), 227–229.

Benner, P. (1984). *From novice to expert: Excellence and power in clinical nursing practice.* Menlo Park, CA: Addison-Wesley.

Benner, P., Sutphen, M., Leonard, V., & Day, L. (2010). *Educating nurses: A call for radical transformation.* San Francisco, CA: Jossey-Bass.

Benner, P., Tanner, C. A., & Chesla, C. A. (2009). *Expertise in nursing practice: Caring, clinical judgment, & ethics.* New York, NY: Springer.

Blomqvist, L., Pitkälä, K., & Routasalo, P. (2007). Images of loneliness: Using art as an educational method in professional training. *The Journal of Continuing Education in Nursing, 38*(2), 89–93.

Caffrey, R. A., Neander, W., Markle, D., & Stewart, B. (2005). Improving the cultural competence of nursing students: Results of integrating cultural content in the curriculum and an international immersion experience. *Journal of Nursing Education, 44*(5), 234–240.

Cagle, C. S., Walker, C. A., & Newcomb, P. (2006). Using imaginative literature in clinical courses to improve student outcomes. *The Journal of Theory Construction and Testing, 10*(1), 6–10.

Cannon-Diehl, M. R. (2009). Simulation in healthcare and nursing: State of the science. *Critical Care Nursing Quarterly, 32*(2), 128–136.

Carper, B. A. (1978). Fundamental patterns of knowing in nursing. *Advances in Nursing Science, 1*(1), 13–23.

Casey, B. (2009). Arts-based inquiry in nursing education. *Contemporary Nurse, 32*(1–2), 69–82.

Chan, E. A. (2008). Evaluating narrative pedagogy in nursing education in Hong Kong. *Nursing Science Quarterly, 21*(3), 261–267.

Chinn, P. L., & Kramer, M. K. (2008). *Integrated theory and knowledge development in nursing* (7th ed.). St. Louis, MO: Mosby Elsevier.

Chinn, P. L., & Watson, J. (Eds.). (1994). *Art and aesthetics in nursing.* New York, NY: National League for Nursing Press.

Chirema, K. D. (2007). The use of reflective journals in the promotion of reflection and learning in post-registration nursing students. *Nurse Education Today, 27,* 192–202.

Cooper, J. B., & Taqueti, V. R. (2004). A brief history of the development of mannequin simulators for clinical education and training. *Quality & Safety in Health*

Care, 13(Suppl. 1): i11–8. Erratum in: (2005). *Quality & Safety in Health Care. 14*(1), 72.

Currier, C., Lucas, J., & Saint Arnault, D. (2009). Study abroad and nursing. In R. Lewin (Ed.), *The handbook of research and practice in study abroad* (pp. 133–150). New York, NY: Routledge.

DeDee, L., & Stewart, S. (2003). The effect of student participation in international study. *Journal of Professional Nursing, 19*(4), 237–242.

De Leon Siantz, M. L., & Meleis, A. I. (2007). Integrating cultural competence into nursing education and practice: 21st century action steps. *Journal of Transcultural Nursing, 18*(Supplement), 86S–90S.

DiBartolo, M., & Seldomridge, L. (2008, September/October). A review of intervention studies to promote NCLEX-RN success of baccalaureate students. *Nurse Educator 30*(4, Supplement), 78S–83S.

Diekelmann, N. (2001). Narrative pedagogy: Heideggerian hermeneutical analysis of lived experiences of students, teachers and clinicians. *Advances in Nursing Science, 23*(3), 53–71.

Diekelmann, N. (2002). "Too much content . . ." Epistemologies' grasp and nursing education. *Journal of Nursing Education, 41*(11), 469–470.

Diekelmann, N., & Diekelmann, J. (2000). Learning ethics in nursing and genetics: Narrative pedagogy and the grounding of values. *Journal of Pediatric Nursing, 15*(4), 226–231.

Eifried, S., Riley-Giomariso, O., & Voigt, G. (2001). Learning to care amid suffering: How art and narrative give voice to the student experience. *International Journal of Human Caring, 5*(2), 42–51.

Evanson, T. A., & Zust, B. L. (2004). The meaning of participation in an international service experience among baccalaureate nursing students. *International Journal of Nursing Education Scholarship, 1*(1), 1–14.

Frisch, N. (1990). An international nursing student exchange program: An educational experience that enhanced student cognitive development. *Journal of Nursing Education, 29*(1), 10–12.

Frith, K., Sewell, J., & Clark, D. (2008, September/October). Best practices in NCLEX-RN readiness preparation for baccalaureate student success. *Nurse Educator 33*(6, Supplement), 46S–53S.

Fuzard. B. (1995). *Innovative teaching strategies in nursing* (2nd ed.). Gaithersburg, MD: Aspen.

Gaba, D. M. (2004). The future vision of simulation in healthcare. *Quality Safe Healthcare, 13*, 2–10. doi:10.1136/qshc.2004.009878

Giddens, J., & Brady, D. (2007). Rescuing nursing education from content saturation: The case for a concept-based curriculum. *Journal of Nursing Education, 46*, 65–69.

Goldmark, J. (1923). *Nursing and nursing education in the United States: Report of the Committee for the Study of Nursing Education.* New York, NY: Macmillan Company.

Goodrich, A. W. (1973). The nurse and the university. In A. W. Goodrich (Ed.), *The social and ethical significance of nursing: A series of addresses* (pp. 131–145). New Haven, CT: Yale University School of Nursing. (Original work published 1930).

Green, M. F., & Olson, C. (2003). *Internationalizing the campus: A user's guide.* Washington, DC: American Council on Education.

Gwele, N. S. (1996). The process-product dichotomy in education: Relevance to nursing education. *Curationis, 19*(1), 27–32.

Hagerty, B. M. K. (1992). Development of the applied liberal education competencies scale. *Nursing Research, 41*(3), 132–137.

Hanson, K. S. (1989). The emergence of liberal education in nursing education, 1893–1923. *Journal of Professional Nursing, 5*(2), 83–91.

Hunter, B., White, G. P., & Godbey, G. C. (2006). What does it mean to be globally competent? *Journal of Studies in International Education, 10*(3), 267–285. doi:10.1177/1028315306286930

Ironside, P. M. (2004). "Covering content" and teaching thinking: Deconstructing the additive curriculum. *Journal of Nursing Education, 43*(1), 5–12.

Ironside, P. M. (2006). Using narrative pedagogy: Learning and practising interpretive thinking. *Journal of Advanced Nursing, 55*(4), 478–486.

Issenburg, S. B., McGaghie, W. C., Petrusa, E. R., Gordon, D. L., & Scalese, R. J. (2005). Features and uses of high fidelity medical simulations that lead to effective learning: A BEME systematic review. *Medical Teacher, 27*(1), 10–28.

Jeffries, P. R. (2005). A framework for designing, implementing, and evaluating simulations used as teaching strategies in nursing. *Nursing Education Perspectives, 26*(2), 96–103.

Kawashima, A. (2005). The implementation of narrative pedagogy into nursing education in Japan. *Nursing Education Perspectives, 26*(3), 168–171.

Khosravani, S., Manoochehri, H., & Memarian, R. (2005). Developing critical thinking skills in nursing students by group dynamics. *The Internet Journal of Advanced Nursing Practice, 7*(2). Retrieved from http://www.ispub.com/journal/the_internet_journal_of_advanced_nursing_practice/volume_7_number_2_1/article/developing_critical_thinking_skills_in_nursing_students_by_group_dynamics.html

Kidd, L. I., & Tusaie, K. R. (2004). Disconfirming beliefs: The use of poetry to know the lived experience of student nurses in mental health clinicals. *Issues in Mental Health Nursing, 25*, 403–414.

Knowles, M. S. (1968). Andragogy, not pedagogy. *Adult Leadership, 16*(10), 350–352, 386.

Knowles, M. S., Holton, E. F., & Swanson, R. A. (1998). *The adult learner: The definitive classic in adult education and human resource development* (5th ed.). Woburn, MA: Butterworth-Heinemann.

Kolb, D. A. (1984). *Experiential learning: Experience as the source of learning and development.* Englewood Cliffs, NJ: Prentice-Hall.

Langdon, M. G., & Cunningham, A. J. (2007). High-fidelity simulation in postgraduate training and assessment: An Irish perspective. *Irish Journal of Medical Science, 176*(4), 267–271.

Lasater, K. (2007). High-fidelity simulation and the development of clinical judgment: Students' experiences. *Journal of Nursing Education, 46*(6), 269–276.

Lee, N. J. (2004). The impact of international experience on student nurses' personal and professional development. *International Nursing Review, 51*, 113–122.

Leininger, M. M. (1988). Leininger's theory of nursing: Cultural care diversity and universality. *Nursing Science Quarterly, 1*(4), 152–160.

Lockyer, J., Gondocz, S. T., & Thivierge, R. L. (2004). Knowledge interpreter: The role and place of practice reflection. *The Journal of Continuing Education in the Health Professions, 24*, 50–56.

Lysaught, J. P. (1970). *An abstract for action.* New York, NY: McGraw-Hill.

March, K., & Ambrose, J. (2010). Rx for NCLEX-RN Success: Reflections on development of an effective preparation process for senior baccalaureate students. *Nursing Education Perspectives, 31*(4), 230–232.

Mezirow, J. (2000). *Learning as transformation.* San Francisco, CA: Jossey-Bass.

Michael, S., & Candela, L. (2006). Using aesthetic knowing to teach diversity of the chronic illness experience to nursing students. *Home Health Care Management & Practice, 18*(6), 439–443.

Montag, M. L. (1951). *The education of nursing technicians.* New York, NY: G.P. Putnam.

National Council of State Boards of Nursing (2009). NCLEX-RN® Test Plan: Effective April 2010. Retrieved March 3, 2010, from https://www.ncsbn.org/2010_NCLEX_RN_TestPlan.pdf

Nehrig, W. M., & Lashley, F. R. (2004). Using the Human Patient Simulator in nursing education. *Annual Review of Nursing Education, 2*, 163–181.

Nehrig, W. M., & Lashley, F. R. (2007). U.S. boards of nursing and the use of high fidelity patient simulators in nursing. *Journal of Professional Nursing, 24*(2), 109–117.

Niemer, L., Pfendt, K., & Gers, M. (2010). Problem-based learning in nursing education: A process for scenario development. *Nurse Educator, 35*(2), 69–73. doi: 10.1097/NNE.0b013e3181ced891

Ost, D., DeRosiers, A., Britt, J. E., Fein, A. M., Lesser, M. L., & Mehya, T. C. (2001). Assessment of a bronchoscopy simulator. *American Journal of Respiratory and Critical Care Medicine, 164*(12), 2248–2255.

Raingruber, B. (2003). Integrating aesthetics into advanced practice mental health nursing: Commercial film as a suggested modality. *Issues in Mental Health Nursing, 24*, 467–495.

Sakalys, J. A. (2002). Literary pedagogy in nursing: A theory-based perspective. *Journal of Nursing Education, 41*(9), 386–392.

Scheckel, M. M., & Ironside, P. M. (2006). Cultivating interpretive thinking through enacting narrative pedagogy. *Nursing Outlook, 54*, 159–165.

Sohn, K. S. (1986). General education in nursing: Current practices and faculty attitudes. *Nursing Papers/Perspectives on Nursing, 18*(4), 41–57.

Tanner, C. A. (2006). Thinking like a nurse: A research-based model of clinical judgment in nursing. *Journal of Nursing Education, 45*, 204–211.

Tanner, C. A. (2010). From mother duck to mother lode: Clinical education for deep learning. *Journal of Nursing Education, 49*, 1–3.

Thompson, K., Boore, J., & Deeny, P. (2000). A comparison of an international experience for nursing students in developed and developing countries. *International Journal of Nursing Studies, 37*(6), 481–492. doi: 10.1016/S0020-7489(00)00027-4

Visconti, C. (2010). Problem-based learning: Teaching skills for evidence-based practice. *Perspectives on Issues in Higher Education, 13*(1), 27–31.

Wallin, C., Meurling, L., Hedman, L., Hedegard, J., & Fellander-Tsai, L. (2007). Target-focused medical emergency team training using a human patient simulator: Effects on behavior and attitude. *Medical Education, 11*(6), 705–714.

Walsh, L. V., & De Joseph, J. (2003). "I saw in a different light": International learning experiences in baccalaureate nursing education. *Journal of Nursing Education, 42*(6), 266–272.

Wasylko, Y., & Stickley, T. (2003). Theatre and pedagogy: Using drama in mental health nurse education. *Nurse Education Today, 23*, 443–448.

Wikström, B-M., & Svidén, G. (2007). Student nurses in dialogues with hypothetical patients regarding paintings. *Journal of Research in Nursing, 12*(4), 403–413.

Wong, C. K., & Blissett, S. (2007). Assessing performance in the area of cultural competence: An analysis of reflective writing. *Journal of Physical Therapy Education, 21*(1), 40–47.

Wong, F. K. Y., Kember, D., Chung, L. Y. F., & Yan, L. (1995). Assessing the level of student reflection from reflective journals. *Journal of Advance Nursing, 22*, 48–57.

Zorn, C. R. (1996). The long-term impact on nursing students of participation in international education. *Journal of Professional Nursing, 12*(2), 106–110.

14

RELATIONAL LEARNING AND ACTIVE ENGAGEMENT IN OCCUPATIONAL THERAPY PROFESSIONAL EDUCATION

Patricia Schaber, Lauren Marsh, and Kimerly J. Wilcox

Occupational therapy (OT) is a health care discipline that originated in the aftermath of World War I to teach convalescent soldiers in military hospitals preindustrial skills (Kidner, 1925, p. 188) and invalids residing in asylums "decent habits of living" (Slagle, 1924, p. 98). Emerging out of the Age of Enlightenment's "moral treatment" movement, which humanized those with insanity by eradicating the notion that they were possessed by the devil (Bing, 1981), the early founders of the profession discovered that engagement in activity or *occupation* could contribute to healing, health, and well-being (Bockoven, 1971).[1] Asylums or psychiatric hospitals incorporated activities such as basketry into the daily structure of the institution to "occupy" residents with meaningful activity (hence the term, *basket case* to describe someone in an institutional setting who would benefit from occupational therapy). Veterans were trained in work skills, such as woodworking or floor loom weaving, as part of their rehabilitation from physically disabling conditions. Aligned with a medical model, OT was prescribed by physicians as an alternative or complement to other therapies.

OT practice is grounded in the belief that the health and life quality of an individual is to be understood in the context of his or her capacities as an occupational being, as *Homo faber*, man the fabricator (Arendt, 1958). Health and well-being are outcomes of full participation in daily life activities and optimal performance in one's chosen occupations. The occupational therapist, in partnership with the client/patient, designs activities in order to achieve outcomes for occupational performance or participation in daily life. Thus, occupational therapy is rooted in the belief that *we are what we do*. This belief has guided pedagogical as well as clinical practice. In fact, OT pedagogical practice mirrors therapeutic practice and is informed by the same philosophy and professional values. As a scientific approach to rehabilitating people with physical and psychological disabilities, the key feature of occupational therapy practice and training has been "learning by doing." From the beginning, occupational therapy practitioners shared their knowledge, skills, and expertise drawn from firsthand experience; attitudes and values—especially the value of human dignity in any state of the human condition—were imparted through a mentor–mentee relationship in an apprenticeship model.

After World War II, when the demand for occupational therapy was spearheaded by returning soldiers, the teaching of these rehabilitative skills moved into universities affiliated with medical centers; "learning by doing" took the form of classroom-based (didactic) education along with fieldwork training. Associated with medical schools and run by physicians, occupational therapy education programs were located in proximity to clinics and hospitals. As early as 1948, actively engaging with clients was viewed as core to the pedagogy: "The proximity of the hospital to the classroom has other advantages, making it possible for instructors [to instruct] not only through demonstration but by actual practice" (University of Wisconsin, 1948, p. 34). This contextual approach has been the standard pedagogy of occupational therapy education, with training programs integrating the classroom with Level I fieldwork in the didactic portion and Level II fieldwork after the didactic portion. Fieldwork education has been cited as "the proving ground of the profession" (Presseller, 1983, p. 163). Learning by doing embodied within the mentor–mentee relationship continues to function as one of the signature pedagogies that shape the educational experience, in the field and in the classroom. This chapter will review occupational therapy's signature pedagogies and explore the challenges and conflicts that these foundational pedagogies give rise to in the context of new trends in higher education, including distance education and the emergence of the virtual classroom.

Occupational Therapy Educational Goals

The goal of OT education is professional identity formation and transformation of the student into a practitioner who embodies interpersonal sensitivity, empathy, respect for the dignity of each human life, concern for justice, and open-mindedness (AOTA, 2009; Hooper, 2008; Peloquin, 2005). A century after the emergence of occupational therapy, the signature pedagogies used to effect this transformation continue to reflect the principles upon which it was founded: relational learning privileges the teacher–student relationship through mentorship, apprenticeship, and modeling. By modeling empathy and caring, as well as touch and handling, educators, whether in the classroom or fieldwork setting, guide students toward a professional identity. A key feature of relational pedagogy is affective learning—the realm of learning that impacts a change in students' attitudes and beliefs. Highly contextualized, active engagement provides the philosophical underpinnings of the therapeutic approach and describes the pedagogical model for training occupational therapy students, who learn by doing. Since the early 20th century, the field of OT—both practice and education—has undergone cycles of change and renewal. Currently, the field is undergoing transformation in ways that map to trends in 21st-century education, trends that create challenges to developing mentoring relationships and actively engaging with students.

Educational Approaches: A History

The first professional schools opened in 1918, and standards for education were published in 1923 (Woodside, 1971). In the first 50 years of the profession, OT practices were based on experience in the field and transferred to students through an apprenticeship model in a hospital setting. As education became formalized, OT practitioners became the educators and contributed to the relational pedagogy and design of active learning experiences. These educational practices and processes were embraced by the larger professional organization (American Occupational Therapy Association [AOTA]), became the standard, and were widely accepted, but were not the subject of inquiry. Therefore, the pedagogical literature around OT professional identity formation remained relatively sparse until the 1950s, when the seminal *American Journal of Occupational Therapy* began publishing articles on all facets of the field, including educating future professionals.

Some of the earliest studies were on the trait-based selection of students. As early as 1948, students were selected based on personal qualities. It was believed that through proper selection of students, those entering the field would already embody the affective qualities expected in a therapist, then be nurtured through ongoing mentoring by professionals in the classroom and field. Therefore, for many years, little research was done to determine the effectiveness of educational strategies or mentoring relative to professional identity formation.

Literature related to teaching and learning in OT, particularly around teaching affective learning, really emerged in the 1970s, as it became evident that trait selection alone was not enough to ensure professional identity development: Instruction was required, and various approaches were investigated, with small-group learning gaining popularity. Several studies examined these, focusing on interpersonal and communication skills (Delworth, 1972), self-awareness, feelings, and reactions and their impact on others (Maynard & Pedro, 1971), and personal growth/personality modification (Posthuma & Posthuma, 1972). Other active, small peer-group instructional methodologies emerged, such as Learning Through Discussion (LTD; Hill, 1973), which purports to provide personal growth along with content mastery. Unfortunately, although students rated the small group experiences favorably, robust measures of learning were not employed.

In spite of this lack of rigorous evaluation, small-group methods remained highly popular. Problem-Based Learning (PBL), in which learning is motivated by internal curiosity and through peer interactions, supported OT curricula and the development of team-building skills with peers (Hammel et al., 1999). Case-based learning, another small-group, peer-dependent strategy, was effectively used to develop clinical reasoning and reflective thinking skills in OT students (VanLeit, 1995). Cooperative learning methods, using interdependent peer groups, were also integrated into professional training (Nolinske & Millis, 1999) but once again, their effectiveness was not studied. Not all activities used to mold a professional identity were group based; for example, journals were used to elicit personal awareness and change attitudes toward practicing occupational therapy in mental health settings (Tryssenaar, 1995).

The 1970s also saw a movement of OT practice beyond the hospital and related environs into community settings. This led to additional studies that scrutinized methods of socializing students into the professional culture with a focus on practical learning or fieldwork. The apprenticeship or brief (Level I) fieldwork experiences occurring during the didactic portion of student education were found to positively impact student attitudes in working with various client groups, specifically older adults (Cole, 1985), and in mental health settings (Lyons, 1997). A more recent study found that fieldwork, along with discussions, developed "a discerning viewpoint of evidence-based practice" in students (Stube & Jedlicka, 2007). Other studies have measured fieldwork effectiveness in various locations, such as community agencies, clinics, or emerging practice areas, and determined who is qualified to provide the instruction (Johnson, Koenig, Piersol, Santalucia, & Wachter-Schutz, 2006). The movement of OT practice into the community expanded the "social model," which was integrated into OT education. The idea that others beyond the classroom instructor could serve in a mentoring role opened the door for creating multiple exposures to practicing clinicians in diverse settings. The relational pedagogy approach became "multi-relational," encompassing many people engaged in guiding student learning during the professional development process: peers, fieldwork supervisors, other professionals, clients, and so on (Nolinske, 1995).

This expansion into community settings also provided opportunities for active learning beyond fieldwork in traditional settings. Creative, "authentic," designed learning experiences linked classroom to field, using a variety of models. A community service model evaluated in 1972 described a partnership between Loyola University and New Orleans Crippled Children's Hospital (Cahn & Hayden, 1972). This type of collaborative service-learning within a community health setting impacted the students' sense of social responsibility and appreciation of the interprofessional team. Fieldwork placement in a correctional facility in eastern Michigan (Platt, Martell, & Clements, 1977) and in the Allegheny County Jail (Provident & Joyce-Gaguzis, 2005) effectively educated students in community health practice models. Active engagement in the community has even taken the form of "compulsory volunteering," serving clients while learning core concepts (Jenkins, Douglas, & Chamberlain, 2008, p. 38). Aligning education with community agencies allowed for direct experiences between students and clients but resulted in less formal management or structure for learning.

Present Educational Approach

In the last decade, OT professional education has continued to support relational pedagogies, with the "desired ways of being" communicated through the culture of the program, in order to mold a student into an occupational therapist (Peloquin, 2005). Hooper (2008) suggested that this occurred through the "implicit" curriculum ("the rituals, rites, patterns of relating, artifacts, spaces, and social organization—the culture—of the program") rather than the explicit curriculum ("the actual courses, sequences, teaching methods, and field experiences afforded a group of students," [Berg et al., 2009, p. 5]). However, the decade has also brought many challenges to the implicit curriculum: The role of the instructor is evolving from dispenser of knowledge to designer of learning experiences, and there is pressure for increased student enrollment and satellite campuses, producing a need to expand the reach of faculty already strained for time and opportunity for relational development. To meet these challenges, instructors and programs have turned to technology, in the form of video instruction, blended learning, and myriad technology-enhanced activities. This pedagogical shift has focused on the explicit curriculum as the starting point of the learning experience rather than the nature of the teacher–student relationship (Hooper, 2006). For example, one recent study tested the effects of engaging in online discussion on students' clinical reasoning processes, finding that this platform for learning can enhance the ability to critique or judge knowledge or perspectives (Scanlan & Hancock, 2010). Another study found that using a cyclical, intentional online course design was effective in teaching critical thinking skills in an occupational therapy theory course (Schaber & Shanedling, 2010). For relational learning, yet another study compared outcomes in the face-to-face classroom to online learning outcomes using a mix of educational technologies, such as video interviews and voice-activated discussions, and found both formats increased students' perceived understanding of topics related to affective learning (Schaber, Wilcox, Whiteside, Marsh, & Brooks, 2010). More studies like these are needed to support educational strategies that promote relational learning in a 21st-century environment.

Traditional Signature Pedagogies

The AOTA, the national OT association, stated that "Professional [educational] programs are highly influenced by the professions they serve" (Coppard et al., 2007, p. 672). In OT, the "profession" comprises both OT educators and current practitioners working in a variety of sites that offer occupational therapy; many of them are represented by AOTA. Through its membership, AOTA negotiates national standards for program accreditation and certifies students; these standards have evolved with the profession as it has responded to society's changing needs. AOTA released a model curriculum in 2010 that will refocus scholarship agendas on meeting accreditation standards through innovative course designs and efficient methods of educational delivery. This represents a significant departure from AOTA's historical focus on content and competencies.

The emphasis of this section is on the signature pedagogies through which these standards are communicated. In the course of writing this chapter, we have realized that the traditional pedagogies that characterize the origins of occupational therapy continue to be the signature pedagogies that necessarily inform educational practice. Shulman (2005) emphasizes that signature pedagogies in professional education define not only the knowledge base but how that knowledge becomes known. In this section we will describe these pedagogies, and, in the next, describe the ways they are being adapted in the face of challenges posed by the changing educational landscape. OT signature pedagogies are relational, in support of affective learning, as well as active and highly contextualized. The approach is traditionally "high touch," with emotional and physical connections, using person-to-person mentoring and peer learning within clinical, community, and industry partnerships.

Relational Learning

Occupational therapy education from its inception has embraced relational learning, reflecting an intimate tie between educator and student. Through this relationship, emotional intelligence is developed, transforming or "socializing" students to align with the professional standards and a common set of attitudes, values, beliefs, and behaviors (Mechanic, 1990). Emotional intelligence is an outcome of personal sharing; in OT, it's called "sharing our stories." There is a great deal of emphasis placed on bringing educators' experience to the classroom. Stories provide a valuable connection to clinical practice; they provide content for a case-based approach to learning and engage students emotionally with that content. Through storytelling, and through the more structured approach to case analysis, faculty personify the kind of professional attitudes and values expected of students and demonstrate ways of thinking and behaving. Provided with a complicated case, the instructor challenges students to develop an intervention. After students struggle with this and share their work, the instructor, as expert, shares the details and clinical reasoning processes in handling the case, providing a dialogue in acknowledging key points of the case, in the selection of assessments, pros and cons of specific interventions, and anticipated outcomes. Instructors help shape professional behavior by modeling reasoning, process, and affect.

Affective Learning

Affective learning involves teaching topics, such as empathy or grief, which generate an emotional reaction leading to a change in student attitudes and beliefs. In the classroom, affective learning is scaffolded and provides the structured engagement that moves the student from a focus on the self to a focus on others through the lens of professional identity. For example, initially the instructor creates student interest using a brief introductory exercise designed to challenge the students to think differently about the topic, setting a tone that communicates that the environment is safe, supportive, confidential, and reflective; this allows students to reflect on their own experiences. Then topic content is delivered through readings, followed by lecture or guest presentations; guests are often clients who have the role of self-advocate. Students then have guided disclosure and discussion in small groups. Finally, they reconvene as a large group for instructor-led, large-group discussion and summary (Schaber et al., 2010). Affective learning is built upon in every course from multiple perspectives. In Level II fieldwork, after the didactic portion of the curriculum is completed, through real-time experience, the scaffolding is dismantled gradually as students draw from their own professional identities rather than depending on external supports.

Contextualized Learning

Professional acculturation also occurs through active and highly contextualized learning experiences guided by professionals in the classroom and in the field. Occupational therapy classroom educators have been or are researchers, clinicians, community practitioners, school-based therapists, entrepreneurs, and even clients, all, for the most part, from the ranks of the profession. Clinical practice settings originated in hospitals, rehabilitation centers, and outpatient clinics in long-term care facilities as part of the medical model. In the past two decades, a social model has expanded OT into community practice settings, including agencies that provide services to at-risk families with children, community-based mental health and substance abuse treatment centers, home care, and adult day services, all areas with increased needs for occupational therapy services. These sites typically have been available to students with supervision provided by experienced occupational therapists. The idea that others beyond the classroom instructor could serve in a mentoring role emerged and opened the door for creating multiple exposures to practicing clinicians in diverse settings and accepting instructional methods that used community facilitators. This has extended the definition of faculty mentors to the community of OTs who share a role in student development. There are variations in student experiences that are site-specific, such as work ethic, productivity levels, level of experience of the supervisor, time allotted to student mentoring, diversity of client diagnoses, interdisciplinary team activities, and so on; these might change frequently, putting many factors beyond the control of the educational program.

Students experience "learning by doing" in classroom and fieldwork settings, individually and in groups, in the context of reflective learning, case-based or problem-based learning, simulations, classroom practice sessions (labs), practical exams, in-class activities, such as group presentations, and instructor demonstrations followed by students' hands-on engagement, as well as service-learning. In OT intervention, the medium is engagement in occupation (activity), the outcome, occupational performance and participation. In OT education, we replicate the OT process by applying it to students: They, like clients, learn by doing. Active learning, designed around a cycle of learning content, applying the content, and sharing discussion to reflect on the experience incorporates the key tenets of professional practice.

Trends, Challenges, and Strategies for Moving Forward

Occupational therapy has relied on relational pedagogies to effectively align students with the values and standards of the profession. However, in the 21st century, the discipline is confronted with higher education trends that constrain this traditional pedagogical approach, driven by the need for occupational therapy services in outlying geographic areas or with diverse populations in urban areas. The resulting pressure to graduate more students has focused attention on distance education; hybrid or blended learning is being explored to accommodate more students. Seen through the lens of OT's signature relational pedagogy, distance education is just that—a geographic separation and a potential chasm affecting the teacher–student relationship.

The virtual classroom and increasing numbers of students represent a radical disruption of traditional relational pedagogy: Intensive teacher–student interaction cannot be sustained in the absence of frequent face-to-face meetings or in the face of larger class sizes. In the short term, this has been experienced as a crisis. Anxieties abound for instructors who feel that the intensity of the mentor–mentee relationship has been diminished, and who feel they have lost autonomy and control, as well as the forum for hands-on demonstration and the modeling that have characterized the classroom experience. Furthermore, the increased number of students strains the availability of fieldwork placement sites, where students can work with qualified and experienced fieldwork supervisors. As a result, the weakening ties between the educational program and the master professionals who provide supervision and training in the field could be a prime challenge to grooming future ranks.

Yet new models and opportunities are emerging. Online and hybrid learning require us to reimagine traditional pedagogies in order to create powerful and engaging learning experiences that have the transformative effect needed to "create practitioners who think, perform and act with integrity" (Shulman, 2005, p. 52). Insofar as relationships and interpersonal communication skills are central to OT education, educators must design learning environments and leverage Web-based tools and strategies that meet these needs. How can effective pedagogies be sustained in different modalities without disrupting the learning process or compromising effectiveness? We'd like to offer some examples.

Engagement with practitioners and client self-advocates has always been the bedrock of the OT educational experience: Now, video allows clients and professionals to share their stories online. Voice is particularly powerful in supporting learning through personal sharing. Students can hear and respond to one another using any number of audio tools that support both synchronous (video/audio chat) and asynchronous communication (threaded discussions that support audio, podcasts). Reflection and collaboration are supported by discussion boards embedded in learning management systems as well as the ever-increasing number of cloud-based tools such as Google Apps. Demonstrations can be broadcast through video conferencing, or captured using video, or created using animation software. In all of these cases, instructors and students need support in order to become comfortable with these new ways of teaching and learning. Instructors need familiarity with a model of course design wherein they begin by identifying learning outcomes or competencies and work backward to design assessments and activities (Fink, 2003; Wiggins & McTighe, 1998). Instructors will need guidance in choosing technologies that best support various activities and will need awareness of the student experience in the online environment in order to anticipate students' support needs. In other words, faculty development must be part of the plan for moving forward.

The online environment might also present challenges for active engagement, particularly traditionally kinesthetic activities. For this reason, OT education is likely to remain hybrid rather than completely online, at least for the near future. Educators are actively exploring which skills can be taught online and which require face-to-face engagement. For instance, an instructor at the University of Minnesota is conducting a study comparing learning outcomes of a video anatomy lab versus a face-to-face, cadaver-based lab (V. Mathiowetz, personal communication, January 21, 2011). Because best practices in online education will necessarily remain a moving target, as technologies change rapidly and new opportunities are constantly presenting themselves, both educators and students need to develop skills for orienting themselves in emerging learning environments (naturally, this is a challenge for the university community as a whole). And of course, all of these changes offer opportunities for instructors to engage in the scholarship of teaching and learning as they implement new strategies and activities.

Whereas relational learning originally involved the student and a mentor/instructor, going forward we must develop an "it takes a community" approach to teaching and learning by reframing and refining instruction to emphasize other relationships: a "multi-relational" pedagogy. To the extent that the role of the instructor is changing, the role of the student is also changing. The weakening of the classroom instructor/student bond also represents an opportunity to increase the expectations of students in guiding their own learning. This expectation includes changing the student role so that students are active agents in seeking learning opportunities and cocreating learning experiences. Students should begin patterning a lifelong-learning habit in the academic environment that extends beyond the disciplinary program. Whereas evaluation was once solely the area of instructors, students are now developing and measuring their own professional behaviors.

It is clear that, if instructors are to design for relational learning, relational learning now must be elevated from its status as implicit curriculum—

that which is foundational but goes without saying (and remains unsaid)—and made part of the explicit curriculum. "The implicit curriculum may include what faculty members believe is most important to know, what intentions they hold for students, what teaching processes they value, and what content they do or do not avail students with opportunities to learn . . . students grasp what kind of person they are to be as occupational therapists" (Hooper, 2008, p. 229). This, then, requires designing learning experiences in which students intentionally incorporate ways of being into their repertoire of professional behaviors.

Changes in the nature of education and pressures to provide more occupational therapists are creating challenges to occupational therapy's well-established signature pedagogies, yet OT educators are adapting, using the affordances of the online environment to extend their signature pedagogies into the 21st century.

Note

1. The early founders of the "moral treatment" movement included a psychiatrist, two architects, a social services worker, a nurse, and an arts and crafts teacher (Schwartz, 2003).

References

American Occupational Therapy Association (AOTA). (2009). Occupational therapy fieldwork education: Value and purpose. *American Journal of Occupational Therapy, 63*(6), 821–822.

Arendt, H. (1958). The human condition. In K. Schaff (Ed.), *Philosophy and problems of work* (pp. 23–42). Lanham, MD: Roman & Littlefield Publishers.

Berg, C., Black, R., Fazio, L., Finlayson, M., Hooper, B., Krishnagiri, S., Padilla, R., Rapp, C. Q., Harvison, N., & Rotert, D. (2009). *Occupational therapy model curriculum.* The American Occupational Therapy Association, Inc. Retrieved from http://www.aota.org/Educate/EdRes/COE/Other-Education-Documents/OT-Model-Curriculum.aspx

Bing, R. K. (1981). Occupational therapy revisited: A paraphrastic journey. *American Journal of Occupational Therapy, 35,* 499–518.

Bockoven, J. S. (1971). Occupational therapy—a historical perspective. Legacy of moral treatment—1800's to 1910. *American Journal of Occupational Therapy, 25*(5), 223–225.

Cahn, L., & Hayden, J. (1972). A combined approach. Educator and occupational therapist. *American Journal of Occupational Therapy, 26*(5), 249–251.

Cole, M. (1985). Starting a Level I fieldwork program. *American Journal of Occupational Therapy, 39*(9), 584–588.

Coppard, B. M., Dickerson, A., & Commission on Education. (2007). A descriptive review of occupational therapy education. *American Journal of Occupational Therapy, 61*(6), 672–677.

Delworth, U. M. (1972). Interpersonal skill development for occupational therapy students. *American Journal of Occupational Therapy, 26*(1), 27–29.

Fink, L. D. (2003). *Creating significant learning experiences: An integrated approach to designing college courses.* San Francisco, CA: Jossey–Bass.

Hammel, J., Royeen, C. B., Bagatell, N., Chandler, B., Jensen, G., Loveland, J., & Stone, G. (1999). Student perspectives on problem-based learning in an occupational therapy curriculum: A multiyear qualitative evaluation. *American Journal of Occupational Therapy, 53*(2), 199–206.

Hill, W. F. (1973). Democratization of the instructional program. *American Journal of Occupational Therapy, 27*(3), 127–137.

Hooper, B. (2006). Beyond active learning: A case study of teaching practices in an occupation-centered curriculum. *American Journal of Occupational Therapy, 60*(5), 551–562.

Hooper, B. (2008). Stories we teach by: Intersections among faculty biography, student formation, and instructional processes. *American Journal of Occupational Therapy, 62*(2), 228–241.

Jenkins, G., Douglas, F., & Chamberlain, E. (2008). Compulsory volunteering: Using service learning to introduce occupation to occupational therapy students. *British Journal of Occupational Therapy, 71*(1), 38–40.

Johnson, C. R., Koenig, K. P., Piersol, C. V., Santalucia, S. E., & Wachter-Schutz, W. (2006). Level I fieldwork today: A study of contexts and perceptions. *American Journal of Occupational Therapy, 60*(3), 275–287.

Kidner, T. B. (1925). The hospital pre-industrial shop. *Occupational Therapy and Rehabilitation, 4*(3), 187–194.

Lyons, M. (1997). Understanding professional behavior: Experiences of occupational therapy students in mental health settings. *American Journal of Occupational Therapy, 51*(8), 686–695.

Maynard, M., & Pedro, D. (1971). One day experience in group dynamics in an occupational therapy assistant course. *American Journal of Occupational Therapy, 25*(3), 170–171.

Mechanic, D. (1990). Commentary. The role of sociology in health affairs. *Health Affairs, 9*, 85–97.

Nolinske, T. (1995). Multiple mentoring relationships facilitate learning during fieldwork. *American Journal of Occupational Therapy, 49*(1), 39–43.

Nolinske, T., & Millis, B. (1999). Cooperative learning as an approach to pedagogy. *American Journal of Occupational Therapy, 53*(1), 31–40.

Peloquin, S. (2005). 2005 Eleanor Clarke Slagel Lecture—Embracing our ethos, reclaiming our heart. *American Journal of Occupational Therapy, 59*(6), 611–625.

Platt, N. P., Martell, D. L., & Clements, P. A. (1977). Level I field placement at a federal correctional institution. *American Journal of Occupational Therapy, 31*(6), 385–387.

Posthuma, B. W., & Posthuma, A. B. (1972). The effect of a small-group experience on occupational therapy students. *American Journal of Occupational Therapy, 26*(8), 415–418.

Presseller, S. (1983). Fieldwork education: The proving ground of the profession. *American Journal of Occupational Therapy, 37*(3), 163–165.

Provident, I. M., & Joyce-Gaguzis, K. (2005). Creating a level II fieldwork experience in a county jail setting. *American Journal of Occupational Therapy, 59*(1), 101–106.

Scanlan, J. N., & Hancock, N. (2010). Online discussions develop students' clinical reasoning skills during fieldwork. *Australian Journal of Occupational Therapy, 57*(6), 401–408. doi: 10.1111/j.1440–1630.2010.00883.x

Schaber, P., & Shanedling, J. (2010, April). *Teaching higher level critical thinking skills in an online occupation-based theory course.* Poster session presented at the World Federation of Occupational Therapy, Santiago, Chile.

Schaber, P., Wilcox, K. J., Whiteside, A. L., Marsh, L. J., & Brooks, D. C. (2010). Designing learning environments to foster affective learning: Comparison of classroom to blended learning. *International Journal of the Scholarship of Teaching and Learning.* Retrieved from http://academics.georgiasouthern.edu/ijsotl/v4n2.html

Schwartz, K. B. (2003). History of occupation. In P. Kramer, J. Hinojosa, & C. B. Royeen (Eds.), *Perspectives in human occupation* (pp. 18–31). Philadelphia, PA: Lippincott, Williams & Wilkins.

Shulman, L. S. (2005). Signature pedagogies in the professions. *Daedalus, 134*(3), 52–59.

Slagle, E. C. (1924). A year's development of occupational therapy in New York State Hospitals. *Modern Hospital, 22*(1), 98–104.

Stube, J. E., & Jedlicka, J. S. (2007). The acquisition and integration of evidence-based practice concepts by occupational therapy students. *American Journal of Occupational Therapy, 61*(1), 53–61.

Tryssenaar, J. (1995). Interactive journals: An educational strategy to promote reflection. *American Journal of Occupational Therapy, 49*(7), 695–702.

University of Wisconsin. (1948). The University of Wisconsin course in occupational therapy. *American Journal of Occupational Therapy, 2*(1), 34–35.

VanLeit, B. (1995). Using the case method to develop clinical reasoning skills in problem-based learning. *American Journal of Occupational Therapy, 49*(4), 349–353.

Wiggins, G., & McTighe, J. (1998). *Understanding by design.* Alexandria, VA: Association for Supervision and Curriculum Development.

Woodside, H. H. (1971). The development of occupational therapy 1910–1929. *American Journal of Occupational Therapy, 25*(5), 226–230.

15

TOWARD A COMPREHENSIVE SIGNATURE PEDAGOGY IN SOCIAL WORK EDUCATION

La Vonne J. Cornell-Swanson

The profession of social work began as social welfare in the United States as far back as the 19th century. As social welfare evolved from charity organizations and informal care to formalized care, social work as a profession was established. Along with the establishment of social work as a profession came the establishment of standards of practice, including a professional code of ethics and the development of social work education as a separate field of study. The most commonly accepted definition of the social work profession is provided by the International Federation of Social Workers (IFSW):

> The social work profession promotes social change, problem solving in human relationships and the empowerment and liberation of people to enhance well-being. Utilizing theories of human behavior and social systems, social work intervenes at the points where people interact with their environments. Principles of human rights and social justice are fundamental to social work. (IFSW, 2000)

By framing social work's commitment to the respect for the dignity and worth of all people and the profession's quest for social justice, core values of social work emerged, setting the standards and a code of professional ethics to protect recipients of care. The National Association of Social Workers (NASW) Code of Ethics (1999) proscribe the professional values that guide social work practice including service, social justice, the dignity and worth of the person, the importance of human relationships, integrity, and competence.

The Council on Social Work Education (CSWE), which has been accrediting undergraduate and graduate social work programs since 1974 and overseeing what and how social work is taught, describes the purpose of social work in the following way:

> The social work profession is to promote human and community well-being. Guided by a person and environment construct, a global perspective, respect for human diversity, and knowledge based on scientific inquiry, social work's purpose is actualized through its quest for social and economic justice, the prevention of conditions that limit human rights, the elimination of poverty, and the enhancement of the quality of life for all persons. (CSWE, 2008, p. 1)

As the accrediting body, CSWE also establishes the core curriculum requirements in social work education, published in the Educational Policy and Accreditation Standards (EPAS) document. For many years the EPAS-mandated curriculum offered by accredited social work programs has included content on professional values and ethics, diversity, populations at risk, human behavior and the social environment, social welfare policy and services, social work practice research, field placement for graduate programs, and advanced curriculum content (CSWE, 2001). Central to the mandated curriculum was the generalist social work practice model of theoretical constructs, practice skills sets, and ethical codes of conduct to prepare students to think and behave as social workers. For instance, part of the 2001 curriculum mandate included the requirement that accredited social work programs provide preapproved field internships as the capstone of each graduate's educational experience.

The focus in this chapter is to describe the unique habits and methodologies of teaching social work and articulate how social work education's signature pedagogy is more comprehensive than the senior capstone field placement.

Social Work Education and the Scholarship of Teaching and Learning (SoTL)

The field of social work education has two major peer reviewed journals, CSWE's *Journal of Social Work Education (JSWE)* and Rutledge's *Journal of Teaching Social Work*. Although both journals feature articles on teaching strategies, these publications focus more on assessment of clinical practice, teaching practice, and curriculum. What is missing is strong representation of articles that use the SoTL approach to assess what students are learning. A review of the literature in both SoTL and signature pedagogies reveals a dearth of publications written by social work educators about social work education. The SoTL articles available include a chapter in *GAUISUS: Selected Sources on SoTL at Illinois State University 2004–2009* by Ressler and Zosky on how LGBTQ students experience the campus climate at Illinois State University (Ressler & Zosky, 2009), one article in the *Journal of the Scholarship of Teaching and Learning (JoSoTL)* by Williamson and Chang (2009) on problem-based learning, and one article from the United Kingdom (UK) published in *Transformative Dialogues* by Cooper and Pickering (2008) on practice-based learning in social work education. This lack of SoTL publications reflects the profession's heavy emphasis on social work curriculum, rather than *how* students are learning.

Social Work Educational Policy and Standards 2008 and the Search for Signature Pedagogy

As recently as 2008, CSWE made changes to the EPAS requirements that represent a dramatic shift from mandated content curriculum. The new EPAS requirements consist of four curriculum features, program mission and goals, and an explicit curriculum, including field education, implicit curriculum, and assessment (EP, 10.17.2008 ADP p. 1). Central to the new EPAS requirements is a set of 10 competencies, creating the opportunity to support a stronger focus on systematic assessment of student learning. These competencies include

> identity as a professional social worker, application of the ethical principles to guide professional social work practice, application of critical thinking, engage diversity and difference in practice, advance human rights and social and economic justice, engage in research informed practice and practice informed research, apply knowledge of human behavior and the social environment, engage in policy practice, attend to contexts, and engage, assess, intervene and evaluate with individuals, groups, organizations and communities. (Holloway, Black, Hoffman, & Pierce, 2009, p. 2)

Along with this shift from content to competency-based curriculum, EPAS described the final apprenticeship field placement as part of the explicit curriculum and declared it as the signature pedagogy of social work education.

Although the definition of signature pedagogy adopted in EPAS references Shulman's groundbreaking concept (2005), the literature in social work education reveals a lack of research about "default pedagogies" (Gurung, Chick, & Haynie, 2009) used in social work education. Since 2008 there have been a few new articles in social work journals that have adopted the term *signature pedagogy* to describe field education (Dedman, 2008; Holloway et al., 2009; Homonoff, 2008; Lager & Robbins, 2004). Missing from these publications is the connection of Shulman's (2005) descriptions of the "temporal patterns" and deep structures that emerged in his study of signature pedagogies within the professions and related publications (Calder, 2006; Golde, 2007; Shulman, 2005). Without these connections, the literature lacks a comprehensive description of the signature pedagogy that is central to social work education.

According to the literature on signature pedagogies in social work (Dedman, 2008; Homonoff, 2008), field placement is the heart of social work education, suggesting that interning in a social work field setting will help students learn how to be social workers and teach them the professional field's values, knowledge, manner of thinking, and worldview. Holloway, Black, Hoffman, and Pierce (2009) suggest that the purpose of defining field placement as signature pedagogy was to elevate its role and recognize field placement as intrinsic to social work education and critical to the process of becoming a professional social worker. They claim that social work field placement was never meant to be an apprentice program, or one in which student learning is based exclusively on replicating the work of a supervisor or master practitioner (Holloway, Black, Hoffman, & Pierce, 2009)—a definition of apprenticeship that differs from the comprehensive descriptions of apprenticeship as discussed in Sullivan, Colby, Wegner, Bond, and Shulman (2007).

Central to the concept of signature pedagogies in the professions are three typical, temporal patterns: the pervasive initial pedagogy that frames and prefigures professional preparation; the pervasive capstone apprenticeships; and the sequenced and balanced portfolio (Shulman, 2005; Sullivan et al., 2007). The ideas that support social work's field placement as a pervasive capstone apprenticeship include the apprenticeship of identity and purpose. It is the very place where students are introduced to the purposes, attitudes, and experiences guided by the ethics and values they are taught through dramatic pedagogies of practice simulation prior to field placement. Field placement involves the integration of learning between courses and the social agency in which the student is placed.

Although I agree that field placement is a central component of social work's signature pedagogy, I believe it represents only one of the three temporal patterns of a signature pedagogy—"the pervasive capstone apprenticeship" (Shulman, 2005, p. 55)—and alone does not acknowledge that students engage in a pervasive initial pedagogy that "frames and prefigures professional preparation" and the "sequenced and balanced portfolio" (Shulman, 2005, p. 55) that provides students with simulated practice situations to develop the competencies necessary for field placement. The pervasive initial pedagogy and the sequenced and balanced portfolio is broader, happens much earlier, and includes teaching theoretical constructs, practice skills sets, and ethical codes of conduct that prepare students to think and behave like social workers and can be recognized in the profession as the traditional ways of teaching social work. As social work educators redesign curricula around the 10 competencies identified in EPAS, they should recognize and build upon a comprehensive signature pedagogy that combines all three temporal patterns that define what counts in social work and "how things become known" (Shulman, 2005): how social workers analyze, critique, accept, or discard knowledge, as well as how social workers define the functions of expertise and value clients as the authority in their care (Shulman, 2005).

The First Apprenticeship of Learning: Habits of the Mind and Heart

What teaching practices have social work educators used when teaching habits of the mind and heart? This process begins with the prerequisite general education courses in anthropology, psychology, sociology, political science, human biology, and communications, followed by required courses developed within the major that include human behavior and the social environment across the life span, as well as seminar courses in child and family development. Also included in the major core are courses on social welfare policy, community development, and research. The common signature pedagogy threaded throughout the curriculum at this stage is the application of case study, the "surface structure" (Shulman, 2005, p. 54). Case examples are largely based on real-life experiences of social work practitioners but revised to protect the anonymity of clients. The case studies are used to illustrate client situations within the context of their environment and place the social work student in the position of engaging in case dialogue with faculty and their peers. Case applications are used to engage students in dialectical discussions about the case before considering the potential interventions and solutions. Often the pedagogy is active and interactive, combining lecture, paired discussions, small-group interaction, and large-classroom dialogue. Students are expected to be accountable to faculty and peers in their responses, commentaries, and introduction of opposing or supportive data, a process that slowly introduces them to the necessity of public performance that increases in the second apprenticeship of learning.

Social workers draw from many diverse theoretical perspectives to explain and understand why people behave as they do, to better understand "how the environment affects behavior, guides intervention strategies, and predicts the potential of a particular social work intervention" (Greene & Ephross, 1999, p. 5). Acquiring a broad knowledge base grounded in the social sciences is the first dimension involved in social work education. Theoretical knowledge is the deep structure in social work signature pedagogy and lays the groundwork for training students to assess all situations from an ecological and empowerment perspective, including but not limited to ecosystems theory, strengths-based practice, social constructionism, and cross-cultural practice.

Ecosystems theory combines core concepts from ecological and general systems theories. Ecology focuses on how things fit together and how they adapt to one another. In ecological terms, adaptation is "a dynamic process between people and their environments as people grow, achieve competence, and make contributions to others" (Greif, 1986, p. 225). Within ecosystems, persons and environments are not separate but exist in ongoing transactions with each other: "The ecosystems view is compatible with various theories of human behavior making it particularly useful as an organizational tool for synthesizing the many perspectives that social workers apply in practice" (Miley, O'Melia, & DuBois, 2009, p. 32).

Within an ecosystems framework, the terms *maladaptive* and *dysfunctional* don't really apply. One of the habits of mind for social workers is to understand adaptation to the environment from a strength-based perspective. Building on a client's strengths calls attention to the capacities and competencies of human beings. Social work students are trained to understand that practicing from a strengths orientation means that

> everything you do as a social worker will be predicated in some way on helping to discover and embellish, explore and exploit clients' strengths and resources. In the service of assisting them to achieve their goals, realize their dreams and shed the irons of their own inhibitions and misgivings, and society's domination. This is a versatile practice approach, relying heavily on the ingenuity and creativity, the courage and common sense of both clients and their social workers. (Saleebey, 2002, p. 1)

Social constructionism addresses how people construct meaning in their lives, emphasizing social meaning as generated through language, cultural beliefs, and social interaction (Gergen, 1994). This approach allows students to consider people within the contexts of their social situation.

Habits of the Heart: Values, Ethics and Cultural Competence

> Action indeed is the sole medium of expression for ethics.
>
> —Jane Addams, Social Worker, Activist

Teaching the values and ethics of the profession represents the defining characteristics of social work's signature pedagogy. Values shape the thinking, which guides action and development of practice principles. The values include acceptance, individualization, nonjudgmentalism, objectivity, self-determination, access to resources, confidentiality, and accountability. Both personal and professional values are part of what it means to think like a social worker, because they have embodied a social worker's frame of reference since the beginning of the profession (Reamer, 2008).

Valuing the inherent human dignity and worth of all people reflects a nondiscriminatory view of human kind. The NASW (2001) Standards for Cultural Competence indicate that

> cultural competence is the process by which individuals and systems respond respectfully and effectively to people of all cultures, languages, classes, races, ethnic backgrounds, religious and other diversity factors in a manner that recognizes, affirms and values the work of individuals, families, and communities, and protects and preserves the dignity of each. (p. 11)

Culturally sensitive practice shifts the emphasis from acquiring static knowledge about various cultural groups toward developing the worker's attitude of acceptance, respect, and appreciation for each client's cultural uniqueness. In maintaining an open and inquisitive approach, workers become lifelong learners about human diversity, defining multicultural competence as a process of becoming rather than an achievement or end product (Castex, 1994; Green, 1999; Sue & Sue, 2003). Cultural responsiveness, on the other hand, accentuates key practice skills as a method to achieve multicultural competence: "The worker's expertise lies in applying the skills necessary to access the client's cultural expertise. The ability to elicit and accept client stories without imposing the worker's assumptions, biases, or interpretations is the starting point" (Miley et al., 2009, p. 72).

The Second Apprenticeship of Learning in Social Work Education: Habits of the Hand

Taught by master social workers, practice courses represent the apprenticeship of learning, where students are exposed to and required to develop and practice the social work skills needed to become skilled technicians in their profession. In this second apprenticeship, students are engaged in hands-on simulated micro, mezzo, and macro practice experiences with individuals, families, small groups, community- and government-based organizations, and public meetings. Micro practices develop skills such as "relationship building, the effectual use of verbal and non verbal behavior, and proficiency in interviewing" (Kirst-Ashman & Hull, 2009, p. 46). Mezzo practice "requires both group knowledge and skills to facilitate a conversation with a collection of people with shared interests who come together to pursue individual, group, organization, and/or community goals" (Kirst-Ashman & Hull, 2009, p. 116). Macro practice involves expanding assessment and intervention on behalf of whole groups or populations of clients and might include challenging major social issues and global organizational policies (Kirst-Ashman & Hull, 2009).

Although approaches to teaching social work practice skills at all three levels can vary, they often include lab classes designed to teach interviewing, assessment, and facilitation skills, followed by application of these skills to simulated cases. Within the lab classes, students are often engaged in simulated practice situations that are videotaped for ongoing observation and critiqued by faculty, peers, and themselves. The critique process is designed to further the skills of observation. Embedded in the simulated case examples are ethical dilemmas that challenge students to apply the values, ethics, and cultural competence standards of the profession in simulated and live interviews.

Effective communications skills for interviewing provide the core skill set in social work practice. According to Kadushin and Kadushin (1997), "An interview resembles a conversation in many ways. Both involve verbal and non verbal communication between people during which they exchange ideas, attitudes, and feelings" (p. 4). The specific communications skills social work students are taught include eye contact, attentive listening, use of facial expressions, body positioning, and the ability to convey warmth, empathy, and genuineness (Kirst-Ashman & Hull, 2009, p. 53). The process by which these skills are taught can vary by program. Some practice courses ask students to interview their peers and be interviewed by their peers about personal life situations in an effort to simulate the experience of being both the social worker and the potential client. This process helps the student recognize the difficulties of revealing one's personal stories and understand the importance of maintaining professional standards. It should be a guided practice in all lab classes to require students abide by NASW's Code of Ethics and the Federal Educational Rights to Privacy Act (FERPA).

Micro skills create the foundation for working with mezzo and macro systems. Scaffolding occurs within the curriculum of lab courses, often beginning with learning how to interview a single person, assess his or her strengths and concerns, and develop a basic intervention plan. The practice with individuals is often followed by mezzo practice, expanding the skill set involved in interviewing families and facilitating small group process. In the mezzo practice course, students are engaged in applying their interviewing skills with a group of peers who simulate a family in need of services. The role of social worker and family member rotates to allow each student the full experience. The mezzo practice lab course often includes teaching the practice skills of facilitating small groups of peers, simulating a support or educational group. Creative models might even include outdoor adventure team-building skills and leadership development. Included in these teaching practices is the skill of critique. Often videotaped, the practice simulations provide students and their peers the opportunity to learn how to effectively critique the interview process and strive to meet models of best practice. As students progress in the mezzo skills course, they become prepared for leadership roles and community-based macro practice.

In macro practice skills lab courses, students are often given both simulated opportunities to facilitate meetings and challenged to enter the community to observe and participate in public meetings that address social policy initiatives. At this level, the focus shifts from the individual and family to an organizational model. As students are taught the skills needed to assess community infrastructures, they begin integrating theory and practice. Often the structure of a macro course includes seminar discussions to compare and contrast what is learned in the classroom to what is practiced in the world. It is at this stage that a broader integration of the knowledge, values, ethics, and skills begins to emerge, indicating the student is ready for field placement.

Supervised Field Placement: Social Works' Third Apprenticeship, The Pervasive Capstone

The third apprenticeship, referred to by Sullivan et al. (2007) as the apprenticeship of identity and purpose, introduces students to the purposes and attitudes guided by the values for which the professional community is responsible. It opens the student to the critical public dimension of professional life as a social worker. The essential goal is to teach the skills and inclinations, along with the ethical standards, social roles, and responsibilities that mark the professional social worker. Not unlike the definition of legal education, in field placement

> students have the opportunity to test what they have learned in the classroom; integrate theory with practice; evaluate the effectiveness of interventions; contend with the realities of social, political, and economic injustice; strive for cultural sensitivity and competence; deliberate on the choices posed by ethical dilemmas; develop a sense of self in practice; and build a connection to and identity with the profession. (Lager & Robbins, 2004, p. 3)

In essence, field placement becomes the pervasive capstone of their degree and creates the opportunity to prepare for successful licensure or certification and career employment. Although field placement is recognized as the third apprenticeship of learning in the social work profession, it is not without challenges for student learning. According to the research, field education has encountered challenges both in academia and in community agencies that serve as field placement sites. Identified challenges of supervising social work field students include the following:

> Teaching a wide variety of skills of assessment and intervention; balancing the teaching of these skills with the encouragement of reflection; teaching interns to connect theory with practices; developing an integrative model of supervision; applying research to practice; showing appropriate support to interns; and upholding the mission of field education in the face of fiscal retrenchment and pressures for accountability. (Homonoff, 2008, p. 135)

Of possibly even greater concern is the loss of agency placements to support training of social work interns (Donner, 1996; Globerman & Bogo, 2003), which has increased because of fiscal constraints and increased concerns over professional liability (Homonoff, 2008).

Ultimately, though, to be successful in a field setting, students must be well prepared in the knowledge and skills of the profession. Although field placement is the pinnacle of the social work degree, without the first two apprenticeships of learning, the social work's signature pedagogy would be incomplete.

Expanding the Teaching Commons in Social Work Education

In *The Advancement of Learning: Building the Teaching Commons*, Mary Taylor Huber and Pat Hutchings say that

> though employed in different ways and to different degrees, the scholarship of teaching and learning entails basic but important principles. It means viewing the work of the classroom as a site for inquiry, asking and answering questions about students' learning in ways that can improve one's own classroom and also advance the larger profession of teaching. (2005, p. 1)

The time for social work to expand the teaching conversation and contribute to the knowledge on student learning through SoTL is now. As we consider the changes to the accreditation requirements with a focus on competencies, there will need to be further assessment of the accepted signature pedagogy in social work and how effectively students learn from it. The time is ideal to develop stronger signature pedagogies with both implicit and explicit structures and a sequenced balanced portfolio of student learning in social work based on the competencies set by the profession. The new call for competency-based education in social work education and resulting set of accreditation standards creates the perfect opportunity for social work programs to launch new assessments of student learning that can be designed with SoTL methodologies and contribute to the body of SoTL knowledge that has developed in other disciplines.

References

Calder, L. (2006). Uncoverage: Toward a signature for the history survey. *Journal of American History, 92*(4) 1358–1370.

Castex, G. M. (1994). Providing services to Hispanic/Latino populations: Profiles in diversity. *Social Work, 39*, 288–297.

Cooper B., & Pickering, M. (2008). Dialogues in widening participation: Transition to professional qualification and the importance of self directed learning. *Transformative Dialogues: Teaching and Learning Journal 1*(3), 1–13.

Council on Social Work Education (CSWE). (2001). *Educational policy and accreditation standards*. Retrieved August 10, 2010, from http://www.cswe.org/File.aspx?id=14115

Council on Social Work Education (CSWE). (2008). *Educational policy and accreditation standards*. Retrieved August 10, 2010, from http://www.cswe.org/Accreditation/Handbook.aspx

Dedman, D. E. (2008). Social work field instructors' perceptions of on-line training. *Dissertations Abstracts International, A: The Humanities and Social Sciences, 69*(07), 1–113.

Donner, D. (1996). Field work crisis: Dilemmas, dangers and opportunities. *Smith College Studies in Social Work* I, *66*(13), 317–331.

Gergen, K. J. (1994). *Realities and relationships: Soundings in social construction*. Cambridge, MA: Harvard University Press.

Globerman, J., & Bogo, M. (2003). Changing times: Understanding social workers' motivation to be field instructors. *Social Work, 48*(1), 65–73.

Golde, C. M. (2007). Signature pedagogies in doctoral education: Are they adaptable for the preparation of educational researchers? *Educational Researcher, 36*(6), 344–351.

Green, J. W. (1999). *Cultural awareness in the human services: A multi-ethnic approach* (3rd ed.). Boston, MA: Allyn & Bacon.

Greene, R. R., & Ephross, P. H. (1999). *Human behavior theory and social work practice* (2nd ed.). New York, NY: Aldine De Gruyter.

Greif, G. L. (1986). The ecosystems perspective "Meets the press." *Social Work, 31*, 225–226.

Gurung, R., Chick, N., & Haynie, A. (Eds.). (2009). *Exploring signature pedagogies: Approaches to teaching disciplinary habits of the mind.* Sterling, VA: Stylus Publishing, LLC.

Holloway, S., Black, P., Hoffman, K., & Pierce, D. (2009). *Some considerations of the import of the 2008 EPAS for curriculum design.* Retrieved August 12, 2010, from http://www.cswe.org/File.aspx?id=31578

Homonoff, E. (2008). The heart of social work: Best practitioners rise to challenges in field instruction. *The Clinical Supervisor, 27*(2), 135–169.

Huber, M. T., & Hutchings, P. (2005). *The advancement of learning: Building the teaching commons.* San Francisco, CA: Josey-Bass.

International Federation of Social Workers. (2000). *Definition of social work.* Retrieved August 10, 2010, from www.ifsw.org/en/p38000208.html

Journal of Social Work Education (JSWE). (2010). Retrieved August 10, 2010, from www.cswe./Publications/JSWE/SubmittingtoJSWE.aspx

Journal of Teaching Social Work (JoTSW). (2010). Retrieved August 10, 2010, from http://www.tandf.co.uk/journals/WTSW

Kadushin, A., & Kadushin, G. (1997). *The social work interview.* New York, NY: Columbia University Press.

Kirst-Ashman, K., & Hull, G., Jr. (2009). *Understanding generalist social work practice* (4th ed.). Pacific Grove, CA: Brooks Cole Publishing Co.

Lager, P., & Robbins, V. (2004). Field education: Exploring the future, expanding the vision. *Journal of Social Work Education, 40*(1), 3–11.

Miley, K. K., O'Melia, M., & DuBois, B. (2009). *Generalist social work practice: An empowering approach* (6th ed.). Boston, MA: Allyn & Bacon.

National Association of Social Workers (NASW). (1999). *Code of ethics of the National Association of Social Workers.* Washington, DC: Author.

National Association of Social Workers (NASW). (2001). *NASW standards for cultural competence in social work practice.* Washington, DC: Author.

Reamer, F. (2008). Ethics and values. In T. Mizrahi & L. E. Davis (Eds.), *Encyclopedia of social work, 2*(20), pp 143–151. Washington, DC: NASW Press.

Ressler, P., & Zosky, D. (2009). LGBTQ students experience Illinois State University as benignly heteronormative. In K. McKinney & P. Jarvis (Eds.), *GAUISUS: Selected sources on SoTL at Illinois State University 2004–2009* (pp. 31–39). Illinois State University.

Saleebey, D. (2002). *The strengths perspective in social work practice* (3rd ed.). Boston, MA: Allyn & Bacon.

Shulman, L. S. (2005, Summer). Signature pedagogies in the professions. *Daedalus, 134*, 52–59.

Sue, D. W., & Sue, D. (2003). *Counseling the culturally different* (4th ed.). New York, NY: John Wiley & Sons.

Sullivan, W., Colby, A., Wegner, J. W., Bond, L., & Shulman, L. S. (2007). *Educating lawyers: Preparation for the profession of law.* Stanford, CA: John Wiley & Sons.

Williamson, S., & Chang, V. (2009). Enhancing the success of SoTL research: A case study using modified problem-based learning in social work education. *Journal of the Scholarship of Teaching and Learning, 9*(2), 1–9.

16

TOWARD A SIGNATURE PEDAGOGY IN TEACHER EDUCATION

Linda K. Crafton and Peggy Albers

> The concern of teacher educators must remain normative, critical, and even political—neither the colleges nor the schools can legislate democracy. But something can be done to empower teachers to reflect upon their own life situations, to speak out in their own ways about the lacks that must be repaired; the possibilities to be acted upon in the name of what they deem decent, humane, and just.
>
> —Greene, 1978, p. 71

Everyone has experience with teaching and being taught, whether it's through school or home. Therefore, many believe that they know how students should be taught, especially those who believe that education should serve a larger purpose (e.g., getting a good job, developing a career). However, as those of us in teacher education know, articulating a signature pedagogy for teacher education requires a thoughtful exploration of various tenets around which we believe good teacher preparation occurs. As teachers of teachers, we embrace a vision of a signature pedagogy that, as is true in many disciplines, has not yet been fully realized. Ours is a field that recognizes the far reaches of our work into the social, cultural, and political contexts of public schools and into the society beyond.[1]

Parker Palmer (1998) argues that teaching is intimately connected to knowing oneself and that only through this knowing can teachers reach out meaningfully to their students, which is when good teaching occurs. But self-knowledge, like effective teaching and learning, does not reside only or primarily within the individual, nor does it reside solely in knowledge of a disciplinary field. It is through the "interaction and interdependence" (p. 25) of disciplinary knowledge, theories of learning, ways of interpreting and constructing knowledge, and reflecting on one's practice, that teachers can teach who they are and examine the significance of their profession and the important work they do with students. To understand teaching in this way suggests that teachers assume both a moral and an ethical commitment, along with the ongoing intellectual explorations that help teachers shape our craft as we shape our selves. Led by an undivided self, we seek to find ways in which the personal and professional are fused and, in the process, identities are shaped and transformed—our own as well as those whom we teach.

In this chapter, we will define the field of teacher education, lay out the traditional pedagogy of this field, and propose a signature pedagogy that responds to 21st-century teachers and learners who live their lives as citizens in a democracy.

Defining Teacher Education: Training or Educating Teachers?

Teacher education is an applied field of study that draws from a range of familiar disciplines, including sociology, anthropology, linguistics, semiotics, psychology, political science, and others. At the same time, teacher education has several intellectual traditions that have guided the construction of learning experiences for new teachers. Zeichner and Gore (1990) describe them in terms of functionalist, interpretive, and critical. All three explain how and why teachers are socialized into particular practices, an important background for a field's signature pedagogy.

The functionalist tradition is based in positivism in which reality can be identified, named, and passed along in an objective manner. Subjectivity cannot enter into any definition of the knowledge to be transmitted, because it must pass from one person to another in a pure, neutral fashion. There is a mechanical, impersonal dimension to this view of learning. The phrase *teacher training* is a direct extension of a perspective that sees teaching as a simple, straightforward transmission of information and teachers as disconnected technicians (Shannon, 1993). In the 19th century, the concept of training described how both those preparing to be teachers and practicing teachers were educated. However, by the late 1930s, educators began to reject the idea of training in favor of education that involved *understanding*. In 1938, Alan Valentine argued that teachers who are "trained" will only train children, whereas teachers who are educated will then educate children (Spearman, 2009). Today's educators, like Valentine, see training as a deficit concept, so narrow that it reduces teachers to "low-level technicians who obediently carry out the plans of those removed from the classroom without exercising their judgment and making adaptations to the specific needs of their pupils" (Zeichner, 2006, p. 329).

The interpretive and critical traditions give the profession of teaching far more respect. The interpretive tradition recognizes the importance of an individual's subjective experience in understanding the social world. Unlike the functionalist tradition, which seeks an *explanation*, the interpretive tradition seeks an *understanding*. However, like the functionalist, neither tradition challenges the status quo, as they work toward a "sociology of regulation," which emphasizes the need to explain that which unifies and makes cohesive aspects of society (Burrell & Morgan, 1979, p. 17).

In contrast to the interpretive and functionalist traditions, the critical tradition emphasizes the role of production and reproduction, as well as agency and structure (Zeichner & Gore, 1990). In this tradition, the individual has agency to transform within the often deeply rooted structures that comprise the field of education (e.g., teacher as educated vs. teacher as trained, standardized vs. student-centered curriculum). With teaching historically perceived as "women's work," a critical perspective would make conscious the fact that those in leadership roles are often males who exert power over classroom teachers (often women) and over the decisions that women make regarding classroom practice.

How teacher education is defined depends on which tradition is invoked: All three traditions offer insight into how teachers have been socialized into particular ways of knowing and practicing based on the core beliefs that underpin these traditions. In such traditions, we want to ask who benefits when particular traditions are in place? How are teachers implicated in terms of their practice and their education (or training)?

Traditional Teacher Education Programs and Approaches to Pedagogy

At the end of the 20th century, a knowledge base in psychology and pedagogy had emerged to a degree that criteria for good teaching could be named and measured in observable teacher skills and student outcomes, and to make teacher education seem more rigorous, scientific theory was added. The tradition of training teachers, then, became a matter of translating theory into practice through large sets of skills, with the universities providing the theories and related methods, the schools providing the contexts, and potential teachers moving, often unsteadily, between the two (Korthagen, 2001). A major difficulty of this model is that university courses are often loosely connected, if at all, and teacher education programs often are not able to develop and maintain a high level of control over the match between what they are teaching and students' clinical experiences in the public schools. This often results in what Sorensen and Sears (2005) call "induction into a culture of poor practice and weak pedagogy" (p. 621).

Another troubling norm or tradition in teacher education is the emphasis on deep content knowledge. Conventional wisdom suggests that the more content knowledge one has, the better one can teach. Although there is a great deal of support for this position, the National Teacher Examinations (NTEs) found no consistent relationship between this measure and how well a teacher performed in class, especially when viewed from student outcomes and supervisory ratings (Darling-Hammond, 2010). Certainly teachers must be knowledgeable in their content;[2] however, this is not the only criterion around which good teacher preparation should happen.

Pedagogical knowledge has been given far less weight than content knowledge. In fact, in many states, preservice teachers can apply for a provisional teaching certification to teach if they have taken enough university or college hours in a particular disciplinary field. There remains the perception that content and pedagogy, while connected, remain primarily separate, teachers learn *what* to teach and then *how* to teach it. In traditional programs, the assumption is that disciplinary content is neutral, a static, decontextualized body of knowledge, floating around waiting for pedagogical decisions to bring it to life. However, pedagogy does not begin with the decision to instruct students in particular content in a particular way. Pedagogy begins each time a teacher makes a decision regarding what content to present and what content to leave out. What children in the United States *should* know has been hotly debated, especially with the publication of Hirsch's (1988) *Cultural Literacy: What Every American Needs to Know,* a text that has been widely used to guide content in curriculum, a text that scholars like Macedo (2006) have argued is a form of dominant cultural reproduction that circumvents independent thinking.

Perhaps the primary flaw in traditional models of teacher education is that they are not based on what we currently know about how people learn and change (particularly the trajectory of novices becoming more expert) or the crucial personal, institutional, cultural, and political supportive structures that are necessary for change to occur. A signature pedagogy would account for these interdependent systems and the underlying processes that are invisible to the uninitiated. A signature pedagogy in teacher education would move far beyond a view that sees teaching and learning to teach as the simple acquisition and transfer of skills. A signature pedagogy would transform "hierarchical dispensations of wisdom to shared inquiries into practice" (Hargreaves & Fullan, 2000, p. 54).

Toward a Signature Pedagogy in Teacher Education

In outlining a vision for a signature pedagogy in teacher education, we think it wise to begin, as Wiggins and McTighe (2005) instruct, with the end in mind. What is it that we hope to achieve as teacher educators? We see this end through a statement made by Harste: "Curriculum is a metaphor for lives we want to lead and the people we want to be" (Egawa & Harste, 2001, p. 8). How do we envision a signature pedagogy in terms of values and ways of thinking, knowing, and doing? What do we consider significant and critical experiences for teachers who prepare K–12 classrooms for the 21st century?

We identify four broad areas that make up a signature pedagogy in teacher education: the need for a deep understanding of how people learn, the importance of communities of practice and the development of identities within them, the significance of semiotic practices, and the recognition that the aim of education is to create critical and democratic spaces of learning.

Views of Learning

In order for teachers to teach well, a signature pedagogy must invite them to consider the many ways in which theories of learning inform practice. Views of learning in social contexts driven by personal and collective inquiries date back to Dewey (1938), who helped us understand that people "learn as they do," while engaged in meaningful work. Constructing knowledge as one learns through participation is an important intellectual activity and is a form of cognitive apprenticeship (Rogoff, 1990; Wells, 1999). One of Vygotsky's (1986) central contributions to psychological thought and development was his emphasis on socially meaningful activity as crucial to human consciousness. Cultural mediation is a key premise of Vygotsky's theories along with the understanding that language is central to learning. His zone proximal development has helped educators understand that by recognizing an individual's potential for learning and providing support beyond what that person can do on her or his own, students can engage in meaningful collaboration on mutual tasks. This understanding is the foundation for a signature pedagogy and how teachers are apprenticed into the profession.

Communities of Practice and Professional Identity

As people pursue a shared inquiry, over time, practices unique to that endeavor are generated, and members of the community construct particular identities within it. Wenger (1998, p. 56) states that participation shapes not only our experience and competence, but it shapes the community as well. Participation in practice not only becomes a part of what we do, it becomes a part of who we are. This is the infrastructure that becomes the primary means by which educators construct the knowledge, skills, and dispositions of the profession. And because learning "transforms who we are and what we can do, it is an experience of identity" (p. 215).

Teacher identity has in the past 20 years become of great interest to teacher educators (see Akkerman & Meijer, 2011; Alsup, 2006; Rogers & Scott, 2008). No longer seen as an overarching and unified framework with static characteristics, teacher identities are multiple, discontinuous, and shaped by the social worlds in which they engage (Rogers & Scott, 2008). Our identities include a strong view of ourselves as professional learners engaged in continuous cycles of collaborative inquiry to better understand ourselves, our views of the world, our students, and especially our practices. Our knowledge and identity construction thus occur within communities of practice we have developed over time. As Palmer (1998) suggested in our introduction, in order to teach well, a teacher must know her or himself. A signature pedagogy requires that teachers reflect on the shifting nature of school contexts and the students whom they serve, their pedagogical approaches, and how content is selected and presented.

One of the ongoing difficulties in teacher education is the vulnerability beginning teachers often feel as they enter their own classrooms. Many leave during the first few years, crushed under the weight of imposed demands by external stakeholders (e.g., principals, district-mandated curriculum, textbook publishers, legislators) as well as their own perceived lack of effectiveness. Experienced teachers burn out by working in isolation with little energy or opportunity to renew themselves by learning more and becoming more. Instead of a steady growth toward competence, as Zeichner and Tabachnick (1981) showed, many conceptions developed during preservice teacher education were "washed out" during field experiences. In contrast, communities of practice offer support to teachers from their initial entry into the profession until retirement, developing into fully participating members who understand the work, the people, and their ways of knowing.

As preservice teachers and teacher educators move into K–12 classrooms to work alongside in-service teachers, a school-wide culture of collaborative inquiry can be constructed to support ongoing changes in practice as well as a scholarship of teaching and learning. Preparing new teachers who can research their own practice and work collaboratively with colleagues are essential elements in a signature pedagogy. Such a framework can simultaneously and powerfully demonstrate the habits of mind and values of professional educators. These tools and ways of thinking and doing include close observation, qualitative data collection of student artifacts and processes, reasoned analysis, critical reflection, and making research-informed practice public. As communities of cross-generational teacher research pose questions together and pursue shared inquiries, continuous dialogue around their unfolding insights provides "newcomers" as well as "oldtimers" (Wenger, 1998) with the linguistic, intellectual, social, and analytical tools that qualitative scholars in the field have been using for decades to create new knowledge. Building on the extensive literature of teacher research (see Mohr, Rogers, Sanford, Nocerino, MacLean, & Clawson, 2004), insider knowledge is co-constructed as educators at all levels become pedagogical scholars together. Darling-Hammond (2010) also calls for teacher education programs to venture out from their campus homes into public school classrooms and the school as a whole to engage in a mutual transformation agenda with their K–12 colleagues.

One 30-year example of sustained learning communities and teacher transformation of self and practice comes from the National Writing Project where teachers become writers themselves and return to their classrooms to implement writing curriculum developed through a process of collaboration and self-reflection. Here, there is very little change that is "washed out"; in fact, the teachers tracked by Lieberman and Wood (2003) not only used the strategies they learned in the Writing Project but became students of their own practice, many going public with their work for the first time. With the ability to construct multimedia representations of teaching and share those with distant online colleagues, the whole experience of the induction years and ongoing professional development changes.

Semiotic Practices

To understand learning deeply, a signature pedagogy must recognize how meaning is expressed and interpreted across time and place and find ways to empower teachers to learn and teach with this in mind. In the field of teacher education, expression and meaning-making through written and oral language have commanded the most attention. They are the two forms of communication that dominate our schools, through which teachers primarily learn how to teach. Curriculum has focused largely on supporting students' construction of knowledge through print-based texts, where students share this knowledge through written texts.

As early as 1984, Harste, Woodward, and Burke encouraged a different, semiotic approach to designing curricula, in particular, literacy curriculum. They wrote, "our program of research forced us to abandon what in retrospect might be termed a 'verbocentric' [Eco, 1976] view of literacy and to adopt a semiotic one, in which the orchestration of all signifying structures from all available communication systems in the event have a part" (p. 208). Semiotics is a theory that explores the nature and function of signs. In brief, it is a study of signs and sign systems, or language systems, that have distinct grammars, including art, music, language, math, movement, and dance. Semiotics offers a way of thinking about meaning in which meaning-making is mediated and represented within and across sign systems.

Arising from semiotics, other theories have influenced teacher education, including Gardner's (1983) theory of multiple intelligences, which posits that intelligence is evident in multiple ways (spatial, mathematical, artistic, verbal, musical, kinesthetic, logical); multiliteracies (The New London Group, 1996) in which the increasing cultural and linguistic diversity in the world requires the use of multiple communication sources (Internet, visual, sound, etc.); and multimodal learning (Jewitt & Kress, 2003), in which design, production, materiality, and mode are central to one's interpretation and production of meaning. To teach in a 21st-century world, teachers must not only know these theories through ongoing experiences but also implement them in their practices.

Current pedagogical work (Albers, 2007; Albers, Vasquez, & Harste, 2008; Crafton, Brennan, & Silvers, 2007; Rowsell & Pahl, 2007) locates semiotics as significant in curriculum design. For example, the idea of the Focused Study (Burke, 2004) was realized in Albers's (2006) work with English teachers and the Harlem Renaissance. In a community of practice, Albers's teachers lived this Focused Study through music, art, drama, literature, and writing and expressed their learning in semiotic ways (multimedia projects, expressions, poetry, etc.). From this experience, teachers designed semiotic curricula for their own classrooms, curricula that would engage their students across sign systems. Teachers reflected on how and why teaching practices informed by semiotics offered deeper insights into learning. This was a signature pedagogy in action.

Education as a Democratic Endeavor

In the United States, public education should serve the purposes of a democracy. To do this work, a signature pedagogy must engage teachers in critical pedagogy, pedagogy that recognizes the inequities in education that serve some and disenfranchise others. Grounded in Freire's (1970, 1994) emancipatory literacy work in Brazil, Kincheloe (1988) defined critical pedagogy as a set of tenets including an awareness that education is inherently political, or Freire's (1970) concept of *conscientization*, that markers of identity (race, class, sexuality, physical ability, and so on) are important domains of oppression and anti-hegemonic action, and that the education should alleviate oppression, human suffering, and the practice of blaming students for the (lack of) knowledge they bring to class. In teacher education, all involved must engage and share in ongoing reflection related to white privilege and socially constructed views of race, class, and gender.

Positioning students as social agents contributes to changing inequities in the community and beyond. Students must see how their own experiences (their own situatedness) have conditioned them to make certain meanings rather than others. Students must understand how texts work and how it is that texts work to get things done in the world (Comber & Kamler, 1997). Lakoff (2004) argued that we need to help students understand what "frames" are being used and how these frames support certain interpretations rather than other interpretations. Work such as Vasquez, Albers, and Harste (2010), asking Canadian teachers to engage in a critical inquiry into social issues within their own community (e.g., poverty, racism, vandalism) and use new technologies to design and share their insights, is but one example of the powerful engagements that will, over time, transform the discipline of teacher education.

Conclusion: A New Professionalism

The discourse around teacher education has tended to be both functionalist and content-driven, leaving teachers' apprenticeships into the profession in everyone's hands but their own. Learning to teach and improving one's practice are ultimately processes of becoming, best nurtured "through practice (learning as doing), through meaning (learning as intentional), through community (learning as participating and being with others), and through identity (learning as changing who we are)" (Lieberman & Pointer Mace, 2008). Although there are many arguments for and examples of the dimensions that could inform a national effort for reform of teacher education, the visions and processes that are being promoted on a wide scale have more to do with narrow, outdated views of teaching and learning and high-stakes accountability measures that do not respond to what we know about learning, teaching, and social responsibility. The manner of thinking in teacher education—its signature pedagogy—must be both critical and complex, based on the best that we know about how people learn with one another, promoting the ongoing collaborative inquiries within learning communities. Further, it must involve knowledge of one's discipline and must invite a willingness to engage teachers and students in interpreting, producing, and critiquing a range of texts, print and non-print. It is within professional communities of practice committed to teaching for a democracy that new and experienced teachers move their pedagogy forward.

Notes

1. We wish to acknowledge Carolyn Burke for her invaluable contributions to our thinking in the early stages of this chapter.

2. Bransford, Derry, Berliner, Hammerness, and Beckett (2005) remind us that there is also a downside to having a great deal of knowledge about one's subject matter, because the content can become so intuitive that experts can lose sight of what it was like to be a novice (p. 48).

References

Akkerman, S., & Meijer, P. (2011). A dialogical approach to conceptualizing teacher identity. *Teaching & Teacher Education, 27*(2), 308–319.

Albers, P. (2006). Imagining the possibilities in multimodal curriculum design. *English Education, 38*(2), 75–101.

Albers, P. (2007). Visual discourse analysis: An introduction to the analysis of school-generated visual texts. In D. W. Rowe, R. T. Jimenez, D. L. Compton, D. K. Dickinson, Y. Kim, K. M. Leander, & V. J. Risko (Eds.), *56th Yearbook of the National Reading Conference* (pp. 81–95). Oak Creek, WI: NRC.

Albers, P., Vasquez V. M., & Harste, J. C. (2008). A classroom with a view: Teachers, multimodality and new literacies. *Talking Points, 19*(2), 3–13.

Alsup, J. (2006). *Teacher identity discourses. Negotiating personal and professional spaces.* Mahwah, NJ: Lawrence Erlbaum Associates, Inc.

Bransford, J., Derry, S., Berliner, D., Hammerness, K., & Beckett, K. (2005). Theories of learning and their roles in teaching. In L. Darling-Hammond & J. Bransford (Eds.), *Preparing teachers for a changing world: What teachers should learn and be able to do* (pp. 40–87). San Francisco, CA: Jossey-Bass.

Burke, C. (2004, November). *Curriculum as inquiry.* Presentation at the Annual Conference of the National Council of Teachers of English, San Francisco, CA.

Burrell, G., & Morgan, G. (1979). *Sociological paradigms and organizational analysis.* London, UK: Heinemann.

Comber, B., & Kamler, B. (1997). Critical literacies: Politicising the language classroom. *Interpretations, 30*(1), 30–53.

Crafton, L. K., Brennan, M., & Silvers, P. (2007). Critical inquiry and multiliteracies in a first grade classroom. *Language Arts, 84*(6), 510–518.

Darling-Hammond, L. (2010). Constructing 21st century teacher education. In V. Hill-Jackson & C. W. Lewis (Eds.), *Transforming teacher education: What went wrong with teacher training, and how we can fix it* (pp. 223–249). Sterling, VA: Stylus.

Dewey, J. (1938). *Experience and education.* New York, NY: Collier Books.

Egawa, K., & Harste, J. C. (2001). Balancing the literacy curriculum: A new vision. *School Talk, 7*(1), 1–8.

Freire, P. (1970). *Pedgagogy of the oppressed.* London: Penguin.

Freire, P. (1994). *Pedagogy of hope: Reliving pedagogy of the oppressed.* New York: Continuum.

Gardner, H. (1983). *Frames of mind: Theories of multiple intelligences.* New York, NY: Basic Books.

Greene, M. (1978). *Landscapes of meaning.* New York, NY: Teachers College Press.

Hargreaves, A., & Fullan, M. (2000). *Mentoring in the New Millenium.* Toronto, Ontario: University of Toronto Press.

Harste, J., Woodward, V., & Burke, C. (1984). *Language stories and literacy lessons.* Portsmouth, NH: Heinemann.

Hirsch, E. D. (1987). *Cultural literacy: What every American needs to know.* New York, NY: Vintage Books.

Jewitt, C., & Kress, G. (Eds.). (2003). *Multimodal literacy.* New York, NY: Peter Lang.

Kincheloe, J. L. (1988). Fighting professional amnesia: Building strong academic backgrounds for teachers. *The High School Journal, 72*(1), 1–7.

Korthagen, F. (2001). *Linking practice and theory: The pedagogy of realistic teacher education.* Mahway, NJ: Lawrence Erlbaum.

Lakoff, G. (2004). *Don't think of an elephant: Know your values and frame the debate.* White River Junction, VT: Chelsea Green Publishing.

Lieberman, A., & Pointer Mace, D. (2008). Making practice public: Teacher learning in the 21st century. *Journal of Teacher Education, 61*(1–2), 77–84.

Lieberman, A., & Wood, D. (2003). *Inside the national writing project.* New York, NY: Teachers College Press.

Macedo, D. (2006). *Literacies of power: What Americans are not allowed to know.* Boulder, CO: Westview Press.

Mohr, M., Rogers, C., Sanford, B., Nocerino, M. A., MacLean, M., & Clawson. (2004). *Teacher research for better schools.* New York, NY: Teachers College Press.

New London Group. (1996). *A pedagogy of multiliteracies: Designing social futures.* From: http:wwstatic.kern.org/filer/blogWrite44ManilaWebsite/paul/articles/A_Pedagogy_of_Multiliteracies_Designing_Social_Futures.htm.

The New London Group. (1996). A pedagogy of multiliteracies: Designing social futures. *Harvard Educational Review, 66*(1), 60–92.

Palmer, P. J. (1998). *The courage to teach: Exploring the inner landscape of a teacher's life.* San Francisco, CA: Jossey-Bass.

Rogers, C. R., & Scott, K. H. (2008). The development of the personal self and professional identity in learning to teach. In M. Cochran-Smith, S. Feiman-Nemser, D. J. McIntyre, & K. E. Demers (Eds.), *Handbook of research on teacher education* (pp. 732–755). New York, NY: Routledge.

Rogoff, J. (1990). *Apprenticeship in thinking: Cognitive development in social context.* New York, NY: Oxford University Press.

Rowsell, J., & Pahl, K. (2007). Sedimented identities in texts: Instances of practice. *Reading Research Quarterly, 42*(3), 388–404.

Shannon, P. (1993). Developing democratic voices. *The reading teacher*, 47(2), 86–95.

Sorensen, P., & Sears, J. (2005). Collaborative practice in initial teacher education: The use of paired subject placements in school practicum. *International Journal of Learning, 14*, 619–631.

Spearman, M. (2009). O. L. Davis, and the history of teacher education. *Curriculum and Teaching Dialogue, 11*(1–2), 53–59.

Vasquez, V., Albers, P., & Harste, J. C. (2010). From the personal to the worldwide Web: Moving teachers into positions of critical interrogation. In B. Baker (Ed.), *The new literacies: Multiple perspectives on research and practice* (pp. 265–284). New York, NY: Guildford Press.

Vygotsky, L. (1986). *Thought and language*. Boston, MA: The MIT Press.

Wells, G. (1999). *Dialogic inquiry: Toward a socio-cultural practice and theory of education.* Cambridge, UK: Cambridge University Press.

Wenger, E. (1998). *Communities of practice*. Cambridge, UK: Cambridge University Press.

Wiggins, G., & McTighe, J. (2001). *Understanding by design*. New York, NY: Prentice Hall.

Zeichner, K. M. (2006). Reflections of a university-based teacher educator on the future of college- and university-based teacher education. *Journal of Teacher Education, 57*(3), 326–340.

Zeichner, K., & Gore, J. (1990). Teacher socialization. In W. R. Houston (Ed.), *Handbook of research on teacher education* (pp. 329–348). New York, NY: Macmillan.

Zeichner, K. M., & Tabachnik, B. R. (1981). Are the effects of teacher education "washed out" by our school experience? *Journal of Teacher Education, 32*(3), 7–11.

ABOUT THE AUTHORS

Peggy Albers holds a PhD from Indiana University and is a professor of language education at Georgia State University (Atlanta), where she works with doctoral students, preservice teacher preparation in English education, and in-service teachers in literacy and English education. Albers has published widely in such journals as *Journal of Early Childhood Education*, *Journal of Literacy Research*, *Language Arts*, *English Education*, *Talking Points*, and *The Reading Teacher*, and has authored or edited three books: *Literacies, the Arts, and Multimodalities* (with Jennifer Sanders; National Council of Teachers of English), *Finding the Artist Within* (International Reading Association), and *Telling Pieces: Art as Literacy in Middle Grades Classes* (with Sharon Murphy; Lawrence Erlbaum Associates).

Jeffrey L. Bernstein is professor of political science at Eastern Michigan University. He holds a BA from Washington University and an MA and PhD from the University of Michigan. His research interests include public opinion and political behavior, citizenship education, and the scholarship of teaching and learning. Bernstein was a 2005–2006 Carnegie Scholar with the Carnegie Foundation for the Advancement of Teaching. He is coeditor and contributing author of *Citizenship Across the Curriculum* (Indiana University Press, 2010). His work has appeared in *Political Research Quarterly*, *Politics and Gender*, the *Journal of Political Science Education*, and in numerous edited volumes.

Stephen Bloch-Schulman is an associate professor of philosophy at Elon University. He works in political philosophy and the scholarship of teaching and learning and is particularly interested in the intersection of education and democracy. He presents widely and has published in, among others, *The Journal of Speculative Philosophy* and the *Journal of Higher Education Outreach and Engagement* (with Spoma Jovanovic). He coordinates and is a research scholar for the inaugural Elon Research Seminar on Engaged

Undergraduate Learning (focused on teaching democratic thinking) and is coordinator for the Hannah Arendt Circle.

Karen R. Breitkreuz, EdD, MSN, RN, is assistant professor of nursing at Boise State University and focuses on global pediatric nursing. Her specialty is pediatric nursing, and her research areas are international nursing education and children's health. She has served as resident director and international studies assistant director for two years at the University of Connecticut.

Ruth Bridgstock is vice-chancellor's research fellow at the Australian Research Council's Centre of Excellence for Creative Industries and Innovation, hosted by Queensland University of Technology in Australia. Her research addresses career development in the arts and creative industries and the role of higher education in preparing artists for 21st-century work. Bridgstock is involved in research about arts graduates' expectations of the education-to-work transition, one-to-one pedagogies within the music conservatoire, characteristics and career trajectories of outstanding innovators, early career artists' identity development, and arts entrepreneurship education. She also teaches developmental psychology, career development, and entrepreneurship, supervises doctoral students, and performs in musical theater.

Nancy L. Chick is professor of English at the University of Wisconsin–Barron County. She holds a BA from the University of New Mexico and an MA and PhD from the University of Georgia. Her research interests include teaching and learning literary studies, signature pedagogies, feminist pedagogies, and scholarship of teaching and learning (SoTL). She codirects the UW System Teaching Fellows and Scholars Program, sits on the ISSoTL (International Society for the Scholarship of Teaching and Learning) Board of Directors, and coedited the first volume of *Exploring Signature Pedagogies*, for which she wrote the chapter on literary studies. Her work has appeared in *Pedagogy*, *IJ-SoTL*, and *Teaching English in the Two-Year College*, among other journals and edited volumes.

Anthony (Tony) A. Ciccone (PhD SUNY–Buffalo) is professor of French, director of the Center for Instructional and Professional Development at the

University of Wisconsin–Milwaukee, and recipient of several teaching awards. Ciccone is past director of the Carnegie Academy for the Scholarship of Teaching and Learning (CASTL) and has authored a book and several articles on Molière, and coauthored two French language textbooks. Ciccone has presented SoTL nationally and internationally and published SoTL research in *Arts and Humanities in Higher Education.* With Pat Hutchings and Mary Huber, he coauthored *The Scholarship of Teaching and Learning Reconsidered: Institutional Impact and Integration* (Jossey-Bass).

La Vonne J. Cornell-Swanson is the director of the Office of Professional and Instructional Development for the University of Wisconsin System, through which she meets the professional development needs for faculty, instructional staff, and leadership at 15 university institutions and 26 campuses. Her SoTL focuses on the impact of creating safe classroom environments, and she presents frequently on creating classroom and community dialogues on diversity, cross-cultural practice, and ethics and boundaries in social work. Prior to her director position, Cornell-Swanson was an associate professor of social work at the University of Wisconsin–Eau Claire. She has a master's degree in social work from the University of Oklahoma and a PhD in cultural and linguistic anthropology from the University of Wisconsin–Milwaukee.

Linda K. Crafton is associate professor of communication at the University of Wisconsin–Parkside and teaches and researches teacher education and language/literacy processes. Before then, Crafton was a professor in reading education at Northeastern Illinois University–Chicago and a lecturer in the Graduate School of Education and Social Policy at Northwestern University. Crafton has published in *Language Arts* (NCTE), *Journal of Early Childhood Literacy*, and *Improving Schools* and also authored three books: *Whole Language: Getting Started, Moving Forward* (Richard C. Owen), *Standards in Practice* (NCTE), and *Challenges of Holistic Teaching: Answering the Tough Questions* (Christopher-Gordon). Crafton's current research interests include multi-literacies, critical media literacy, and communities of practice.

Desiree A. Diaz, PhD, RN-BC, is a clinical assistant professor in the School of Nursing at the University of Connecticut. She has a PhD in nursing from the University of Connecticut, an MD in nursing from the University of

Connecticut, and an MD in education from St. Joseph College of Maine. Her BA in nursing comes from the University of Connecticut. She is board certified as a medical/surgical nurse. Her specialty areas are orthopedics and pediatrics. Her primary areas of research are in simulation and limited English–proficient patient populations.

Arthur J. Engler, DNSc, NNP-BC, APRN, is an associate professor in the School of Nursing at the University of Connecticut. He received his BSN from the University of Akron (Ohio), his MS in pediatric primary care and baccalaureate nursing education from the University of Maryland–Baltimore, and his DNSc from the Catholic University of America, Washington, DC. His practice and research interests center around the care and well-being of newborns and their families.

Linda Essig was founding director of the School of Theatre and Film in the Herberger Institute for Design and the Arts at Arizona State University, where she currently serves as director of and professor in ASU's arts entrepreneurship program, p.a.v.e., the performing arts venture experience. A professional lighting designer, Essig has designed lighting for theaters throughout the country and has exhibited her work in the United States, the Czech Republic, and Canada. She has authored numerous articles on lighting design and on arts entrepreneurship, holds an MFA from New York University, and is working on the third edition of *Lighting and the Design Idea* (Wadsworth).

Matthew A. Fisher is an associate professor of chemistry at Saint Vincent College. He received a PhD in biochemistry from the University of Wisconsin–Madison in 1990 and spent four years as a chemistry professor at Randolph-Macon College before joining the Saint Vincent faculty in 1995, where he served for seven years as the director of Saint Vincent College's Teaching Enhancement and Mentoring Program. He is a senior fellow with the National Center for Science and Civic Engagement, the parent organization for the NSF-funded SENCER (Science Education for New Civic Engagement and Responsibility) Project. Fisher is a 2005 Carnegie Scholar focusing on redesigning an undergraduate biochemistry course for integrative learning.

Steven Gravelle is an associate professor of chemistry who has been teaching at Saint Vincent College in Latrobe, Pennsylvania, for 20 years. He earned his PhD in physical chemistry from Northwestern University. He currently teaches general chemistry (freshmen), quantitative analysis (sophomores), and physical chemistry (juniors), along with the associated lab courses. He has used process-oriented guided inquiry learning in his lecture courses since 2000 and has incorporated the science writing heuristic into his lab courses since 2005.

Regan A. R. Gurung is professor of human development and psychology at the University of Wisconsin–Green Bay. He has published articles in *Psychological Review*, *Personality and Social Psychology Bulletin*, and *Teaching of Psychology* and is the coauthor/coeditor of six books, *Exploring Signature Pedagogies* (Gurung, Chick, & Haynie, 2009), Getting Culture (Gurung & Prieto, 2009), Optimizing Teaching and Learning (Gurung & Schwartz, 2009), Culture & Mental Health (Eshun & Gurung, 2009), *The Psychology of Teaching* (Schwartz & Gurung, in press) and *An Easy Guide to APA Style and Format* (Schwartz, Landrum, & Gurung, 2012). His textbook *Health Psychology: A Cultural Approach* (Cengage) relates culture, development, and health.

Jennifer Ham is associate professor of German and humanistic studies in the Modern Languages Program at the University of Wisconsin–Green Bay, where she teaches courses on German literature, culture, and language. She holds a PhD in German from Rutgers University and has presented and published on Frank Wedekind, animal studies, Nietzsche, femininity, German cinema, language teaching, and the philosophy of education. As both a UW System Wisconsin teaching fellow and then scholar, she has explored challenges students face traversing the language-literature disciplinary divide. Her current research explores literary and filmic depictions of schooling and the intersection of turn-of-the-twenty-first-century German educational theory and the practices of nation building.

Holly Hassel is associate professor of English at the University of Wisconsin–Marathon County and chair of the UW Colleges Women's Studies Program. She regularly teaches courses in women's studies, literature, and composition. Her current scholarly interests and publications include feminist approaches to popular culture, with recent articles focusing on children's science fiction films, the television show *Lost,* and the *Harry Potter* series;

underprepared writers in the first-year college classroom, particularly multilingual writers; writing program development and faculty development at two-year colleges; and scholarship of teaching and learning in women's studies. She earned her PhD in English from the University of Nebraska–Lincoln in 2002.

Aeron Haynie is associate professor of English and humanities at the University of Wisconsin–Green Bay and director of the Center for the Advancement of Teaching and Learning. She coedited *Exploring Signature Pedagogies* (Gurung, Chick, & Haynie), *Beyond Sensation: Mary Elizabeth Braddon in Context* (Gilbert, Tromp, & Haynie), and *A Memoir of the New Left: The Political Autobiography of Charles A. Haynie* (Haynie & Miller).

Christina Hong, PhD, is the assistant dean (teaching and learning), Creative Industries Faculty, Queensland University of Technology, Brisbane, Australia. Hong has previously served as an executive head of the School of Performing and Screen Arts, as a curriculum specialist for the New Zealand Ministry of Education, and as principal lecturer in teacher education and arts education consultant. She has presented and published on arts education in K–12 and higher education and has contributed to academic communities as a visiting scholar in the United States and Hong Kong. Hong's current research includes inquiry into curriculum and pedagogies in the arts, arts entrepreneurship, assessment for better learning, and arts-based leadership in higher education.

Thomas Lawrence Long, associate professor-in-residence at the University of Connecticut, has a joint appointment in the School of Nursing and Department of English. He chairs the School of Nursing's Education Innovation Research Nursery team. He is the author of articles and papers on reading and on writing instruction in the general education undergraduate curriculum.

Mark H. Maier, professor of economics at Glendale Community College (California), is coauthor of *Just-in-Time Teaching* (with S. Simkins) and *Introducing Economics* (with J. Nelson) and author of *The Data Game* and *City Unions*. He is coprincipal investigator (with K. McGoldrick and S. Simkins) for the National Science Foundation (NSF) project "Starting Point:

Teaching and Learning Economics" and principal investigator for the NSF project "Adapting Effective Outreach and Workshop Practices to Improve Community College Economics Instruction." He has published widely on the adaptation of economics to research-based pedagogies, including just-in-time teaching, interactive lecture demonstrations, context-rich problems, and structured small groups.

Lauren Marsh is manager of the Faculty Development and Consultation Services in the Office of Information Technology at the University of Minnesota. Since joining the team in 2003, she has worked with faculty, departments, and colleges to help them plan the thoughtful application of learning technologies. She is comanager, along with Kimerly Wilcox, of the OIT Faculty Fellowship Program, an 18-month, multidisciplinary program that promotes faculty leadership and scholarship in the area of technology-enhanced learning. She has published and presented on faculty development and technology-enhanced learning. She received her PhD in English from the University of Minnesota.

KimMarie McGoldrick is the Joseph A. Jennings chair in business at the University of Richmond. Her pedagogic research has appeared in numerous academic journals, including the *Journal of Economic Education* and the *International Review of Economic Education*, covering topics including service-learning, cooperative learning, cheating in the classroom, economics as liberal education, and developing critical inquiry skills. Along with Mark Maier and Scott Simkins, she has developed *Starting Point: Teaching and Learning Economics*, an economics pedagogical portal funded by the National Science Foundation. She is coeditor (with Gail Hoyt) of the *International Handbook on Teaching and Learning Economics* (Elgar Press). She currently serves as an associate editor of the *Journal of Economic Education* and on the American Economic Association Committee on Economic Education. Dr. McGoldrick has received several university, disciplinary, and statewide teaching awards.

John J. McNulty, MS, RN, is a clinical instructor at the University of Connecticut. He has an MS in nursing (administration) from the University of Connecticut, a BSN from American International College, and an RN diploma from Saint Francis Hospital School of Nursing. He has held positions as a staff nurse, nurse manager, quality improvement coordinator, utilization review and in nursing administration. He is an experienced nurse educator, having taught in RN pre-licensure programs for more than 20 years. His specialty area is adult medical-surgical nursing in acute care settings. He remains active in clinical nursing practice, serving as a clinical resource coordinator at Saint Francis Hospital and Medical Center in Hartford, Connecticut.

Susan M. Mountin holds a PhD in education from Marquette University, where she is an administrator and adjunct professor, teaching journalism, theology, and education courses since 1977. She teaches courses on Dorothy Day and the Catholic Worker Movement, Ignatian spirituality, social justice/social activism, and Christian discipleship. She has been published in *America, St. Anthony Messenger, Jesuit Journeys, MOMENTUM,* and *US CATHOLIC* and has a chapter in *Dorothy Day and the Catholic Worker Movement,* which she coedited with William Thorn and Phil Runkel.

Nerissa Nelson is a librarian/associate professor at the University of Wisconsin–Stevens Point and coordinator of the Women's and Gender Studies Program. She is a reference and instruction librarian, and she coordinates outreach for the library and the Foundation Collection. Her research interests include media concentration, information literacy, and scholarship of teaching and learning in women's studies. She earned her MA in communication from the University of Wisconsin–Stevens Point in 2001 and her MA in library and information studies from the University of Wisconsin–Madison in 1997.

Rebecca S. Nowacek is associate professor of English and director of the Ott Memorial Writing Center at Marquette University. She teaches writing, the teaching and tutoring of writing, and drama. She is the author of *Agents of Integration: Understanding Transfer as a Rhetorical Act* (Southern Illinois University Press) and coeditor—with Michael B. Smith and Jeffrey L. Bernstein—of *Citizenship Across the Curriculum* (Indiana University Press). Her scholarship has appeared in *College Composition and Communication, College English, JGE: Journal of General Education,* and *Research in the Teaching of English.* Rebecca was a 2005–2006 Carnegie Scholar with the Carnegie Academy for SoTL.

Sheila O'Driscoll is director of disability studies at the Centre for Adult Continuing Education, University College Cork (UCC) Ireland. A guidance counselor by profession, she is responsible for developing disability studies programs on campus and in outreach centers throughout Ireland, and also teaches women's studies and social studies. More recently, her interests have extended to adult education and lifelong learning in a European context and the European Grundtvig Programmes, aimed at improving teacher training of adult educators and disseminating good practice throughout Europe. Her interest in SoTL began as a participant in the Masters in Teaching and Learning in Higher Education program in UCC.

Carol Polifroni is a nurse, administrator, educator, and consultant. She directs pre-licensure programs in the School of Nursing at the University of Connecticut, where she has been employed since 1981. Carol's research is in health policy focused on engaged learning, transitions from one role to another, and workplace environment issues. She is the coeditor and author of the only anthology of the philosophy of science in the discipline of nursing. Carol is a professor at the University of Connecticut School of Nursing and earned her baccalaureate degree from Saint Anselm College, her master's from New York University, and her doctorate from Rutgers: The State University of New Jersey.

Patricia Schaber is an associate professor in the Program in Occupational Therapy at the University of Minnesota, teaching courses in professionalism, theory, and occupational therapy process with families and small groups. She received her PhD in family social science, with a minor in gerontological research from the University of Minnesota, a master's in pastoral studies from the University of St. Thomas, and a BS in occupational therapy from the University of Minnesota. In addition to studies in SoTL, her investigation is in assessment and intervention of adults with Alzheimer's disease and related disorders.

Jeanne Schueller has been an applied linguist in the Department of German at the University of Wisconsin–Madison since 2010. She teaches undergraduate and graduate courses in German language and applied linguistics/second language acquisition. A focus of her research is the use of authentic materials (print and film) in language learning. She is the author of *Cinema for German Conversation* (2009) and is working on *Cineplex*, an intermediate

German textbook that didacticizes full-length feature films to provide learners with authentic cultural, historical, and linguistic input. She has had a special interest in SoTL since she was a 2005 Wisconsin teaching fellow.

Alison Shreeve is head of the School of Design, Craft and Visual Arts at Buckinghamshire New University. She has a PhD in educational research, exploring the relationship between teaching and creative practice. She previously directed the Creative Learning in Practice Centre for Excellence in Teaching and Learning at the University of the Arts London, United Kingdom.

Scott P. Simkins is the director of the Academy for Teaching and Learning and associate professor of economics at North Carolina A&T State University. His pedagogic research has appeared in book chapters and academic journals, including the *Journal of Economic Education*, and focuses on pedagogical innovation and cross-disciplinary sharing of educational research and pedagogical practices. He has co-led multiple National Science Foundation–supported economic education research projects, most recently the Web-based *Starting Point: Teaching and Learning Economics* (with Mark Maier and KimMarie McGoldrick). Dr. Simkins is coeditor (with Mark Maier) of *Just-in-Time Teaching: Across the Disciplines, Across the Academy* (2009) and serves as an executive editor of *College Teaching*.

Ellen Sims is a senior educational developer at the University of the Arts London, United Kingdom. She is currently undertaking a doctorate in education and is researching academic and professional practice in art and design in higher education.

Jennifer Casavant Telford is an assistant professor in the School of Nursing at the University of Connecticut. She has a PhD in the history of nursing from the University of Virginia, a master's degree as an acute care nurse practitioner from Yale University, and a bachelor's degree in nursing from the University of Connecticut. Her primary areas of research are in the history of nursing, particularly the history of nursing practice during wartime.

Kimerly J. Wilcox received her PhD in the biological sciences in 1982 from the University of Cincinnati. While teaching biology at the University of

Minnesota in the 1990s, she became interested in the educational potential of new technologies and the World Wide Web. In 2000, she joined the Office of Information Technology (OIT) at the University of Minnesota as a senior educational technology consultant, working with instructors on effective uses of educational technology, coordinating consultation services, participating in faculty development programs, and comanaging (with Lauren Marsh) the OIT Faculty Fellowship Program. Her interests include active, student-centered learning, learning/cognitive science, new learning environments, and science, technology, engineering and mathematics (STEM) education.

Dugald Williamson is associate professor in the School of Arts at the University of New England, Armidale, Australia. Previously, he taught at Griffith University, Brisbane. He teaches and researches in the interdisciplinary fields of communication, media, and writing studies. Since the mid-1990s, he has published a range of papers on SoTL that promote collaborations between faculty, librarians, and educational developers to enhance student learning in the context of changing communication technologies. A theme of his publications is the links among communication, education, and formations of personal and civic identity. His most recent book is the coauthored *Australian Documentary: History, Practices and Genres* (Cambridge University Press).

INDEX

Also available from Stylus

Exploring Signature Pedagogies
Approaches to Teaching Disciplinary Habits of Mind
Edited by Regan A. R. Gurung, Nancy L. Chick, Aeron Haynie
Foreword by Anthony A. Ciccone

"*Exploring Signature Pedagogies* is a remarkable achievement that is sure to find its way onto everyone's short shelf of essential books on teaching and learning. Here we see more evidence that the scholarship of teaching and learning can no longer be described as an 'emergent' field, but is well into its prime and yielding some of the most exciting and potentially transformative discoveries in higher education today. The ambition of the project is breathtaking: to give fourteen Cook's tours of selected disciplines across the arts and sciences, highlighting each field's distinctive habits of head, hand, and heart and how these habits form—or more often, fail to inform—how teaching and learning is done with undergraduates. But the real contribution of the volume lies in the authors' recommendations for how disciplinary fields might develop signature pedagogies that enact and perform the disciplines' core concerns. This is the perfect book to give to faculty members who are dubious of 'faddish' education research. It also belongs in the hands of every beginning teacher or anyone wanting a good road map to the problems and possibilities of teaching the liberal arts."—***Lendol Calder***, *Associate Professor of History at Augustana College, currently represents the Organization of American Historians on the board of the National Council on History Education.*

Engaging Student Voices in the Study of Teaching and Learning
Edited by Carmen Werder and Megan M. Otis
Foreword by Pat Hutchings and Mary Taylor Huber

"*Engaging Student Voices in the Study of Teaching and Learning* illustrates the pedagogical power of extending the teaching and learning relationship to form an engaged and interactive partnership inside and outside the classroom. Not only does this book ground the practices of engaging students in developing and implementing the learning process theoretically, it illustrates the successes and challenges of establishing a shared responsibility for conceptualizing and constructing knowledge and ways of knowing. A must read for those teachers seeking to increase student engagement and to enhance each student's self-authorship in the learning process."—***Barbara Mae Gayle***, *Academic Vice President, Viterbo University*

"Readers will bring their own experiences, questions, even skepticism to this collection, but we hope they will take from it, as we do, an expanded and more nuanced sense of the roles that students can play in this work, and a renewed sense of hope and possibility for how this work can enrich the educational experience of students—and teachers—as well. What is clear is the power for students and faculty alike of looking closely at the twists and turns, the messy, emergent business of moving from not knowing to fuller understanding."—***Pat Hutchings and Mary Taylor Huber***

22883 Quicksilver Drive
Sterling, VA 20166-2102

Subscribe to our e-mail alerts: www.Styluspub.com